ArtScroll Series®

Rabbi Nosson Scherman / Rabbi Meir Zlotowitz

General Editors

A Translation and Explanation of all the Amidah prayers of Rosh Hashanah and Yom Kippur

Plus: Ten suggestions on how to merit a favorable judgement.

Published by

Mesorah Publications, ltd

PATHWAY TO PRAYER

קונטרס עבודת התפלה

Rosh Hashanah ראש השנה
Yom Kippur יום כפור

Rabbi Mayer Birnbaum

FIRST EDITION
First Impression … September 2000

Published and Distributed by
MESORAH PUBLICATIONS, LTD.
4401 Second Avenue / Brooklyn, N.Y 11232

Distributed in Europe by
LEHMANNS
Unit E, Viking Industrial Park
Rolling Mill Road NE32 3DP
Jarow, Tyne & Wear,
England

Distributed in Israel by
SIFRIATI / A. GITLER
10 Hashomer Street
Bnei Brak 51361

Distributed in Australia and New Zealand by
GOLDS WORLD OF JUDAICA
3-13 William Street
Balaclava, Melbourne 3183
Victoria Australia

Distributed in South Africa by
KOLLEL BOOKSHOP
Shop 8A Norwood Hypermarket
Norwood 2196, Johannesburg, South Africa

ARTSCROLL SERIES
PATHWAY TO PRAYER — ROSH HASHANAH AND YOM KIPPUR
© Copyright 2000, by MESORAH PUBLICATIONS, Ltd.
4401 Second Avenue / Brooklyn, N.Y. 11232 / (718) 921-9000 / www.artscroll.com

Typography by CompuScribe at ArtScroll Studios, Ltd.

Printed in the United States of America by Noble Book Press Corp.
Bound by Sefercraft, Quality Bookbinders, Ltd., Brooklyn N.Y. 11232

This book is dedicated to the memory of

William & Celia Hecht
Paul & Jeanne Serotta

*Who were the very definitions of what
parents and grandparents should be.
They taught us that love comes in many forms,
but it originates in our devotion to
and understanding of our heritage.*

*Blessed be their memories
for they shall be an inspiration for generations to come.*

William Hecht
וועוועל בן ר׳ ישעיה יצחק הכהן ע״ה
8 Tishrei 5737

Celia Hecht
צפורה בת ר׳ מיכאל הלוי ע״ה
30 Nisan 5760

Paul Serotta
פסח בן ר׳ דוד הכהן ע״ה
3 Adar II 5755

Jeanne Serotta
שיינדל בת ר׳ הרשל ע״ה
24 Kislev 5755

**Howard & Carol Hecht Serotta
Andrew, Stephani, Sydney & Carly Serotta
Judd & Linda Serotta
William Serotta**

✑§ Table of Contents

HASKAMAH TO THE HEBREW EDITION

אלעזר מנחם מן שך
קרית הישיבה
בני ברק

הנה ראיתי מאת הרה"ג היקר מהור"ר מאיר הלוי בירנבוים שיחי' **קונטרס "עבודת**
התפלה" אשר בו מבאר ומפרש כל מילה מתפלת שמונה עשרה שלא יהי' ח"ו מהדברים
העומדים ברומו של עולם ובני אדם מזלזלין. וכל מה שפירש וביאר ממקורות מוסמכים. ואף
שגודל מעלת התפילה מבואר בחז"ל אבל כמה ההרגל גורם שנאמר התפילה כמתעסק ובלא
כוונה ובמהירות וחושב שיוצא ידי חובתו. לזה הוא בא לעורר ולהסביר שכל אחד ואחד
ימצא בו יותר מהחיוב לתת עיונו בתפלה. וכאשר נוכחתי לדעת שהדברים יוצאים אך ורק
לשם שמים בודאי יכנסו בלב כאו"א וישפיעו הרבה.

ואשר בברכה מרובה שיזכה שיפוצו דבריו ברבים ויתקבלו.

מנאי המכבדו ומוקירו

אלעזר מנחם מן שך

HASKAMAH TO THE HEBREW EDITION

I have seen **Kunteres Avodas Hatefillah** by Rabbi Mayer Birnbaum, in which he translates and explains each word of the *Shemoneh Esrei,* to insure that this exalted prayer not be treated lightly, Heaven forbid. All that he has written is based on reliable sources

Although our sages have described the great significance of prayer, the regular repitition of the prayers often causes people to pray by rote, saying the words quickly and without concentration, yet thinking that they have prayed properly. The author has come to inspire people so they will understand the need to pray with greater concentration.

I know that the author is publishing this work solely for the sake of Heaven, so he will certainly succeed in inspiring and having a great influence on all.

I close with the blessing that the author's words should be widely spread and accepted.

From me, who honors and respects him,

Elazar Menachem Mann Shach

אברהם פאם
RABBI ABRAHAM PAM
582 EAST SEVENTH STREET
BROOKLYN, NEW YORK, N. Y.
11218

בס"ד

הנה הרה"ג ר' מאיר בירנבוים שליט"א נתעורר על נחיצות הענין
לתרגם ולפרש את תפלת שמונה עשרה. דברתי קצת עם המחבר בעניני
תרגום וראיתי שמדקדק טובא. וגם כבר איתמחי גברא בחיבורו "קונטרס
עבודת התפלה" שנתקבל ברצון בעולם התורה, ועכשיו בא לתרגם את ספרו
לאנגלית לצורך אלו שקשה להם להבין לשון הקודש.

הנה באמת זהו ענין חשוב מאד לרומם ערך התפלה שעיקרה עבודה
שבלב, ובודאי ספר זה יעזור שיהיו התפלות נאמרות יותר כתיקונן.

אברהם יעקב הכהן פאם

Rabbi Mayer Birnbaum has realized the importance of translating and explaining the *Shemoneh Esrei* prayer. I have spent some time with the author discussing matters relating to translation, and I have seen that he is extremely meticulous.

The author has already established his reliability through his *Kunteres Avodas Hatefillah* that has been warmly received in the Torah world, and he is now translating his work into English for those who have difficulty understanding Hebrew.

This undertaking to elevate the appreciation of *tefillah* — which is primarily a service of the heart — is indeed an important endeavor, and this *sefer* will surely help people pray more meaningfully.

Avrohom Yaakov HaKohen Pam

HASKAMAH TO *PATHWAY TO PRAYER — SHEMONEH ESRAY*

400 MT. WILSON LANE • BALTIMORE, MARYLAND 21208 • (410) 484-7200
FAX: (410) 484-3060

בס״ד

Rabbi Meyer Birnbaum has enriched the Jewish world of prayer with his works illuminating the prayers. His concise comments and guide to the meaning of the prayers have been accepted and are used universally.

Rav Birnbaum has now undertaken to provide an English version of his inspiring works. We are deeply grateful to him for doing so.

The English version will enable a wider range of Jews involved in service of Hashem to benefit from the mind opening guides of this gifted work.

With deepfelt blessings to the author and deep longing for the ultimate service in the Beis Hamikdosh.

Rabbi Yaakov S. Weinberg
Rosh HaYeshiva

YSW:mg

₰ Preface

I thank Hashem with all my heart for having granted me the opportunity to present this *sefer, Pathway to Prayer — Rosh Hashanah/Yom Kippur,* to the English-speaking public. This volume is a free translation of the Hebrew works that I published *b'ezras Hashem* several years ago — *Kuntres Avodas HaTefillah* on Rosh Hashanah and Yom Kippur — which are elucidations of every phrase of the *amidah* prayers of these Holy Days. Those *sefarim* (already in their seventh edition) have been enthusiastically received both in Israel and in America, and I have received numerous requests to translate them into English, to allow a wider audience to benefit from those concise, practical works.

The previous volume, *Pathway to Prayer — Shemoneh Esrei* (published in 1997), has also been very well received, and many have asked that I continue this series to provide a High-Holiday companion for those who want more understanding of the special words of the prayers of Rosh Hashanah and Yom Kippur. I have written this work for them. My hope is that the special thoughts and words of the prayers which the Sages composed for these Holy Days will be understood clearly, and enter the hearts of the readers, to inspire them to repent fully, which is the ultimate purpose of these days. It is only through this that we can hope to be inscribed and sealed for a good new year.

As an aid to reaching this objective, I thought it beneficial to add a list of "Ten Suggestions on How to Merit a Favorable Judgment," which I collected from the discourses of the great Ponevezher *Mashgiach,* R' Yechezkel Levenstein, *zt''l.* This list can be found at the end of this work, in Appendix II.

This volume is the result of extensive research into all available commentators on the High Holiday prayers, including many out-of-print and rare commentaries (such as *machzorim* from Bologna, 1540; Cracow, 1585; Venice, 1599; and *Siddur R' Hirtz Shatz* from Tohegan, 1560). Every effort has been made to find a commentary on every phrase, and although usually the earliest commentary was followed, where another commentary seemed to fit into the words more easily, the latter has been chosen. (The source for every interpretation can be found in the Hebrew edition.)

I began the format of these works with the prayers of Rosh Hashanah while still a student in the **Yeshivah of Staten Island.** I want to take this opportunity to thank the *menahalim* and *rebbeim* of the Yeshivah of Staten Island for having taught me the ways of the Torah, and for having guided me from the day I came to the yeshivah (over 20 years ago) until this day. A special *hakaras hatov* is due to my Rebbe, R' Moshe Boruch Newman, *shlita,* for all his encouragement, guidance, and patience. It is impossible to describe how much I have gained from him. I also feel a special *hakaras hatov* to the *Mashgiach,* R' Chaim Mintz, *shlita,* who has been a tremendous encouragement particularly since I left the yeshivah, and who has been of special guidance to me in the position that I have held the past seven years as *Mashgiach* of the Yeshivah Gedolah of Bayonne.

It was also a great privilege to spend Rosh Hashanah and Yom Kippur together with the *Rosh Yeshivah,* **HaGaon HaRav Moshe Feinstein,** *zt''l,* for many years. Being in the presence of the *Gadol Hador* for the *Yamim Nora'im* left an indelible impression on all of us. Through watching his every action, especially how he stood during *tefillah* like a servant before his Master, one could learn what it means to be a true servant of Hashem. I want to mention two stories of the *Rosh Yeshivah* from those days that made a great impression on me:

> When I came to the yeshivah, the Rosh Yeshiva was already over 80, and nevertheless he was careful never to sit within four amos (7' 1'') of the chazzan during the repetition of the tefillah (as the halachah dictates; except that for weak people there is a leniency). But since he wanted to sit for part of the lengthy prayer, the Rosh Yeshivah moved to sit in someone else's empty seat, although everyone knew he was weak.

> Similarly, the Rosh Yeshivah was careful to never sit down in the Beis Midrash when the Aron Kodesh was open, although it is not a halachah, just a good practice (see Igros Moshe, O.C. V 38). Nevertheless, during Ne'ilah, when the custom is to keep the Aron Kodesh open for the entire prayer, when the Rosh Yeshivah needed to sit, he went out of the Beis Midrash and sat down next to the door, on the outside, in order not to weaken even an iota the custom of standing!

Also, a special *hakaras hatov* is due to my dear friend, R' Shimon Shain, *shlita,* who has been a *chaver tov* in the true sense of the words (see *Rabbeinu Yonah on Avos* 1:6). His inspiration and friendship have been, and are, a great *chizuk* for me. May he have *siyata d'Shmaya* to continue growing in Torah and *yiras Shamayim,* and may he come to share his wellsprings of Torah with many others.

I also want to express my great appreciation to Yeshivas Ner Yisrael in Baltimore where I studied in *kollel* for nine years. I benefited greatly from being there, especially from the *shmuessen* (*mussar* discourses) of the *Rosh Yeshivah,* HaGaon HaRav Yaakov Yitzchok Ruderman, *zt"l,* and from the many private conversations I had with this *gadol.* I was also greatly moved by the amazing *eimas hadin* (fear of the Divine judgment) shown by Rav Ruderman on Rosh Hashanah. Every year he would address the yeshivah before the blowing of the *shofar;* once, when he quoted R' Yisrael Salanter's famous letter stating that the awesome moment of judgment is at the time of the *shofar*-blowing, he was literally crying and it greatly inspired the entire assemblage.

Also, a special *hakaras hatov* to R' Naftali (Herman) Neuberger, *shlita,* who has been of great help to me whenever it was needed. His example of selfless care and concern for all has left an indelible impression on me.

There are numerous people who helped me write the original Hebrew *sefer* which is the basis of this work. I would particularly like to thank those who were the main editors of that work: R' Menachem Moshe Oppen, R' Mayer Goldstein, and R' Abba Tzvi Naiman.

A special thanks to Mrs. Tova Finkelman whose skillful editing has tremendously improved this translation. Also a special thanks to my long-time friend R' Avrohom Biderman, as well as to the entire Artscroll staff, for the meticulous care that they have given this work. May all their efforts be blessed.

Of course, I owe a tremendous *hakaras hatov* to my parents, Rabbi and Mrs. Naftali Birnbaum, *shlita,* for bringing me up to appreciate Torah and *tefillah.* Their encouragement and help in everything has enabled me to reach thus far, *b'ezras Hashem.* I would also like to thank my parents-in-law, R' and Mrs. Reuven Shnidman, for their encouragement in all my projects. May Hashem bless them all with long life in good health and much *Yiddishe nachas* from all their children and grandchildren.

And last, but certainly not least, my great appreciation and *hakaras hatov* to my wife Rochel, whose tireless efforts, selflessness and encouragement have enabled me to spend the countless hours that it took to complete this work. May Hashem give us *siyata d'Shmaya* to serve Him properly and bless us with much *Yiddishe nachas* from all of our children.

Mayer Birnbaum
Nissan 5760 / April 2000

Rosh Hashanah / The Day of Judgement

The Prayers of Rosh Hashanah

The main concept of Rosh Hashanah is *Malchiyos,* accepting God as King over ourselves. This thought is the conclusion of the central blessing of the prayer, which is representative of the fundamental idea of the day. The great Lakewood *Rosh Yeshivah,* R' Aharon Kotler, *zt"l,* said that there are two parts to *Malchiyos*: (1) recognizing God's sovereignty, meaning that everything is from the Creator and He dominates everything; and (2) realizing that we are His servants and are obligated to serve Him. All this is included in the statement of the *Gemara* (*Rosh Hashanah* 16a): God said that we should say *Malchiyos* "in order that you should accept My sovereignty upon yourselves."

Although we are not ruled by kings *today,* and therefore it is very difficult for us to comprehend exactly what our relationship toward a king should be, nevertheless, the Sages have given us a text — the middle blessing of the *Mussaf Shemoneh Esrei* — which should help us acquire this feeling. However, as R' Elya Lopian, *zt"l,* said, it is not the mere saying of these words that endows us with this thought of making God our king; rather, it is concentrating on what we are saying, and contemplating it, that imbues us with the proper attitude.

R' Hirtz Shatz wrote in his introduction to the prayers of the High Holidays (printed in 1560), "Every person is obligated to **concentrate completely** in his prayers, blessings and every holy word . . . He must increase his concentration and examine his deeds. He should seek mercy from the King Who is sitting now to judge all of His creations, with the books of life and death before Him . . . One who does not concentrate is not considered as having prayed, as it says (*Yeshayahu* 29:13), 'with his lips he has honored Me, but his heart is far from Me.' " [See *Pathway to Prayer — Shemoneh Esrei,* Introduction, for an elaboration on this thought.]

Yesod VeShoresh HaAvodah reminds us that we should be very careful about saying the Names of God with proper concentration. [It should be noted that every Name of God has a meaning, a connotation one must think about when saying it, as outlined in *Shulchan Aruch, Orach Chaim* Ch. 5, and therefore the meaning of every Name has been written out in the translation, to facilitate proper concentration.]

Chayei Adam writes that one must pray with **great concentration,** and certainly be careful not to forget the additions that were instituted in the blessings, like *"Zachreinu,* Remember us." [It is interesting to note a converse thought written by the *Meiri (Chibur HaTeshuvah,* p. 263): Since this is a time when one must stir himself to the highest level, the Sages instituted additions in all the blessings (except *Retzei,* see ibid. as to why) to awaken the person, for when there is something new one naturally concentrates more.]

Besides concentration on the words of the *tefillah,* there is another important thought one should have in mind throughout the entire prayer, and it is so critical that it caused the Sages to modify the requirement for the type of *shofar* to be blown on Rosh Hashanah. The *Tur (Orach Chaim,* Ch. 586) writes that based on Torah sources, a *shofar* may be bent or straight; however, the Sages decreed that one should use a bent *shofar.* The *Yerushalmi* explains that this signifies that they should "bend their hearts" (i.e., humble themselves) in prayer. It is obvious from here that it is prayer that is the central focus of Rosh Hashanah, and therefore the Sages mandated that we use the type of *shofar* which will influence everyone to humble themselves — in prayer. We see from here the importance of feeling very humble during prayer on Rosh Hashanah.

Pele Yo'eitz combines both of these and writes, "One should pray with **great concentration, exceeding humbleness,** with a crying voice, pleasant expression and clear, exact pronunciation of every letter of the prayer." This short description defines how our prayer ought to really be on Rosh Hashanah.

In his discourse to the yeshivah on *erev* Rosh Hashanah in 1983, R' Ruderman, *zt"l,* the Rosh Yeshivah of Ner Yisrael in Baltimore, quoted the *Gemara (Rosh Hashanah* 18a) which relates that two people were summoned to court accused of capital crimes, and their punishment was to be the same, but one was saved and the other one was not saved, [for] one prayed and was answered and the other one prayed and was not answered. The *Gemara* asks: Why was one answered and the other was not? The *Gemara* answers: One prayed a complete prayer and was therefore answered; the other one did not pray a complete prayer so he was not answered. *Rashi* explains that "complete prayer" means that he had *concentrated* on the words he had said. R' Ruderman pointed out that on Rosh Hashanah we are all standing in judgment for our lives; this *Gemara* teaches us that one can be saved from a decree of death by praying with concentration. From here we see the urgency of straining ourselves to pray with concentration on Rosh Hashanah.

We can also see the great power of the prayers of Rosh Hashanah from that which R' Dovid Kronglas, *zt"l,* once said in the name of the *Tzlach* [R'

Yechezkel Landau, better known as the *Noda BiYehudah*]: If one says the prayers of Rosh Hashanah **with concentration,** it uplifts and rectifies all the prayers that one had said without concentration the entire year, and then all those prayers which were previously rejected will be accepted. [See *Mo'ed LeChol Chai* 13:3 (by *R' Chaim Palagi*) for a similar statement.]

Since the prayers of Rosh Hashanah are so important, for they not only rectify the past, but our entire future depends on them, it behooves us to say them with tremendous concentration. Without preparing oneself by studying the meaning of the prayers beforehand, it will be extremely difficult to concentrate properly. Furthermore, one will not derive the full benefit of this book without prior study, since simply familiarizing oneself with the material will preoccupy his mind, precluding proper concentration in prayer.

Therefore it is incumbent upon us to prepare ourselves before Rosh Hashanah by learning the meaning of the prayers so that we can recite them fluently; then our prayers will come up before God "for a good remembrance."

Maariv, Shacharis, and Minchah
for the Day of Judgment[1]

AT MINCHAH ADD:

When I call in the name of the Master of all	**כִּי** שֵׁם יהוה אֶקְרָא
you should ascribe greatness to the Master of all strength, Who is able to do anything and Who takes care of us with Divine Providence.	הָבוּ גֹדֶל לֵאלֹהֵינוּ.

Master of all[2] — in particular, My Master	אֲדֹנָי
please open my lips (because I am afraid and ashamed to open them)	שְׂפָתַי תִּפְתָּח
and [help me pray with concentration, so] my mouth will [be able to] tell Your true praise.	וּפִי יַגִּיד תְּהִלָּתֶךָ.

אבות

Our God and the God of Our Fathers,
Who Created Everything, and Protected Abraham[3]

You are the source of blessing (an expression of praise)[5]	**בָּרוּךְ** אַתָּה[4]
Master of all (Who always was, is, and will be)	יהוה

---

1. R' Dovid Kronglas pointed out that although one's natural tendency might be to concentrate more on the part of the prayers which are special to Rosh Hashanah, the truth is that the first *brachah* is the most crucial, for if one does not concentrate on every word of the first blessing he has not fulfilled his obligation to pray (unlike the other *brachos*, where lack of concentration does not invalidate the prayer). And therefore, especially on Rosh Hashanah when our lives lie in the balance, we have to exert ourselves to concentrate on the first *brachah* more than any other, for it is the main one. [See note 3.]

2. The *Mesillas Yesharim* (Ch. 19) writes that a person should think about three things when he begins to pray. It is possible that these three thoughts are hinted at in these three phrases that introduce the *Shemoneh Esrei*:
   (a) he is standing in front of Hashem — "Master of all";
   (b) the exaltedness of Hashem — "Open my lips because I am afraid";
   (c) the lowliness of man — "And help me tell Your true praise."

3. As noted above, one must be very careful to concentrate when saying this *brachah,* because otherwise he does not fulfill his obligation to pray. It is noteworthy that the *Mishnah Berurah* [the authoritative halachic work] (101:4) states that if one did not yet say בָּרוּךְ אַתָּה ה' at the end of this *brachah,* he may go back to אֱלֹהֵי אַבְרָהָם and repeat from there with concentration, thereby rectifying his previous lack of concentration.

4. The *Beis Elokim* explains that we bow at the beginning and end of this *brachah* because it contains a summary of all the praises of Hashem and His all-encompassing powers which signify His Oneness. Recognizing this, we bow down to Hashem in humility.

5. See Appendix concerning the reason for this translation, rather than the common translation "blessed."

the Master of all strength, Who is able to do anything
and Who takes care of us with Divine Providence,

אֱלֹהֵינוּ

and the God Who took care of our
Fathers with Divine Providence
(and made a covenant with each of them)

וֵאלֹהֵי אֲבוֹתֵינוּ

the God Who made a covenant with our father
Abraham (who excelled in kindness)

אֱלֹהֵי אַבְרָהָם

the God Who made a covenant with our father
Isaac (who excelled in service of God)

אֱלֹהֵי יִצְחָק

and the God Who made a covenant with our father
Jacob (who excelled in learning Torah)

וֵאלֹהֵי יַעֲקֹב

He is the Almighty (all power is His,
especially in exercising the attribute of mercy)

הָאֵל

Who is the Great One (all greatness is His,
especially in exercising the attribute of kindness)

הַגָּדוֹל

(and) He is the Strong One (all strength is His,
especially in exercising the attribute of judgment)

הַגִּבּוֹר

and He alone deserves to be feared (because
no being has the ability to do good or bad except Him)

וְהַנּוֹרָא

for He is the supreme God Who is the ultimate cause
of everything

אֵל עֶלְיוֹן

Who always does kindnesses that are
purely good

גּוֹמֵל חֲסָדִים טוֹבִים

and He recreates everything, constantly, every day

וְקוֹנֵה הַכֹּל

and every day He recalls for our benefit
the kindnesses performed by the forefathers

וְזוֹכֵר חַסְדֵי אָבוֹת

and He constantly brings the Redeemer closer

וּמֵבִיא גוֹאֵל

to the forefathers' children's children (even though
the merit of the forefathers might already be used up)

לִבְנֵי בְנֵיהֶם

for the sake of His Name (which will be
sanctified at the time of the Redemption)

לְמַעַן שְׁמוֹ

[and He will also bring the Redeemer]
because of His great love for the Jewish people.

בְּאַהֲבָה

**Remember us for life in this world
(in order that we may earn the World to Come
by doing *mitzvos* here)**

זָכְרֵנוּ לְחַיִּים

**King, Who desires life
(and not death for a sinner,
but rather that he should repent)[6]**

מֶלֶךְ חָפֵץ בַּחַיִּים

**and write us in the
Book of the Righteous, for life**

וְכָתְבֵנוּ בְּסֵפֶר הַחַיִּים

for Your sake, in order that we may serve You[7]

לְמַעַנְךָ

**the Master of all strength,
Who is able to do anything and is the One
Who apportions life to all.**

אֱלֹהִים חַיִּים

He is the King over all

מֶלֶךְ

Who is the Helper (to help one succeed)

עוֹזֵר

and the Savior (from trouble)

וּמוֹשִׁיעַ

and the Protector (to prevent trouble from coming).

וּמָגֵן

You are the Source of Blessing, Master of all,

בָּרוּךְ אַתָּה יהוה

the Protector of Abraham (and because of Abraham
He continues His protection over us).

מָגֵן אַבְרָהָם.

---

6. R' Hirtz Shatz in his *Siddur* writes that when one says these words he should think
that if he only repents he will live, and should resolve to do *teshuvah*.

7. R' Yechezkel Levenstein said that this word should alert us to the type of life we are
requesting; that is, a life of service to Hashem, the kind of life that Hashem desires, and
not merely a life of self-fulfillment and self-indulgence.

גבורות
The Mighty Acts of God and the Revival of the Dead[8]

You alone are eternally Strong	**אַתָּה** גִּבּוֹר לְעוֹלָם
Master of all	אֲדֹנָי
You even revive the dead (which shows the greatest strength, contradicting all laws of nature)	מְחַיֵּה מֵתִים אַתָּה
[and] You have an abundance of strength with which to save.	רַב לְהוֹשִׁיעַ
He provides all the living with their food and other needs in kindness (not because they are deserving)	מְכַלְכֵּל חַיִּים בְּחֶסֶד
He revives the dead with great mercy (searching for merits with which they would deserve revival)	מְחַיֵּה מֵתִים בְּרַחֲמִים רַבִּים
He supports those who are falling (whether physically, emotionally, or financially)	סוֹמֵךְ נוֹפְלִים
and He heals the sick from all types of illnesses (even when doctors have given up hope)	וְרוֹפֵא חוֹלִים
and He opens the bonds of those who are restricted (e.g., giving movement to our limbs when we awaken)	וּמַתִּיר אֲסוּרִים
and He will keep His promise to those sleeping in the dust (the dead), to revive them.	וּמְקַיֵּם אֱמוּנָתוֹ לִישֵׁנֵי עָפָר
Who is like You (who can do as many mighty deeds, which are infinite, even for one person)?	מִי כָמוֹךָ
— You, to Whom all mighty deeds belong! —	בַּעַל גְּבוּרוֹת

---

8. While reciting this *brachah* we should instill in ourselves perfect belief in the Revival of the Dead, one of the thirteen principles of faith outlined by the *Rambam* [Maimonides].

And who is comparable to You in even one of Your mighty deeds (which are of the highest quality)?	וּמִי דוֹמֶה לָּךְ
You are the King over all	מֶלֶךְ
Who causes death and revival in many respects (such as sleep and awakening, poverty and wealth)	מֵמִית וּמְחַיֶּה
and, like the sprouting of a seed, You bring the Salvation (the Revival of the Dead).[9]	וּמַצְמִיחַ יְשׁוּעָה
Who is like You, who has as much mercy on his sons as You, the Merciful Father, have for us	**מִי כָמוֹךָ אַב הָרַחֲמִים**
(and) remembers His creatures, out of mercy, for life.	**זוֹכֵר יְצוּרָיו לְחַיִּים בְּרַחֲמִים**
And (from the mighty deeds that we mentioned) we see that You are surely trusted to revive the dead.	וְנֶאֱמָן אַתָּה לְהַחֲיוֹת מֵתִים
You are the Source of Blessing, Master of all,	בָּרוּךְ אַתָּה יהוה
the Reviver of all the dead (from Adam until the time of the Revival).[10]	מְחַיֵּה הַמֵּתִים.

---

9. This salvation refers to the Revival of the Dead, which is a major topic in this *brachah*. A similar expression is used in the Shabbos morning prayers where it says, ''And no one is comparable to You, our **Savior,** for the Revival of the Dead'' [R' Yehudah ben Yakar].

This *brachah*'s comparison of the Revival of the Dead to the sprouting of a seed (a comparison found also in *Kesubos* 111b) is explained beautifully by *Dover Shalom* (in *Siddur Otzar HaTefillos*), who says that death is not the end of a person; rather, it is like the burying of a seed, which decomposes in the earth to produce an even greater plant. In the same way, Hashem causes death in order to bring a person back to life in a more glorious form than he had had originally. The *Tiferes Yisrael* (*Or HaChaim* 2a) mentions another analogy to this: The caterpillar crawls around for a short time and then enshrouds itself in a cocoon, which is really like a grave, where it decomposes; but after a few weeks, out comes a creature with beautiful wings that can fly thousands of miles — a butterfly!

10. Even though many bodies have decomposed over thousands of years, and some have been burned and their dust has been scattered, and others have drowned at sea, Hashem with His great might will recognize and recompose the bodies and return to them their original souls (*Yesod VeShoresh HaAvodah*).

קְדוּשַׁת הַשֵׁם
Return of the Glory of God's Kingdom (to Zion)[11]

You, Yourself, are holy (different and separate from everything)	**אַתָּה** קָדוֹשׁ
and Your Name (which comes from Your many acts) reveals holiness	וְשִׁמְךָ קָדוֹשׁ
and the holy ones — Israel —	וּקְדוֹשִׁים
(when *Mashiach* comes) will praise You every day, forever.	בְּכָל יוֹם יְהַלְלוּךָ סֶּלָה.
And then (in the time of *Mashiach*) [may it be speedily in our days]	[12]**וּבְכֵן**
[You shall] put Your fear (which will be a catalyst for repentance)	תֵּן פַּחְדְּךָ
Master of all	יהוה
the Master of all strength, Who is able to do anything and Who takes care of us with Divine Providence,	אֱלֹהֵינוּ
on all Your works (which refers to the Jewish people)	עַל כָּל מַעֲשֶׂיךָ
and (put) Your dread	וְאֵימָתְךָ

11. The *Aruch HaShulchan* (O.C. 582:10) writes that all the special prayers of Rosh Hashanah revolve around the glorification of the Name of God, and since this blessing ends, "the King over all Who is the Holy One," which alludes to the future when God's Kingdom will be revealed to all, therefore, the Sages added these paragraphs beginning, "And then You should put Your fear ...," which speak of the ultimate goal of Creation and the apex of our hopes — the Return of the Glory of God's Kingdom (to Zion).

12. The *Avudraham* notes that the word וּבְכֵן, which is not commonly found in prayer, was chosen here to introduce the Rosh Hashanah prayers to allude to the verse וּבְכֵן אָבוֹא אֶל הַמֶּלֶךְ, *And then I will come to the King* (*Esther* 4:16), so that we should realize that now is the time of judgment and we are coming before the King of Kings! The *Siddur Maggid Tzedek* expounds on this and explains that just as the end of that verse states that Esther was coming unlawfully to King Achashveirosh, so too, we have to consider ourselves unfit to stand in front of the King of the world, and thereby come very humbly.

on all that You have created (which refers to the gentiles).	עַל כָּל מַה שֶּׁבָּרֵאתָ
And then all the Jews will fear You	וְיִירָאוּךְ כָּל הַמַּעֲשִׂים
and all the nations of the world will bow down to You in subjugation	וְיִשְׁתַּחֲווּ לְפָנֶיךָ כָּל הַבְּרוּאִים
and all of mankind will make one group	וְיֵעָשׂוּ כֻלָּם אֲגֻדָּה אֶחָת
to do Your will with a complete heart (submitting all their tendencies to Divine service).	לַעֲשׂוֹת רְצוֹנְךָ בְּלֵבָב שָׁלֵם
As we already know (Your power from the Exodus from Egypt)	כְּמוֹ שֶׁיָּדַעְנוּ
Master of all	יהוה
the Master of all strength, Who is able to do anything and Who takes care of us with Divine Providence,	אֱלֹהֵינוּ
(where You revealed) that dominion is Yours	שֶׁהַשָּׁלְטָן לְפָנֶיךָ
and strength (in the constant running of the world) is in Your (left) hand	עֹז בְּיָדְךָ
and might (to do miracles) is in Your right hand	וּגְבוּרָה בִּימִינֶךָ
and (when You again reveal this in the time of *Mashiach*) Your Name will be revered	וְשִׁמְךָ נוֹרָא
on all the nations of the world.	עַל כָּל מַה שֶּׁבָּרֵאתָ.
And, then, Master of all, give honor to Your nation, Israel	**וּבְכֵן** תֵּן כָּבוֹד יהוה לְעַמֶּךָ
(and cause everyone to) praise those who fear You	תְּהִלָּה לִירֵאֶיךָ
and (give) to those who cling to You the good for which they rely on You	וְתִקְוָה [טוֹבָה] לְדוֹרְשֶׁיךָ

and (give) to those who yearn
for Your salvation, the ability to
praise You as they desire (without fear)

וּפִתְחוֹן פֶּה לַמְיַחֲלִים לָךְ

(and then when they no longer fear anyone) there
will be an inner joy in the land of Israel
(with the ingathering of the exiles)

שִׂמְחָה לְאַרְצֶךְ

and there will be open joy in Your city, Jerusalem,
(where the glory of the Divine Presence will be felt most)

וְשָׂשׂוֹן לְעִירֶךְ

and then the kingdom of the family of
David Your servant will sprout forth
(with the coming of *Mashiach*)

וּצְמִיחַת קֶרֶן לְדָוִד עַבְדֶּךְ

and the influence of the
son of Yishai (father of David)
Your appointed one (*Mashiach*) will spread

וַעֲרִיכַת נֵר לְבֶן יִשַׁי מְשִׁיחֶךָ

(and we ask that this should happen)
speedily in our days (so that we should
witness the return of the honor of God).

בִּמְהֵרָה בְיָמֵינוּ.

And then (when *Mashiach* has come)

וּבְכֵן

the righteous will see (that the glory of God
has returned) and they will have inner joy

צַדִּיקִים יִרְאוּ וְיִשְׂמָחוּ

and the upright ones (who do everything just for
the sake of Heaven) will be inspired to dance from joy

וִישָׁרִים יַעֲלֹזוּ

and the pious (who do more
than they are required to do by the Torah)
will raise their voices in jubilant song

וַחֲסִידִים בְּרִנָּה יָגִילוּ

and all those who do injustice and iniquity
will close their mouths

וְעוֹלָתָה תִּקְפָּץ פִּיהָ

and all evil will vanish like smoke

וְכָל הָרִשְׁעָה כֻּלָּהּ כֶּעָשָׁן תִּכְלֶה

when you remove evil
kingdoms from the earth.

כִּי תַעֲבִיר מֶמְשֶׁלֶת זָדוֹן מִן הָאָרֶץ.

And (then it will be apparent) that You alone, the Master of all, are the only King

וְתִמְלֹךְ אַתָּה יהוה לְבַדֶּךָ

on all Your works (the Jews and the other nations)

עַל כָּל מַעֲשֶׂיךָ

(and Your rule will be especially evident) in the Temple, the place of the manifestation of the Divine Presence,

בְּהַר צִיּוֹן מִשְׁכַּן כְּבוֹדֶךָ

and in Jerusalem which is designated as Your holy city

וּבִירוּשָׁלַיִם עִיר קָדְשֶׁךָ

as it is written in Your holy words (*Tehillim* 146:10):

כַּכָּתוּב בְּדִבְרֵי קָדְשֶׁךָ

"God will reign forever

יִמְלֹךְ יהוה לְעוֹלָם

(that is,) the Master of all strength and the One able to do anything, Who dwells particularly in Zion (the Temple)

אֱלֹהַיִךְ צִיּוֹן

(He will reign) for all generations

לְדֹר וָדֹר

(therefore, Israel) praise God."

הַלְלוּיָהּ.

You are holy (different and separate from everything)

קָדוֹשׁ אַתָּה

and Your Name (which is evident from Your many acts) causes awe

וְנוֹרָא שְׁמֶךָ

and there is no other power except You

וְאֵין אֱלוֹהַ מִבַּלְעָדֶיךָ

as it is written (*Yeshayahu* 5:16):[13]

כַּכָּתוּב

"And the Master of all, Who is the ruler over all the Heavenly and earthly legions, will be exalted

וַיִּגְבַּהּ יהוה צְבָאוֹת

---

13. The fact that this verse is quoted after the previous three lines indicates that it is a biblical support for these three concepts. It appears that the phrase "and the Almighty, Who is holy" parallels **"You are holy"**; "And the Master of all ... when He does judgment on all [he will be exalted]" refers to **"and Your Name causes awe"**; and that which the verse says "Who is the ruler over all the Heavenly and earthly legions" corresponds to **"and there is no other power except You."**

| when He does judgment on all | בְּמִשְׁפָּט |

| and the Almighty, Who is holy (different and separate from everything), | וְהָאֵל הַקָּדוֹשׁ |

| will become more holy in our eyes through the kindness He does with us." | נִקְדַּשׁ בִּצְדָקָה |

| You are the Source of Blessing, Master of all | בָּרוּךְ אַתָּה יהוה |

| **the King, Who is holier than all else.** | **הַמֶּלֶךְ הַקָּדוֹשׁ.** |

קְדוּשַׁת הַיּוֹם
The Holiness of the Day
Revelation of God's Kingdom in the Entire World

| You chose us (the Nation of Israel) from all nations (when You took us out of Egypt) | **אַתָּה** בְחַרְתָּנוּ מִכָּל הָעַמִּים |

| You showed Your love for us (by giving us the Torah) | אָהַבְתָּ אוֹתָנוּ |

| and You showed that You desired us (by giving us the special protection of the Clouds of Glory even though we had sinned with the Golden Calf) | וְרָצִיתָ בָּנוּ |

| and You elevated us from all languages (by giving us the holy language – Hebrew – which is spoken in Heaven)[14] | וְרוֹמַמְתָּנוּ מִכָּל הַלְּשׁוֹנוֹת |

---

14. One may suggest that this second group of phrases is highlighting the special qualities of the three major Festivals, as well as the Days of Awe. The phrase "You chose us from all nations" is supplemented by "You elevated us from all languages," *implying* that God redeemed us from Egyptian bondage (alluding to Pesach) not only in a physical sense, but also spiritually, represented by *lashon hakodesh,* the holy tongue, which conveys the morals and conduct of the Torah (see *Moreh Nevuchim* 3:8). Following this, "You made us holy by giving us the *mitzvos*" expands upon what was stated previously, "You showed your love for us," since the Torah that God gave us (alluding to Shavuos) is not simply a book of knowledge, but rather teaches us how to act in a way which imbues us with holiness. "And Your Name ... You have called on us" develops the earlier phrase "and You showed that You desired us," for God not only showed that He desired us by protecting us with the Clouds of Glory (alluding to Succos), but He also attached His Great and Holy Name to us to signify our uniqueness. We also mention

and You made us holy by giving us the *mitzvos* which permeate us with holiness	וְקִדַּשְׁתָּנוּ בְּמִצְוֹתֶיךָ
and You have brought us close, our King, to Your service	וְקֵרַבְתָּנוּ מַלְכֵּנוּ לַעֲבוֹדָתֶךָ
and Your Name which is great (as we see from Your acts)	וְשִׁמְךָ הַגָּדוֹל
and holy (as we see from Your directing the world with a mastery beyond our comprehension)	וְהַקָּדוֹשׁ
You have called on us — for we are called the Nation of God.	עָלֵינוּ קָרָאתָ.

ON SATURDAY NIGHT ADD:

And You made known to us	**וַתּוֹדִיעֵנוּ**
Master of all, the Master of all strength Who is able to do anything and Who takes care of us with Divine Providence,	יהוה אֱלֹהֵינוּ
Your laws which are proper and understandable	אֶת מִשְׁפְּטֵי צִדְקֶךָ
and You taught us to also do those decrees for which we do not understand the reason, just because they are Your desire.	וַתְּלַמְּדֵנוּ לַעֲשׂוֹת (בָּהֶם) חֻקֵּי רְצוֹנֶךָ
And You gave us (at Mount Sinai),	וַתִּתֶּן לָנוּ
Master of all, the Master of all strength Who is able to do anything and Who takes care of us with Divine Providence,	יהוה אֱלֹהֵינוּ
ethical *mitzvos* that one is commanded to do for his fellow man	מִשְׁפָּטִים יְשָׁרִים
and the teachings of truth of the Written Law and the Oral Law	וְתוֹרוֹת אֱמֶת

"and You have brought us close, **our King,** to Your service," which represents the Days of Awe (note the previous blessing's conclusion of "**the King** Who is holier than all else"), connoting that these special days are meant to bring us closer to the service of God.

(and) *mitzvos* we are obligated
to do for God, whether we understand
their reason or not, all of them are good

חֻקִּים וּמִצְוֹת טוֹבִים

and You gave us as an inheritance the
Festivals at a time of joy because of the season
(spring, or time of harvest or gathering)

וַתַּנְחִילֵנוּ זְמַנֵּי שָׂשׂוֹן

and Festivals that give us an inspiration of holiness
(including Rosh Hashanah and Yom Kippur)

וּמוֹעֲדֵי קֹדֶשׁ

and days that we are permitted to bring voluntary
offerings of donation (i.e., Chol HaMoed)

וְחַגֵּי נְדָבָה

and You gave us as an inheritance the
holiness of the Shabbos (which includes the
additional soul that we are given each Shabbos)

וַתּוֹרִישֵׁנוּ קְדֻשַּׁת שַׁבָּת

and the honor of the Festivals (by
decreeing them as days of rest)

וּכְבוֹד מוֹעֵד

and the sacrifice of *shalmei chagigah*
that was brought on each of the three Festivals
(Pesach, Shavuos and Succos).

וַחֲגִיגַת הָרֶגֶל

And You, Master of all, the Master of all
strength Who is able to do anything and Who takes
care of us with Divine Providence, have separated

וַתַּבְדֵּל יהוה אֱלֹהֵינוּ

between things that are holy and
things that are not holy

בֵּין קֹדֶשׁ לְחוֹל

(and at the time of Creation You separated)
between light and darkness

בֵּין אוֹר לְחֹשֶׁךְ

(and through Torah and *mitzvos* You separated)
between Israel and all the nations of the world

בֵּין יִשְׂרָאֵל לָעַמִּים

(and You separated between)
the seventh day, Shabbos, and
the other days of the week (by forbidding *melachah*)

בֵּין יוֹם הַשְּׁבִיעִי לְשֵׁשֶׁת יְמֵי הַמַּעֲשֶׂה

(and) You separated
between the holiness of
Shabbos and the holiness of the Festivals (when food preparations are permissible)

בֵּין קְדֻשַּׁת שַׁבָּת לִקְדֻשַּׁת יוֹם טוֹב הִבְדַּלְתָּ

and the last day of
Succos (Shemini Atzeres)
You made holier than the six days of Chol HaMoed[15]

וְאֶת יוֹם הַשְּׁבִיעִי מִשֵּׁשֶׁת יְמֵי הַמַּעֲשֶׂה קִדַּשְׁתָּ

and You made Your nation Israel
into three categories — Kohanim,
Levi'im and Yisraelim

הִבְדַּלְתָּ וְקִדַּשְׁתָּ אֶת עַמְּךָ יִשְׂרָאֵל

and You made them all holy with Your holiness.

בִּקְדֻשָּׁתֶךָ.

And the Master of all, the Master of all
strength Who is able to do anything and Who
takes care of us with Divine Providence, gave us

וַתִּתֶּן לָנוּ יהוה אֱלֹהֵינוּ

with love (because of His love for us
He made known to us that today is the Day
of Judgment so we should prepare)

בְּאַהֲבָה[16]

ON WEEKDAYS SAY:

this day of Rosh Hashanah
when everyone is remembered and judged

אֶת יוֹם הַזִּכָּרוֹן הַזֶּה

a day on which there is a *mitzvah*
to blow the *shofar*
(which humbles our hearts to repent)

יוֹם תְּרוּעָה

---

15. The literal translation of this phrase is "and You made holy the seventh day from the six days of work." But this simple meaning makes it a redundancy, since we have already mentioned the separation of Shabbos from the six days of the week. Therefore, the *Rosh* explains [*Pesachim*, Ch. 10 §11] that it refers to the seventh day following the six intermediate days of Succos. That is, according to the Torah Succos has six days of Chol HaMoed (although in the Diaspora we have only five days of Chol HaMoed as we keep the first two days of Succos with equal stringency since the Temple era) and on those days one may do *melachah* which if not done, would cause financial loss. However, the would-be seventh day after these six was made holy by God to become another Festival, called Shemini Atzeres, when one may not do those *melachos* permitted on Chol HaMoed, but only those that are permitted on other Festivals (like those of food preparation). That is what is meant here: that God made the last day of Succos (the "seventh day") holier than the six of Chol HaMoed.

16. The reference of this word depends on whether it is Shabbos. On a weekday the obvious reference is to the love with which God gave us the day of Rosh Hashanah. However, on Shabbos when we add "the Shabbos day" before mentioning Rosh Hashanah, the reference is to the love with which God gave us Shabbos, and the words "with love" that we add later ("when we only mention the verses of *teruah* You gave us with love") are referring to Rosh Hashanah, which is mentioned in the same phrase (Rav Avraham Pam).

with love You gave us] this Shabbos
day [which is called a great gift]

אֶת יוֹם הַשַּׁבָּת הַזֶּה

and this day of Rosh Hashanah on
which everyone is remembered and judged

וְאֶת יוֹם הַזִּכָּרוֹן הַזֶּה

a day when we only mention the verses
of *teruah* You gave us with love

יוֹם זִכְרוֹן תְּרוּעָה בְּאַהֲבָה

a day on which we are called and gather
to sanctify ourselves in prayer

מִקְרָא קֹדֶשׁ

(and) it is a day that is a
remembrance of our going out of Egypt
(for on Rosh Hashanah our servitude ended).

זֵכֶר לִיצִיאַת מִצְרָיִם.

The Master of all strength, Who is able to do anything
and Who takes care of us with Divine Providence,

אֱלֹהֵינוּ

and the God Who took care of our
Fathers with Divine Providence

וֵאלֹהֵי אֲבוֹתֵינוּ

may our remembrance and consideration go up

יַעֲלֶה

and come

וְיָבֹא

and reach

וְיַגִּיעַ

and be seen in a good way

וְיֵרָאֶה

and be accepted with desire

וְיֵרָצֶה

and be heard well

וְיִשָּׁמַע

and be considered

וְיִפָּקֵד

and be remembered forever

וְיִזָּכֵר

our remembrance (i.e., our special relationship with You)

זִכְרוֹנֵנוּ

and Your special consideration to do good for us

וּפִקְדוֹנֵנוּ

and the remembrance of the covenants You made with our Fathers	וְזִכְרוֹן אֲבוֹתֵינוּ
and the remembrance of the promise to bring *Mashiach,* a descendant of David Your servant,	וְזִכְרוֹן מָשִׁיחַ בֶּן דָוִד עַבְדֶּךָ
and the remembrance of Jerusalem, the city of Your Holiness, which is now in ruins	וְזִכְרוֹן יְרוּשָׁלַיִם עִיר קָדְשֶׁךָ
and the remembrance of Your nation, the House of Israel, which is now in exile	וְזִכְרוֹן כָּל עַמְּךָ בֵּית יִשְׂרָאֵל
(may all of these remembrances) come before You	לְפָנֶיךָ
for salvation (for all of Israel)	לִפְלֵיטָה
for good (for all of Israel)	לְטוֹבָה
to find favor in Your eyes and in everyone's eyes	לְחֵן
and to grant us our requests (even though we are not deserving)	וּלְחֶסֶד
and for mercy (not punishing us according to our wrongdoings)	וּלְרַחֲמִים
and for life (for all of Israel)	לְחַיִּים
and for peace (for all of Israel)	וּלְשָׁלוֹם
on this day of Rosh Hashanah (when everyone is remembered and judged).	בְּיוֹם הַזִּכָּרוֹן הַזֶּה
Remember us, Master of all	זָכְרֵנוּ יהוה
the Master of all strength, Who is able to do anything and Who takes care of us with Divine Providence,	אֱלֹהֵינוּ
on this day of Rosh Hashanah to give everyone whatever is good for him	בּוֹ לְטוֹבָה

and consider us on this day for
prosperity and success

וּפָקְדֵנוּ בוֹ לִבְרָכָה

and save us on this day (of judgment)
so that we will merit life.

וְהוֹשִׁיעֵנוּ בוֹ לְחַיִּים

And with Your previous promise to
save us and to have mercy on us

וּבִדְבַר יְשׁוּעָה וְרַחֲמִים

have mercy on us because You are our Creator,
and favor us (with salvation)

חוּס וְחָנֵּנוּ

and have mercy on us because of our lowly
nature and save us, even though we are undeserving

וְרַחֵם עָלֵינוּ וְהוֹשִׁיעֵנוּ

because our eyes are looking to You in hope

כִּי אֵלֶיךָ עֵינֵינוּ

because You are the Almighty King over all

כִּי אֵל מֶלֶךְ

and You are gracious and merciful
(even to the undeserving).

חַנּוּן וְרַחוּם אָתָּה.

The Master of all strength, Who is able to do
anything and Who takes care of us with Divine Providence,

אֱלֹהֵינוּ

and the God Who took care of our
Fathers with Divine Providence

וֵאלֹהֵי אֲבוֹתֵינוּ

demonstrate Your Kingship
with the revelation of Your
Divine Presence on the entire creation

מְלוֹךְ עַל כָּל הָעוֹלָם כֻּלּוֹ בִּכְבוֹדֶךָ

and display Your exaltedness on all
the creations on earth through Your kindness

וְהִנָּשֵׂא עַל כָּל הָאָרֶץ בִּיקָרֶךָ

and reveal Your glorious might in judgment

וְהוֹפַע בַּהֲדַר גְּאוֹן עֻזֶּךָ

on all the inhabitants of Your earth.

עַל כָּל יוֹשְׁבֵי תֵבֵל אַרְצֶךָ

And (by Your bringing them
in judgment) even every plant
will know that You made it

וְיֵדַע כָּל פָּעוּל כִּי אַתָּה פְעַלְתּוֹ

and every living being (including
animals) will understand that You created it

וְיָבִין כָּל יָצוּר כִּי אַתָּה יְצַרְתּוֹ

and every living person (even the
wicked) will say

וְיֹאמַר כֹּל אֲשֶׁר נְשָׁמָה בְאַפּוֹ

the Master of all, Who takes care of
Israel with Divine Providence,
is the true King over all

יהוה אֱלֹהֵי יִשְׂרָאֵל מֶלֶךְ

and His Kingdom shall reign over everything.

וּמַלְכוּתוֹ בַּכֹּל מָשָׁלָה.

ON SHABBOS ADD:

The Master of all strength, Who is able to do anything
and Who takes care of us with Divine Providence,

אֱלֹהֵינוּ

and the God Who took care of our Fathers with
Divine Providence

וֵאלֹהֵי אֲבוֹתֵינוּ

let our rest be pleasant before You

רְצֵה בִמְנוּחָתֵנוּ

---

make us holy from Above so that
we should do Your *mitzvos* properly

קַדְּשֵׁנוּ בְּמִצְוֹתֶיךָ

and grant us Divine assistance so that
all of our occupation should be in Torah study

וְתֵן חֶלְקֵנוּ בְּתוֹרָתֶךָ

bestow upon us good in a way that we will be
satisfied with it (and not pursue our physical desires)

שַׂבְּעֵנוּ מִטּוּבֶךָ

and cause us to rejoice through
the salvation that You will bring us

וְשַׂמְּחֵנוּ בִישׁוּעָתֶךָ

ON SHABBOS ADD:

and give us as an inheritance
(the holiness that Shabbos inspires)

וְהַנְחִילֵנוּ

Master of all, the Master of all strength,
Who is able to do anything and
Who takes care of us with Divine Providence,

יהוה אֱלֹהֵינוּ

because of the love with which You loved us
(when You gave us Shabbos)

בְּאַהֲבָה

and because of the desire You have for us
(that You want us to bring sacrifices even on Shabbos)

וּבִרְצוֹן

[give us as an inheritance] the inspiration
of Shabbos, the day that You made holy,

שַׁבַּת קָדְשֶׁךָ

MINCHAH SHACHARIS MAARIV

and (through this inspiration)
You should cause Israel to have
a complete rest on Shabbos

וְיָנוּחוּ בָהּ / בוֹ / בָם יִשְׂרָאֵל

for they sanctify Your Name (by keeping Shabbos)

מְקַדְּשֵׁי שְׁמֶךָ

and (we ask that You) purify
our hearts so that we serve You
sincerely (without other motives)

וְטַהֵר לִבֵּנוּ לְעָבְדְּךָ בֶּאֱמֶת

for You, the Master of all strength
Who is able to do anything,
are truthful (and we should serve You in truth)

כִּי אַתָּה אֱלֹהִים אֱמֶת

and Your word — "and you will be for Me
a nation, and I will be for you a God"
(*Yirmiyahu* 11:4) — is true and will not change forever.

וּדְבָרְךָ אֱמֶת וְקַיָּם לָעַד

You are the Source of Blessing, Master of all,

בָּרוּךְ אַתָּה יהוה

the King over all the inhabitants of the earth

מֶלֶךְ עַל כָּל הָאָרֶץ

ON WEEKDAYS SAY:

Who chose Israel and made them holier
(than the other nations)

מְקַדֵּשׁ יִשְׂרָאֵל

ON SHABBOS SAY:

Who made the Shabbos holier (than the
other days — and gave it to us as a present)
and made Israel holier (than the other nations)

מְקַדֵּשׁ הַשַּׁבָּת וְיִשְׂרָאֵל

(and through Israel) He makes holy the day
of Rosh Hashanah (on which everyone
is remembered and judged).[17]

וְיוֹם הַזִּכָּרוֹן.

17. We should intend here to offer great thanks to God for having given us this day of
Rosh Hashanah, to enable us to earn for ourselves a favorable judgment (*Korban
Aharon*).

עבודה
Return of the Temple Service

Be pleased[18]	רְצֵה
Master of all,	יהוה
the Master of all strength, Who is able to do anything and Who takes care of us with Divine Providence,	אֱלֹהֵינוּ
with Your nation, Israel (because they are praying for the rebuilding of the Temple)	בְּעַמְּךָ יִשְׂרָאֵל
and with their prayer (for the rebuilding of the Temple)[19]	וּבִתְפִלָּתָם
and return the service of the Temple	וְהָשֵׁב אֶת הָעֲבוֹדָה
(even) to the Holy of Holies.	לִדְבִיר בֵּיתֶךָ
And the fire-offerings that they will bring	וְאִשֵּׁי יִשְׂרָאֵל
and the prayer of Israel (which is now in place of the offerings)	וּתְפִלָּתָם
because of Your love for the Jews	בְּאַהֲבָה
accept with desire	תְקַבֵּל בְּרָצוֹן
and help us that it should always be desirable	וּתְהִי לְרָצוֹן תָּמִיד
the service (whether offerings or prayers) of Israel, Your nation.	עֲבוֹדַת יִשְׂרָאֵל עַמֶּךָ

---

18. Before reciting this blessing one should instill in his heart the love of all Jews, regardless of their origin or affiliation, for we ask here that God should be pleased with all of His nation Israel (*Darchei Chaim*). [The saintly Chofetz Chaim wrote (*Ahavas Yisrael*, Ch. 2) that we constantly pray for the rebuilding of the Temple, but we neglect to contemplate the cause of its destruction, which was hatred for an unjustifiable reason. Therefore if we want the Temple to be rebuilt we must first rectify this sin and love all Jews.]

19. Since Jews pray in every *Shemoneh Esrei* for the rebuilding of the Temple (and not only for material things, as is the way of the world), God should accept and answer our prayers (R' Yehudah ben Yakar).

And let us merit to see (the *Shechinah* — Divine Presence) with our own eyes (i.e., soon, in our days)

וְתֶחֱזֶינָה עֵינֵינוּ

when You return Your Presence to the Temple (even if it is) in mercy (and not through our merits).

בְּשׁוּבְךָ לְצִיּוֹן בְּרַחֲמִים

You are the Source of Blessing, Master of all,

בָּרוּךְ אַתָּה יהוה

Who will return His Divine Presence to the Temple.

הַמַּחֲזִיר שְׁכִינָתוֹ לְצִיּוֹן.

הודאה
Thanking God[20]

We give thanks to You, acknowledging

מוֹדִים אֲנַחְנוּ לָךְ

that You are the Master of all

שָׁאַתָּה הוּא יהוה

the Master of all strength, Who is able to do anything and Who takes care of us with Divine Providence,

אֱלֹהֵינוּ

and the God Who took care of our Fathers with Divine Providence

וֵאלֹהֵי אֲבוֹתֵינוּ

(and that You will continue to take care of us) forever.

לְעוֹלָם וָעֶד

[You are] the Rock — Creator and Sustainer — of our lives

צוּר חַיֵּינוּ

[and You are] the Protector Who saves us from all troubles

מָגֵן יִשְׁעֵנוּ

You are the One [Who keeps us alive and saves us] in every generation.

אַתָּה הוּא לְדוֹר וָדוֹר

---

20. The *Beis Elokim* explains that the reason we bow at the beginning and end of this *brachah* is to show humility, recognizing our unworthiness for Hashem's special care, and realizing that our lives and all goodness come from Him.

We will always express our thanks to You	נוֹדֶה לְּךָ
and we will tell Your praise to others	וּנְסַפֵּר תְּהִלָּתֶךָ
for our lives — each breath — that are given over into Your hand	עַל חַיֵּינוּ הַמְּסוּרִים בְּיָדֶךָ
and for our souls that are entrusted to You (while we sleep)[21]	וְעַל נִשְׁמוֹתֵינוּ הַפְּקוּדוֹת לָךְ
and for the hidden miracles that You do for us every day[22]	וְעַל נִסֶּיךָ שֶׁבְּכָל יוֹם עִמָּנוּ
and for Your wonders of "nature" (which You renew constantly)[23]	וְעַל נִפְלְאוֹתֶיךָ
and for Your favors (that You do for us constantly)	וְטוֹבוֹתֶיךָ
that You do in all parts of the day	שֶׁבְּכָל עֵת
in the evening, morning, and afternoon.	עֶרֶב וָבֹקֶר וְצָהֳרָיִם

21. The *Midrash* (*Tehillim* 25) tells us that every night a person gives over his weary soul to God, and He returns it each morning renewed. It is concerning this that we say the *brachah* of "*Elokai Neshamah*" each morning.

22. Rabbeinu Bachai writes in his introduction to *Parshas Ki Sisa*, **"There is no individual in Klal Yisrael for whom hidden miracles don't happen *every day!*"**

23. The wonders of nature that have been revealed by men so far are much too numerous for anyone to think of. But if one thinks about one of the myriad wonders while saying this prayer, it would make the words so much more meaningful. The *Chovos HaLevavos* (*Shaar HaBechinah*, Ch. 5) writes that the wonders in one's own body are the closest to him and are the ones he should investigate.

To cite just one example: A person should appreciate the eyes with which he is reading this. Without eyesight our lives would be extremely difficult and not very pleasurable. And the eye is one of the most wondrous organs. The eye can move to see all around and adjusts its opening according to the light, to let you see in very dim light and in very bright light. A stereo focusing system automatically adjusts the eyes to let you see things that are far away and very close-up with maximum image sharpness; and a sophisticated image-enhancer clarifies tiny blurs in our vision caused by motion or darkness. And what is most amazing is that in *each* eye there are over 137 ***million*** light-sensitive receptor cells crammed into less than one square inch of the retina — sending messages to the brain at about 300 m.p.h. — to let you see the whole picture in detail and in color — instantly! (See *Designer World* [by R' Avrohom Katz], Ch. 11.)

No wonder we make a blessing every morning thanking God for our eyesight — פּוֹקֵחַ עִוְרִים — "Who gives sight to the blind" — so that we should always appreciate the miracle of sight!

You are the ultimate Good One

הַטּוֹב

for Your mercy has never finished —
for You withhold punishment
from those deserving it

כִּי לֹא כָלוּ רַחֲמֶיךָ

and you are the ultimate Merciful One
(Who not only withholds punishment, but ...)

וְהַמְרַחֵם

Whose kindness never ends —
for You even give these undeserving
people additional kindnesses —

כִּי לֹא תַמּוּ חֲסָדֶיךָ

we have always put our hope in You.

מֵעוֹלָם קִוִּינוּ לָךְ

And for all of these wonders and favors that
You do for us constantly

וְעַל כֻּלָּם

[Your Name] should be praised with the recognition
that You are the Source of all Blessing

יִתְבָּרַךְ

and may Your Name (which represents Your acts)
be exalted through the recognition of Your greatness

וְיִתְרוֹמַם שִׁמְךָ

since You are our King (Who takes care of us especially)
[and we desire that Your Name be praised and exalted]

מַלְכֵּנוּ

constantly, every day,

תָּמִיד

forever and ever.

לְעוֹלָם וָעֶד

**And inscribe for a good life
(i.e., life that will be good
for earning the World to Come)**

וּכְתוֹב לְחַיִּים טוֹבִים

all the children of Your covenant.

כָּל בְּנֵי בְרִיתֶךָ

And all the living (those who will come back to life
by the Revival of the Dead)

וְכֹל הַחַיִּים

will thank You constantly forever

יוֹדוּךָ סֶּלָה

and they will praise Your Name (which comes from Your deeds) truthfully, without any other motive	וִיהַלְלוּ אֶת שִׁמְךָ בֶּאֱמֶת
the Almighty	הָאֵל
Who saves us in all our troubles	יְשׁוּעָתֵנוּ
and Who helps us to succeed	וְעֶזְרָתֵנוּ
constantly, forever.	סֶלָה
You are the Source of Blessing, Master of all,	בָּרוּךְ אַתָּה יהוה
Whose Name is "The Good One" (for You are the ultimate good)	הַטּוֹב שִׁמְךָ
and to You alone it is fitting to give thanks (because You are the cause of all goodness).	וּלְךָ נָאֶה לְהוֹדוֹת.

שלום
Peace[24]

FOR MAARIV AND MINCHAH THE FOLLOWING IS SAID
(FOR SHACHARIS SAY שִׂים שָׁלוֹם ON PAGE 28):

An abundant peace (which includes many forms of peace: of mind, in one's house, between Jews, in the country)	שָׁלוֹם רָב
may You place upon Israel, Your nation, forever	עַל יִשְׂרָאֵל עַמְּךָ תָּשִׂים לְעוֹלָם
for You are the King over all	כִּי אַתָּה הוּא מֶלֶךְ
(and) the Master of all forms of peace (You can make peace in any situation).	אָדוֹן לְכָל הַשָּׁלוֹם.

CONTINUE AT וְטוֹב בְּעֵינֶיךָ ON PAGE 29

---

24. The last *Mishnah* states that God found no adequate vehicle for Israel's blessing other than peace. The Sages tell us (*Vayikra Rabbah* 9:9) that peace is so great that it comes at the end of all prayers. As the *Seder HaYom* writes, "Peace encompasses everything and through peace we will merit everything." Therefore, one should concentrate especially on this all-encompassing final *brachah*.

FOR SHACHARIS THE FOLLOWING IS SAID:

Grant peace (which includes peace of mind,
peace in one's house, peace between Jews,
and peace in the country)

שִׂ**ים** שָׁלוֹם

(and grant what is) good for each person

טוֹבָה

and (grant) prosperity and success

וּבְרָכָה

(and) let us find favor
in Your eyes and thereby find favor in the eyes of all who see us

חֵן

and grant our requests
(even though we are not deserving)

וָחֶסֶד

and have mercy on us
(not to punish us according to our wrongdoings)

וְרַחֲמִים

on those of us here (praying together)

עָלֵינוּ

and on all of Israel, Your nation.

וְעַל כָּל יִשְׂרָאֵל עַמֶּךָ

Since You are our Father,
give us an abundance of goodness and success

בָּרְכֵנוּ אָבִינוּ

all of us like one (equally)

כֻּלָּנוּ כְּאֶחָד

with the "light of Your face"
(which is a symbol of Your great love)

בְּאוֹר פָּנֶיךָ

because we already know from
the Revelation at Sinai that with the
"light of Your face" come great things:

כִּי בְאוֹר פָּנֶיךָ

You gave to us as a present
(not because we were deserving),

נָתַתָּ לָּנוּ

Master of all,

יהוה

the Master of all strength, Who is able to do anything
and Who takes care of us with Divine Providence,

אֱלֹהֵינוּ

the Torah that teaches us how to live

תּוֹרַת חַיִּים

and (through it) the love of doing kindness

וְאַהֲבַת חֶסֶד

and (You gave us with the Torah more opportunities for)
reward in the World to Come (by fulfilling the many *mitzvos*)

וּצְדָקָה

and (as reward for keeping the Torah You give us also)
an abundance of goodness and success (in this world)

וּבְרָכָה

and (in the merit of keeping the Torah You give us)
special mercy

וְרַחֲמִים

and (as a reward for keeping the Torah You give us)
a long, healthy life

וְחַיִּים

and (through the Torah we have) peace of body and mind
(because all the ways of the Torah are peaceful).

וְשָׁלוֹם

CONTINUE HERE FOR ALL PRAYERS:

And it should be good in Your eyes

וְטוֹב בְּעֵינֶיךָ

to give an abundance of goodness and
success to Your nation, Israel

לְבָרֵךְ אֶת עַמְּךָ יִשְׂרָאֵל

in all parts of the day

בְּכָל עֵת

and in all hours of each part of the day

וּבְכָל שָׁעָה

with Your peace (which is a complete peace).

בִּשְׁלוֹמֶךָ

In the book of life

בְּסֵפֶר חַיִּים

of abundant goodness and success

בְּרָכָה

and peace between a man and his friend

וְשָׁלוֹם

and a good (ample and easy) livelihood

וּפַרְנָסָה טוֹבָה

may we be remembered

נִזָּכֵר

and may we be inscribed before You	וְנִכָּתֵב לְפָנֶיךָ
we (who are standing together praying)	אֲנַחְנוּ
and all of Your nation, Israel	וְכָל עַמְּךָ בֵּית יִשְׂרָאֵל
(let us be remembered and inscribed) for a truly good life (i.e., a life that will enable us to earn the World to Come)	לְחַיִּים טוֹבִים
and for peace within ourselves (that we should be satisfied with the materialistic things that we have).	וּלְשָׁלוֹם.

THERE ARE DIFFERENT CUSTOMS CONCERNING THE CONCLUSION OF THIS BLESSING AND EVERYONE SHOULD FOLLOW HIS CUSTOM. IF ONE DOES NOT KNOW HIS CUSTOM HE SHOULD RECITE THE VERSION ON THE RIGHT.

You are the Source of Blessing, בָּרוּךְ אַתָּה	You are the Source of Blessing, Master of all, בָּרוּךְ אַתָּה יהוה
Master of all, יהוה	Who gives an abundance of goodness and success הַמְבָרֵךְ
Who makes peace among all. עוֹשֶׂה הַשָּׁלוֹם.	to His nation, Israel, אֶת עַמּוֹ יִשְׂרָאֵל with peace. בַּשָּׁלוֹם.

תחנונים
Personal Requests[25]

The Master of all strength, Who is able to do anything and Who takes care of me with Divine Providence,	אֱלֹהַי
help me to guard my tongue from speaking bad about others (*lashon hara*)	נְצוֹר לְשׁוֹנִי מֵרָע

25. Although this paragraph is designated for personal requests, it is questionable if one should make any personal requests on Rosh Hashanah. The *Maggid Tzedek* (quoted in *Siddur HaGra*) explains that our sole intention in the Rosh Hashanah prayers should be to pray for the glorification of the honor of God, and that is the theme of the additions for Rosh Hashanah. Therefore the Sages did not add any requests for forgiveness or sustenance, only a short prayer for life, and that only because God is "a King who desires life." We should be like a subject coming to a king and saying that even though we have many needs, that is not what is most important; rather, our primary concern

and [help me to guard] my lips
from speaking deceit or falsehood

וּשְׂפָתַי מִדַּבֵּר מִרְמָה

and help me so that my soul
should be silent (and even in thought
I should not get angry) at those who curse me

וְלִמְקַלְלַי נַפְשִׁי תִדּוֹם

and help me so that my soul
should be like dust (very humble)
before everyone (and not mind insults).

וְנַפְשִׁי כֶּעָפָר לַכֹּל תִּהְיֶה

Open up my heart so that it should be
receptive and understand Your Torah

פְּתַח לִבִּי בְּתוֹרָתֶךָ

and help my soul eagerly pursue
Your *mitzvos*

וּבְמִצְוֹתֶיךָ תִּרְדּוֹף נַפְשִׁי

and all those who want to harm me
(whether in mundane matters or spiritual
matters, i.e., to cause me to sin)

וְכֹל הַחוֹשְׁבִים עָלַי רָעָה

quickly annul their plan

מְהֵרָה הָפֵר עֲצָתָם

and ruin their thought
(even before they make plans).

וְקַלְקֵל מַחֲשַׁבְתָּם

Act (take us out of exile)
for the sake of Your Name,
which is desecrated now among the gentiles[26]

עֲשֵׂה לְמַעַן שְׁמֶךָ

act (take us out of exile)
for the sake of Your right hand,[27]
which You have now withdrawn in our exile

עֲשֵׂה לְמַעַן יְמִינֶךָ

---

is Your Name that is being profaned. And with this we may trust that God will take care of our needs, as is explained based on the verse, "I am to my Beloved and my Beloved is to me" (*Shir HaShirim* 6:3): When all my requests are for my Beloved's sake, then my Beloved will take care of me.

26. The *Tur* (*Orach Chaim*, Ch. 122) wrote that anyone who is careful to say these four phrases (starting with this one) will merit to greet the Divine Presence. At the end of our prayers we reiterate that which is most important to us — the honor of God — and therefore we ask God to take us out of exile for His sake, so that the whole world will see His glory. One who says this sincerely will merit greeting the Divine Presence.

27. The "right hand" of God symbolizes His redeeming power (*The World of Prayer*).

act (take us out of exile)
for the sake of Your Holiness
(so that all will know that You lead us with holiness)

עֲשֵׂה לְמַעַן קְדֻשָּׁתֶךָ

act (take us out of exile)
for the sake of Your Torah
(so the Torah can be studied properly and completely)

עֲשֵׂה לְמַעַן תּוֹרָתֶךָ

and in order that Your dear ones, Israel,
should be released from all troubles

לְמַעַן יֵחָלְצוּן יְדִידֶיךָ

save them with (the wonders and miracles that
are attributed to) Your right hand

הוֹשִׁיעָה יְמִינְךָ

and answer (even) me in this prayer.

וַעֲנֵנִי.

Let the words of my prayer
be desirable to You[28]

יִהְיוּ לְרָצוֹן אִמְרֵי פִי

and also the thoughts of my heart which
I cannot express [should be desirable] before You,

וְהֶגְיוֹן לִבִּי לְפָנֶיךָ

Master of all,

יהוה

My Rock, on Whom I rely for all my requests

צוּרִי

and Who will be my Redeemer.

וְגֹאֲלִי.

ONE SHOULD BOW AND GO BACK THREE STEPS
LIKE A SERVANT DEPARTING FROM HIS MASTER

The One Who makes peace in Heaven
(among the angels)

עֹשֶׂה [הַ]שָּׁלוֹם בִּמְרוֹמָיו

may He make peace (for those on earth,
who are naturally quarrelsome)

הוּא יַעֲשֶׂה שָׁלוֹם

on those of us here (praying together)

עָלֵינוּ

and on all of Israel

וְעַל כָּל יִשְׂרָאֵל

---

28. *Seder HaYom* (quoted also in *Mishnah Berurah* 122:8) writes that one should say this verse with great concentration, for it will help considerably that his prayers should not go unanswered.

and (you, the angels who escort me,) agree to my prayer, and say Amen!	וְאִמְרוּ אָמֵן.
May it be Your desire,	יְהִי רָצוֹן מִלְּפָנֶיךָ
Master of all,	יהוה
the Master of all strength, Who is able to do anything and Who takes care of us with Divine Providence,	אֱלֹהֵינוּ
and the God Who took care of our Fathers with Divine Providence,	וֵאלֹהֵי אֲבוֹתֵינוּ
that You should rebuild the Temple (so that we will be able to do the ultimate *avodah* — service to You)	שֶׁיִּבָּנֶה בֵּית הַמִּקְדָּשׁ
quickly and in our lifetime	בִּמְהֵרָה בְיָמֵינוּ
and help us so that all our toil should be in learning Your Torah	וְתֵן חֶלְקֵנוּ בְּתוֹרָתֶךָ
and there, in the Temple, we will bring offerings (the ultimate service) with reverence	וְשָׁם נַעֲבָדְךָ בְּיִרְאָה
as [they brought offerings and served in reverence] in the earlier days (of Moshe)	כִּימֵי עוֹלָם
and as they did in the previous years (of Shlomo *HaMelech*).	וּכְשָׁנִים קַדְמוֹנִיּוֹת.
And then, it will be pleasing to the Master of all	וְעָרְבָה לַיהוה
the offerings that will be brought in the Temple (which is in the portion of Yehudah in Jerusalem)	מִנְחַת יְהוּדָה וִירוּשָׁלָיִם
as [the offerings were pleasing] in the earlier days (of Moshe)	כִּימֵי עוֹלָם
and as they were in the previous years (of Shlomo *HaMelech*).	וּכְשָׁנִים קַדְמוֹנִיּוֹת.

Introduction to מלכיות, זכרונות ושופרות
(from *Sefer HaIkkarim* 1:4)

There are three essential, all-encompassing principles which are funda-mental to Judaism: the existence of God, Divine Providence regarding reward and punishment, and the Divine origin of Torah . . . and the indicator that these are the fundamentals of belief, through which a person can achieve true success, is that the *Anshei Knesses HaGedolah* (Men of the Great Assem-bly) composed the Rosh Hashanah *Mussaf* prayer with three central blessings, מלכיות זכרונות ושופרות, which correspond to these three fundamental princi-ples. The purpose of the three blessings is to instill in us the knowledge that belief in these principles, and all that they encompass, will enable us to emerge from before God with a favorable judgment.

The *brachah* of מלכיות corresponds to the principle of the exis-tence of God, as indicated by the text of the blessing, "Therefore, we trust in You . . . to see, without delay, the glory of Your great strength, to remove idol worship from the earth . . . and everyone will accept the yoke of Your Kingdom to do whatever You command."

The *brachah* of זכרונות refers to God's Divine Providence regard-ing reward and punishment: "You remember all the actions that were done in the world, and You consider the judgment of all the people that have lived (since Creation). Before You everything is revealed, even that which the person himself did not realize he did."

The *brachah* of שופרות alludes to the third principle, which is be-lief in the Divine origin of Torah, and therefore it begins, "You, God, revealed Yourself (at the time of the giving of the Torah) in a cloud that showed Your Divine Presence, to speak with Your holy nation." And since the giving of the Torah was done through the medium of a supernatural *shofar* blast, this blessing is called שופרות.

To hint to the fact that these three principles are the means to successfully achieve our desired goal, *Yeshayahu* [Isaiah] combined them in one verse (*Yeshayahu* 33:22): "For God is our judge, God is our lawgiver, God is our king; He shall save us." "God is our judge" refers to God's Divine Providence [regarding reward and punishment] . . . "God is our lawgiver" hints at the Divine origin of Torah, which is the third principle. "God is our king" refers to the first principle, the existence of God, Who is the king of the entire world . . . And he concludes, "He shall save us," implying that belief in these three principles grants us superiority over the entire world, and therefore it is fitting that He should save us.

Mussaf for the Day of Judgment

When I call in the name of the Master of all	**כִּי** שֵׁם יהוה אֶקְרָא
you should ascribe greatness to the Master of all strength, Who is able to do anything and Who takes care of us with Divine Providence.	הָבוּ גֹדֶל לֵאלֹהֵינוּ.
Master of all — in particular, My Master	אֲדֹנָי
please open my lips (because I am afraid and ashamed to open them)	שְׂפָתַי תִּפְתָּח
and [help me pray with concentration, so] my mouth will [be able to] tell Your true praise.	וּפִי יַגִּיד תְּהִלָּתֶךָ.

אבות
Our God and the God of Our Fathers,
Who Created Everything, and Protected Abraham[1]

You are the source of blessing (an expression of praise)	**בָּרוּךְ** אַתָּה
Master of all (Who always was, is, and will be)	יהוה
the Master of all strength, Who is able to do anything and Who takes care of us with Divine Providence,	אֱלֹהֵינוּ
and the God Who took care of our Fathers with Divine Providence (and made a covenant with each of them)	וֵאלֹהֵי אֲבוֹתֵינוּ
the God Who made a covenant with our father Abraham (who excelled in kindness)	אֱלֹהֵי אַבְרָהָם

1. One must be exceedingly careful to concentrate when saying this *brachah,* because otherwise he does not fulfill his obligation to pray. In the time of the *Gemara* one would have to repeat the *Shemoneh Esrei* if he had not concentrated on it. Nowadays, however, when we are not sure that the second time will yield the proper concentration either, we do not repeat the *Shemoneh Esrei.* [Nevertheless, if one did not concentrate for the first *brachah* he should still finish the prayer (*Kehillos Yaakov, Brachos,* Ch. 26).]

the God Who made a covenant with our father Isaac (who excelled in service of God)	אֱלֹהֵי יִצְחָק
and the God Who made a covenant with our father Jacob (who excelled in learning Torah)	וֵאלֹהֵי יַעֲקֹב
He is the Almighty (all power is His, especially in exercising the attribute of mercy)	הָאֵל
Who is the Great One (all greatness is His, especially in exercising the attribute of kindness)	הַגָּדוֹל
(and) He is the Strong One (all strength is His, especially in exercising the attribute of judgment)	הַגִּבּוֹר
and He alone deserves to be feared (because no being has the ability to do good or bad except Him)	וְהַנּוֹרָא
for He is the supreme God Who is the ultimate cause of everything	אֵל עֶלְיוֹן
Who always does kindnesses that are purely good	גּוֹמֵל חֲסָדִים טוֹבִים
and He recreates everything, constantly, every day	וְקוֹנֵה הַכֹּל
and every day He recalls for our benefit the kindnesses performed by the forefathers	וְזוֹכֵר חַסְדֵי אָבוֹת
and He constantly brings the Redeemer closer	וּמֵבִיא גוֹאֵל
to the forefathers' children's children (even though the merit of the forefathers might already be used up)	לִבְנֵי בְנֵיהֶם
for the sake of His Name (which will be sanctified at the time of the Redemption)	לְמַעַן שְׁמוֹ
[and He will also bring the Redeemer] because of His great love for the Jewish people.	בְּאַהֲבָה
Remember us for life in this world (in order that we may earn the World to Come by doing *mitzvos* here)	**זָכְרֵנוּ לְחַיִּים**

King, Who desires life
(and not death for a sinner,
but rather that he should repent)

מֶלֶךְ חָפֵץ בַּחַיִּים

and write us in the
Book of the Righteous, for life

וְכָתְבֵנוּ בְּסֵפֶר הַחַיִּים

for Your sake, in order that we may serve You[2]

לְמַעַנְךָ

the Master of all strength
Who is able to do anything and is the One
Who apportions life to all.

אֱלֹהִים חַיִּים

He is the King over all

מֶלֶךְ

Who is the Helper (to help one succeed)

עוֹזֵר

and the Savior (from trouble)

וּמוֹשִׁיעַ

and the Protector (to prevent trouble from coming).

וּמָגֵן

You are the Source of Blessing, Master of all,

בָּרוּךְ אַתָּה יהוה

the Protector of Abraham (and because of Abraham
He continues His protection over us).

מָגֵן אַבְרָהָם.

גבורות

The Mighty Acts of God and the Revival of the Dead

You alone are eternally Strong

אַתָּה גִּבּוֹר לְעוֹלָם

Master of all

אֲדֹנָי

You even revive the dead (which shows the
greatest strength, contradicting all laws of nature)

מְחַיֵּה מֵתִים אַתָּה

[and] You have an abundance of
strength with which to save.

רַב לְהוֹשִׁיעַ

---

2. R' Hirtz Shatz in his *Siddur* writes that when one says these words he should think
that if he only repents he will live, and should resolve to do *teshuvah*.

He provides all the living with their food and other needs in kindness (not because they are deserving)	מְכַלְכֵּל חַיִּים בְּחֶסֶד
He revives the dead with great mercy (searching for merits with which they would deserve revival)	מְחַיֶּה מֵתִים בְּרַחֲמִים רַבִּים
He supports those who are falling (whether physically, emotionally, or financially)	סוֹמֵךְ נוֹפְלִים
and He heals the sick from all types of illnesses (even when doctors have given up hope)	וְרוֹפֵא חוֹלִים
and He opens the bonds of those who are restricted (e.g., giving movement to our limbs when we awaken)	וּמַתִּיר אֲסוּרִים
and He will keep His promise to those sleeping in the dust (the dead), to revive them.	וּמְקַיֵּם אֱמוּנָתוֹ לִישֵׁנֵי עָפָר
Who is like You (who can do as many mighty deeds, which are infinite, even for one person)?	מִי כָמוֹךָ
— You, to Whom all mighty deeds belong! —	בַּעַל גְּבוּרוֹת
And who is comparable to You in even one of Your mighty deeds (which are of the highest quality)?	וּמִי דוֹמֶה לָּךְ
You are the King over all	מֶלֶךְ
Who causes death and revival in many respects (such as sleep and awakening, poverty and wealth)	מֵמִית וּמְחַיֶּה
and, like the sprouting of a seed, You bring the Salvation (the Revival of the Dead).	וּמַצְמִיחַ יְשׁוּעָה
Who is like You, who has as much mercy on his sons as You, the Merciful Father, have for us	**מִי כָמוֹךָ אַב הָרַחֲמִים**
(and) remembers His creatures, out of mercy, for life.	**זוֹכֵר יְצוּרָיו לְחַיִּים בְּרַחֲמִים**

And (from the mighty deeds that we mentioned) we see that You are surely trusted to revive the dead.

וְנֶאֱמָן אַתָּה לְהַחֲיוֹת מֵתִים

You are the Source of Blessing, Master of all,

בָּרוּךְ אַתָּה יהוה

the Reviver of all the dead (from Adam until the time of the Revival).[3]

מְחַיֵּה הַמֵּתִים.

קְדוּשַׁת הַשֵּׁם
Return of the Glory of God's Kingdom (to Zion)

You, Yourself, are holy (different and separate from everything)

אַתָּה קָדוֹשׁ

and Your Name (which comes from Your many acts) reveals holiness

וְשִׁמְךָ קָדוֹשׁ

and the holy ones — Israel —

וּקְדוֹשִׁים

(when *Mashiach* comes) will praise You every day, forever.

בְּכָל יוֹם יְהַלְלוּךָ סֶּלָה.

And then (in the time of *Mashiach*) [may it be speedily in our days]

וּבְכֵן

[You shall] put Your fear (which will be a catalyst for repentance)

תֵּן פַּחְדְּךָ

Master of all

יהוה

the Master of all strength, Who is able to do anything and Who takes care of us with Divine Providence,

אֱלֹהֵינוּ

on all Your works (which refers to the Jewish people)

עַל כָּל מַעֲשֶׂיךָ

and (put) Your dread

וְאֵימָתְךָ

---

3. Even though many bodies have decomposed over thousands of years, and some have been burned and their dust has been scattered, and others have drowned at sea, Hashem with His great might will recognize and recompose the bodies and return to them their original souls (*Yesod VeShoresh HaAvodah*).

on all that You have created (which refers to the gentiles).	עַל כָּל מַה שֶּׁבָּרֵאתָ
And then all the Jews will fear You	וְיִירָאוּךְ כָּל הַמַּעֲשִׂים
and all the nations of the world will bow down to You in subjugation	וְיִשְׁתַּחֲווּ לְפָנֶיךָ כָּל הַבְּרוּאִים
and all of mankind will make one group	וְיֵעָשׂוּ כֻלָּם אֲגֻדָּה אֶחָת
to do Your will with a complete heart (submitting all their tendencies to Divine service).	לַעֲשׂוֹת רְצוֹנְךָ בְּלֵבָב שָׁלֵם
As we already know (Your power from the Exodus from Egypt)	כְּמוֹ שֶׁיָּדַעְנוּ
Master of all	יהוה
the Master of all strength, Who is able to do anything and Who takes care of us with Divine Providence,	אֱלֹהֵינוּ
(where You revealed) that dominion is Yours	שֶׁהַשָּׁלְטָן לְפָנֶיךָ
and strength (in the constant running of the world) is in Your (left) hand	עֹז בְּיָדְךָ
and might (to do miracles) is in Your right hand	וּגְבוּרָה בִּימִינֶךָ
and (when You again reveal this in the time of *Mashiach*) Your Name will be revered	וְשִׁמְךָ נוֹרָא
on all the nations of the world.	עַל כָּל מַה שֶּׁבָּרֵאתָ.
And, then, Master of all, give honor to Your nation, Israel	**וּבְכֵן** תֵּן כָּבוֹד יהוה לְעַמֶּךָ
(and cause everyone to) praise those who fear You	תְּהִלָּה לִירֵאֶיךָ
and (give) to those who cling to You the good for which they rely on You	וְתִקְוָה [טוֹבָה] לְדוֹרְשֶׁיךָ

and (give) to those who yearn
for Your salvation, the ability to
praise You as they desire (without fear)

וּפִתְחוֹן פֶּה לַמְיַחֲלִים לָךְ

(and then when they no longer fear anyone) there
will be an inner joy in the land of Israel
(with the ingathering of the exiles)

שִׂמְחָה לְאַרְצֶךְ

and there will be open joy in Your city, Jerusalem,
(where the glory of the Divine Presence will be felt most)

וְשָׂשׂוֹן לְעִירֶךְ

and then the kingdom of the family of
David Your servant will sprout forth
(with the coming of *Mashiach*)

וּצְמִיחַת קֶרֶן לְדָוִד עַבְדֶּךְ

and the influence of the
son of Yishai (father of David)
Your appointed one (*Mashiach*) will spread

וַעֲרִיכַת נֵר לְבֶן יִשַׁי מְשִׁיחֶךְ

(and we ask that this should happen)
speedily in our days (so that we should
witness the return of the honor of God).

בִּמְהֵרָה בְיָמֵינוּ.

And then (when *Mashiach* has come)

וּבְכֵן

the righteous will see (that the glory of God
has returned) and they will have inner joy

צַדִּיקִים יִרְאוּ וְיִשְׂמָחוּ

and the upright ones (who do everything just for
the sake of Heaven) will be inspired to dance from joy

וִישָׁרִים יַעֲלֹזוּ

and the pious (who do more
than they are required to do by the Torah)
will raise their voices in jubilant song

וַחֲסִידִים בְּרִנָּה יָגִילוּ

and all those who do injustice and iniquity
will close their mouths

וְעוֹלָתָה תִּקְפָּץ פִּיהָ

and all evil will vanish like smoke

וְכָל הָרִשְׁעָה כֻּלָּהּ כֶּעָשָׁן תִּכְלֶה

when you remove evil
kingdoms from the earth.

כִּי תַעֲבִיר מֶמְשֶׁלֶת זָדוֹן מִן הָאָרֶץ.

And (then it will be apparent) that You alone, the Master of all, are the only King

וְתִמְלוֹךְ אַתָּה יהוה לְבַדֶּךָ

on all Your works (the Jews and the other nations)

עַל כָּל מַעֲשֶׂיךָ

(and Your rule will be especially evident) in the Temple, the place of the manifestation of the Divine Presence,

בְּהַר צִיּוֹן מִשְׁכַּן כְּבוֹדֶךָ

and in Jerusalem which is designated as Your holy city

וּבִירוּשָׁלַיִם עִיר קָדְשֶׁךָ

as it is written in Your holy words (*Tehillim* 146:10):

כַּכָּתוּב בְּדִבְרֵי קָדְשֶׁךָ

"God will reign forever

יִמְלֹךְ יהוה לְעוֹלָם

(that is,) the Master of all strength and the One able to do anything, Who dwells particularly in Zion (the Temple)

אֱלֹהַיִךְ צִיּוֹן

(He will reign) for all generations

לְדֹר וָדֹר

(therefore, Israel) praise God."

הַלְלוּיָהּ.

You are holy (different and separate from everything)

קָדוֹשׁ אַתָּה

and Your Name (which is evident from Your many acts) causes awe

וְנוֹרָא שְׁמֶךָ

and there is no other power except You

וְאֵין אֱלוֹהַּ מִבַּלְעָדֶיךָ

as it is written (*Yeshayahu* 5:16):

כַּכָּתוּב

"And the Master of all, Who is the ruler over all the Heavenly and earthly legions, will be exalted

וַיִּגְבַּהּ יהוה צְבָאוֹת

when He does judgment on all

בַּמִּשְׁפָּט

and the Almighty, Who is holy (different and separate from everything),

וְהָאֵל הַקָּדוֹשׁ

will become more holy in our eyes through the kindness He does with us."

נִקְדַּשׁ בִּצְדָקָה

You are the Source of Blessing, Master of all

בָּרוּךְ אַתָּה יהוה

the King, Who is holier than all else.

הַמֶּלֶךְ הַקָּדוֹשׁ.

קְדוּשַׁת הַיּוֹם
The Holiness of the Day[4]

You chose us (the Nation of Israel) from
all nations (when You took us out of Egypt)

אַתָּה בְחַרְתָּנוּ מִכָּל הָעַמִּים

You showed Your love for us (by giving us the Torah)

אָהַבְתָּ אוֹתָנוּ

and You showed that You desired us (by giving us the
special protection of the Clouds of Glory even though
we had sinned with the Golden Calf)

וְרָצִיתָ בָּנוּ

and You elevated us from all languages
(by giving us the holy language — Hebrew —
which is spoken in Heaven)

וְרוֹמַמְתָּנוּ מִכָּל הַלְּשׁוֹנוֹת

and You made us holy by giving us the *mitzvos*
which permeate us with holiness

וְקִדַּשְׁתָּנוּ בְּמִצְוֹתֶיךָ

and You have brought us close, our King,
to Your service

וְקֵרַבְתָּנוּ מַלְכֵּנוּ לַעֲבוֹדָתֶךָ

and Your Name which is great
(as we see from Your acts)

וְשִׁמְךָ הַגָּדוֹל

and holy (as we see from Your directing the world
with a mastery beyond our comprehension)

וְהַקָּדוֹשׁ

You have called on us — for we are called
the Nation of God.

עָלֵינוּ קָרָאתָ.

And the Master of all, the Master of all
strength Who is able to do anything and Who
takes care of us with Divine Providence, gave us

וַתִּתֶּן לָנוּ יהוה אֱלֹהֵינוּ

---

4. This *brachah* also includes the *mussaf korbanos* (the additional sacrifices) of Rosh
Hashanah and the special section called מלכיות.

with love (because of His love for us
He made known to us that today is the Day
of Judgment so we should prepare)

בְּאַהֲבָה

ON WEEKDAYS SAY:

this day of Rosh Hashanah
when everyone is remembered and judged

אֶת יוֹם הַזִּכָּרוֹן הַזֶּה

a day on which there is a *mitzvah* to blow the *shofar*
(which humbles our hearts to repent)

יוֹם תְּרוּעָה

ON SHABBOS SAY:

with love You gave us] this Shabbos
day [which is called a great gift]

אֶת יוֹם הַשַּׁבָּת הַזֶּה

and this day of Rosh Hashanah on
which everyone is remembered and judged

וְאֶת יוֹם הַזִּכָּרוֹן הַזֶּה

a day when we only mention the verses
of *teruah* You gave us with love

יוֹם זִכְרוֹן תְּרוּעָה בְּאַהֲבָה

a day on which we are called and gather
to sanctify ourselves in prayer

מִקְרָא קֹדֶשׁ

(and) it is a day that is a
remembrance of our going out of Egypt
(for on Rosh Hashanah our servitude ended).

זֵכֶר לִיצִיאַת מִצְרָיִם.

And because of our sins we have
been exiled from our land (Israel)

וּמִפְּנֵי חֲטָאֵינוּ גָּלִינוּ מֵאַרְצֵנוּ

and we have been exiled even to a place
very distant from our fields (and therefore
cannot keep the laws dependent on the land)

וְנִתְרַחַקְנוּ מֵעַל אַדְמָתֵנוּ

and we (also) cannot bring the
sacrifices that are an obligation on us

וְאֵין אֲנַחְנוּ יְכוֹלִים לַעֲשׂוֹת חוֹבוֹתֵינוּ

in the *Beis HaMikdash* (the Temple)
where You have chosen to rest Your Divine Presence

בְּבֵית בְּחִירָתֶךָ

in the House that is great in a physical sense
and holy in a spiritual sense

בַּבַּיִת הַגָּדוֹל וְהַקָּדוֹשׁ

on which Your name is called — for it is called
the House of God —

שֶׁנִּקְרָא שִׁמְךָ עָלָיו

[we cannot bring our sacrifices]
because of the hand of the enemy
that was sent to destroy Your Temple.

מִפְּנֵי הַיָּד שֶׁנִּשְׁתַּלְּחָה בְּמִקְדָּשֶׁךָ

Let it be a favorable time to let our prayers
enter the Heavens before You,

יְהִי רָצוֹן מִלְּפָנֶיךָ

Master of all,

יהוה

the Master of all strength, Who is able to do anything
and Who takes care of us with Divine Providence,

אֱלֹהֵינוּ

and the God Who took care of our Fathers
with Divine Providence (and made a covenant
with each of them),

וֵאלֹהֵי אֲבוֹתֵינוּ

the King Whose mercy is great,

מֶלֶךְ רַחֲמָן

that You should again have mercy on Israel
(and gather the exiles)

שֶׁתָּשׁוּב וּתְרַחֵם עָלֵינוּ

[and You should again have mercy] on the Temple
(that is destroyed)

וְעַל מִקְדָּשֶׁךָ

with Your great mercy

בְּרַחֲמֶיךָ הָרַבִּים

and build the (future) Temple without delay

וְתִבְנֵהוּ מְהֵרָה

and You should never remove Your Presence from it
and thereby the glory of the Third Temple will be
greater than that of the previous ones.

וּתְגַדֵּל כְּבוֹדוֹ

(If we are like sons) You are our Father,
and (if we are like servants) You are our King (so, please)

אָבִינוּ מַלְכֵּנוּ

reveal the honor of Your Kingdom
on us without delay

גַּלֵּה כְּבוֹד מַלְכוּתְךָ עָלֵינוּ מְהֵרָה

and the glory of Your Kingdom
should be revealed and seen upon
us before the eyes of all the nations

וְהוֹפַע וְהִנָּשֵׂא עָלֵינוּ לְעֵינֵי כָּל חָי

and You should bring close to You all the Jews that were exiled among the nations close to the land of Israel	וְקָרֵב פְּזוּרֵינוּ מִבֵּין הַגּוֹיִם
and also those who were scattered to distant places You should gather, even from the ends of the earth	וּנְפוּצוֹתֵינוּ כַּנֵּס מִיַּרְכְּתֵי אָרֶץ
and bring us to Your city Zion with the sound of joyous songs	וַהֲבִיאֵנוּ לְצִיּוֹן עִירְךָ בְּרִנָּה
and to Jerusalem, where the Temple is,	וְלִירוּשָׁלַיִם בֵּית מִקְדָּשְׁךָ
with ever-lasting joy.	בְּשִׂמְחַת עוֹלָם
And then we will be able to bring (in the Temple)	וְשָׁם נַעֲשֶׂה לְפָנֶיךָ
the obligatory *korbanos*	אֶת קָרְבְּנוֹת חוֹבוֹתֵינוּ
that is, the *tamid* of the morning and the *tamid* of the afternoon in the order they are written in the Torah.	תְּמִידִים כְּסִדְרָם
And the *korbanos mussaf* according to their laws that are written in the Torah.	וּמוּסָפִים כְּהִלְכָתָם
And the *korban mussaf* of	וְאֶת מוּסְפֵי יוֹם

ON SHABBOS ADD:

Shabbos and	הַשַּׁבָּת הַזֶּה וְיוֹם
Rosh Hashanah	הַזִּכָּרוֹן הַזֶּה
we will do all the preparations of the sacrifices and bring them on the Altar with love	נַעֲשֶׂה וְנַקְרִיב לְפָנֶיךָ בְּאַהֲבָה
as You commanded us	כְּמִצְוַת רְצוֹנֶךָ
as You wrote for us in Your Torah	כְּמוֹ שֶׁכָּתַבְתָּ עָלֵינוּ בְּתוֹרָתֶךָ

that Moshe wrote as a messenger
of Yours just as he heard from the
"mouth" of Your Glory

עַל יְדֵי מֹשֶׁה עַבְדֶּךָ מִפִּי כְבוֹדֶךָ

as it is written (for Shabbos — *Bamidbar* 28:9-10)
[for Rosh Hashanah — *Bamidbar* 29:1-2]

כָּאָמוּר

ON SHABBOS ADD:

"And (the *korban mussaf* of) the day of Shabbos is

וּבְיוֹם הַשַּׁבָּת

two sheep within their first year,
without blemish,

שְׁנֵי כְבָשִׂים בְּנֵי שָׁנָה תְּמִימִם

and two-tenths of an
eifah (a measure) of the
finest wheat flour mixed with olive-oil for a *korban minchah*

וּשְׁנֵי עֶשְׂרֹנִים סֹלֶת מִנְחָה בְּלוּלָה בַשֶּׁמֶן

and wine to pour on the Altar for its *nesachim*.

וְנִסְכּוֹ.

This was the *olah* of the *korban mussaf*
for every Shabbos

עֹלַת שַׁבַּת בְּשַׁבַּתּוֹ

which was sacrificed after the *olah*
of the *korban tamid*

עַל עֹלַת הַתָּמִיד

and the wine that was brought with it and poured
on the Altar for its *nesachim*."

וְנִסְכָּהּ.

SOME ALSO SAY THIS PHRASE ON SHABBOS:

[This is the *korban mussaf*
of Shabbos, and the *korban*
mussaf of Rosh Hashanah as it is written in the Torah:]

[זֶה קָרְבַּן שַׁבָּת וְקָרְבַּן הַיּוֹם כָּאָמוּר]

"And on the first day of the seventh
month — Tishrei (Rosh Hashanah)

וּבַחֹדֶשׁ הַשְּׁבִיעִי בְּאֶחָד לַחֹדֶשׁ

you should have a day on which you gather
to make it holy with prayer

מִקְרָא קֹדֶשׁ יִהְיֶה לָכֶם

any creative work [except for food
preparations] you should not do

כָּל מְלֶאכֶת עֲבֹדָה לֹא תַעֲשׂוּ

it is a day when there is a *mitzvah*
to blow the *shofar*.

יוֹם תְּרוּעָה יִהְיֶה לָכֶם.

And (for the additional sacrifice)
you should bring a *korban olah*

וַעֲשִׂיתֶם עֹלָה

for a pleasing aroma for the Master of all

לְרֵיחַ נִיחֹחַ לַיהוה

one young bull

פַּר בֶּן בָּקָר אֶחָד

(and) one ram

אַיִל אֶחָד

(and) seven male sheep in their first year

כְּבָשִׂים בְּנֵי שָׁנָה שִׁבְעָה

(all of which had to be) without blemish.''

תְּמִימִם.

And their accompanying
flour offerings and wine libations
are as it says in the Torah:

וּמִנְחָתָם וְנִסְכֵּיהֶם כִּמְדֻבָּר

"Three-tenths of an *eifah* (a measure)
of fine flour for the bull

שְׁלֹשָׁה עֶשְׂרֹנִים לַפָּר

and two-tenths of an *eifah* of fine flour
for the ram

וּשְׁנֵי עֶשְׂרֹנִים לָאָיִל

and one-tenth on an *eifah*
for each of the seven sheep

וְעִשָּׂרוֹן לַכֶּבֶשׂ

and wine for each one
according to the amount prescribed in the Torah
to pour on the Altar;

וְיַיִן כְּנִסְכּוֹ

and two male goats within their first year
(one for Rosh Hashanah and one for
Rosh Chodesh) to atone for *tumah*[5] in the Temple

וּשְׁנֵי שְׂעִירִים לְכַפֵּר

and the two daily sacrifices (one in the
morning and one in the afternoon) according
to their law that the Torah writes

וּשְׁנֵי תְמִידִים כְּהִלְכָתָם.

---

5. This refers to spiritual impurity, and like all *mussaf* goats, these come to atone for a spiritually impure person who either entered the Temple or ate from an offering (*Rashi*, *Bamidbar* 28:15).

(and all this is) in addition to the
korban olah of Rosh Chodesh and
its accompanying flour offerings

מִלְּבַד עֹלַת הַחֹדֶשׁ וּמִנְחָתָהּ

and the daily sacrifice and its accompanying
flour offerings

וְעֹלַת הַתָּמִיד וּמִנְחָתָהּ

and the wine libations that are poured
on the Altar for each of these sacrifices
according to what is fitting for them

וְנִסְכֵּיהֶם כְּמִשְׁפָּטָם

for a pleasing aroma when these sacrifices
are brought on the fire for the Master of all."

לְרֵיחַ נִיחֹחַ אִשֶּׁה לַיהוה.

ON SHABBOS ADD:

They will rejoice in the revelation of
Your Kingdom (in the future, in the world which
is completely Shabbos)

יִשְׂמְחוּ בְמַלְכוּתְךָ

those who keep the Shabbos (the seventh day)
by abstaining from work

שׁוֹמְרֵי שַׁבָּת

and who make Shabbos a day of delight
(with joyful rest, and delicious food and drinks)

וְקוֹרְאֵי עֹנֶג

the nation (Israel) who sanctifies the Shabbos
(by abstaining from work)

עַם מְקַדְּשֵׁי שְׁבִיעִי

they will all be satisfied, and also
delight in the spiritual good that
You will show in the future

כֻּלָּם יִשְׂבְּעוּ וְיִתְעַנְּגוּ מִטּוּבֶךָ

because You have found favorable
the seventh day and You have made it
holy as a day of rest

וּבַשְּׁבִיעִי רָצִיתָ בּוֹ וְקִדַּשְׁתּוֹ

since it is the most desirous of days

חֶמְדַּת יָמִים

You have called it a name ("Shabbos" —
which means rest)

אוֹתוֹ קָרָאתָ

to commemorate the act of creation
(and that You "rested" on Shabbos).

זֵכֶר לְמַעֲשֵׂה בְרֵאשִׁית.

מלכיות

Accepting on ourselves God's Kingdom

It is an obligation on us to give praise to the Master of all	**עָלֵינוּ** לְשַׁבֵּחַ לַאֲדוֹן הַכֹּל
[and] to ascribe greatness (concerning the running of the world) to the Creator of all	לָתֵת גְּדֻלָּה לְיוֹצֵר בְּרֵאשִׁית
for He did not make the souls of Israel like the souls of the gentiles (but rather of a higher nature)	שֶׁלֹּא עָשָׂנוּ כְּגוֹיֵי הָאֲרָצוֹת
and He did not place us like the families of the world (to seek false ideologies, rather He gave us the Torah).	וְלֹא שָׂמָנוּ כְּמִשְׁפְּחוֹת הָאֲדָמָה
He did not make our portion like theirs (rather, ours is to keep God's *mitzvos*)	שֶׁלֹּא שָׂם חֶלְקֵנוּ כָּהֶם
and He did not put us under the influence of the Heavenly spheres like their multitude (rather we are guided by His special Divine Providence).	וְגוֹרָלֵנוּ כְּכָל הֲמוֹנָם
[For the gentiles bow to idols and to one empty and powerless	שֶׁהֵם מִשְׁתַּחֲוִים לְהֶבֶל וָרִיק]
and they pray to gods that cannot save them.]	וּמִתְפַּלְלִים אֶל אֵל לֹא יוֹשִׁיעַ]
But we bow down on our knees	וַאֲנַחְנוּ כּוֹרְעִים
and prostrate ourselves[6]	וּמִשְׁתַּחֲוִים
and give thanks to Hashem (for our good portion)	וּמוֹדִים
before the King Who rules over even a king of kings[7]	לִפְנֵי מֶלֶךְ מַלְכֵי הַמְּלָכִים

---

6. *Ya'avetz* (on עלינו in weekday prayer) comments that despite what we say here, there are certain reasons we do not actually prostrate ourselves nowadays; nevertheless it is not a falsehood, for we bow as much as we are allowed, bending over very low.

7. The *Siddur Chasidei Ashkenaz* cites the verse (*Yechezkel* 26:7) which refers to the Babylonian monarch Nebuchadnezzar as מֶלֶךְ מְלָכִים, *a king of kings*.

the Holy One (Who is different and separate from everything) הַקָּדוֹשׁ

[and is] the Source of blessing. בָּרוּךְ הוּא.

For He spreads out the sky (around the earth) and establishes the earth (on a solid foundation) שֶׁהוּא נוֹטֶה שָׁמַיִם וְיוֹסֵד אָרֶץ

and His Throne of Glory is in the heavens above וּמוֹשַׁב יְקָרוֹ בַּשָּׁמַיִם מִמַּעַל

and the strength of His Divine Presence is in the highest heaven (above the throne of His Glory) וּשְׁכִינַת עֻזּוֹ בְּגָבְהֵי מְרוֹמִים

He is the Master of all strength, Who is able to do anything and Who takes care of us with Divine Providence, הוּא אֱלֹהֵינוּ

(and) there is no other strength besides Him. אֵין עוֹד

Our King is the ultimate truth אֱמֶת מַלְכֵּנוּ

and there is no one other than Him אֶפֶס זוּלָתוֹ

as it is written in His Torah (*Devarim* 4:39): כַּכָּתוּב בְּתוֹרָתוֹ

"And you should know and contemplate today וְיָדַעְתָּ הַיּוֹם

and (then) you should take to your heart (that you should live based on this perception) וַהֲשֵׁבֹתָ אֶל לְבָבֶךְ

that the Master of All כִּי יְהוָה

He is the Master of all strength Who is able to do anything הוּא הָאֱלֹהִים

His Divine Presence is in the heavens above בַּשָּׁמַיִם מִמַּעַל

and He rules the earth below וְעַל הָאָרֶץ מִתָּחַת

(and) there is no other strength besides Him." אֵין עוֹד.

(Since You are the only power) therefore we trust in You (to save us)	**עַל כֵּן** נְקַוֶּה לְּךָ
Master of all	יהוה
the Master of all strength, Who is able to do anything and Who takes care of us with Divine Providence,	אֱלֹהֵינוּ
(and we hope) to see, without delay, the glory of Your great strength	לִרְאוֹת מְהֵרָה בְּתִפְאֶרֶת עֻזֶּךָ
to remove abominable idolatry from the earth	לְהַעֲבִיר גִּלּוּלִים מִן הָאָרֶץ
and all idols will be totally cut down (destroyed)	וְהָאֱלִילִים כָּרוֹת יִכָּרֵתוּן
(and then) You will return Your Divine Presence to perfect the world with the kingdom of *Shaddai* [8]	לְתַקֵּן עוֹלָם בְּמַלְכוּת שַׁדַּי
and then all of humanity (Jews and gentiles) will call in the Name of Hashem (to serve Him together)	וְכָל בְּנֵי בָשָׂר יִקְרְאוּ בִשְׁמֶךָ
(and we hope that then) all the wicked will repent to serve You.	לְהַפְנוֹת אֵלֶיךָ כָּל רִשְׁעֵי אָרֶץ
Then all the inhabitants of the world will recognize and know (that You alone are the King)	יַכִּירוּ וְיֵדְעוּ כָּל יוֹשְׁבֵי תֵבֵל
(and) all knees will bow down to You (to accept Your Kingdom)	כִּי לְךָ תִּכְרַע כָּל בֶּרֶךְ
(and) in Your Name all nations will swear in truth (and they will no longer mention other gods).	תִּשָּׁבַע כָּל לָשׁוֹן

---

8. *Rokeach* says that this name of Hashem (i.e., *Shaddai*) is used here because that was the name with which Hashem created the world (see *Chagigah* 12a). *Avudraham,* quoting *Midrash Tanchuma* (*Shemos* 20), says that God told Moshe, "When I suspend the sins of man I apply the name *Shaddai*." [We see from here that the original place of *Aleinu* was in the *Mussaf* of Rosh Hashanah; only afterwards was it included at the end of the daily prayers.]

Before You, Master of all, the Master of all
strength Who is able to do anything and
Who takes care of us with Divine Providence,

לְפָנֶיךָ יהוה אֱלֹהֵינוּ

they will bow down on their knees and fall
on their faces in prostration

יִכְרְעוּ וְיִפֹּלוּ

and to the glory of Your Name
they will give great honor

וְלִכְבוֹד שִׁמְךָ יְקָר יִתֵּנוּ

and everyone will accept
the yoke of Your Kingdom
to do whatever You command

וִיקַבְּלוּ כֻלָּם אֶת עוֹל מַלְכוּתֶךָ

and (we ask that) without delay
You reveal Your Kingdom in a way
that they will accept it eternally

וְתִמְלֹךְ עֲלֵיהֶם מְהֵרָה לְעוֹלָם וָעֶד

since the rule of the world is fitting for You
(since You created the world)

כִּי הַמַּלְכוּת שֶׁלְּךָ הִיא

and forever and ever You shall rule
with honor (that is, the entire world
will honor You)

וּלְעוֹלְמֵי עַד תִּמְלוֹךְ בְּכָבוֹד

as it is written in Your Torah (*Shemos* 15:18):[9]

כַּכָּתוּב בְּתוֹרָתֶךָ

"The Master of all

יהוה

will reveal His kingdom in the entire world
forever and ever."

יִמְלֹךְ לְעֹלָם וָעֶד.

And it also says (*Bamidbar* 23:21):

וְנֶאֱמַר

"I (God) have looked well, and I have not seen
any idolatry among the people of Israel

לֹא הִבִּיט אָוֶן בְּיַעֲקֹב

nor have I seen any dishonesty among
the righteous;

וְלֹא רָאָה עָמָל בְּיִשְׂרָאֵל

---

9. Here begin the ten verses of *Malchiyos*. The *Yesod VeShoresh HaAvodah* writes that
when one says each of these verses he should think: "I accept God's Kingdom upon
myself and my descendants until the end of all generations." He should feel great joy,
recognizing that he is ruled by a holy, great and awesome King.

Master of all, the Master of all strength Who is
able to do anything and Who takes care of Israel
with Divine Providence, helps them

יהוה אֱלֹהָיו עִמּוֹ

and the Divine Presence of their King – Hashem –
rests among them (because of His love for them)."

וּתְרוּעַת מֶלֶךְ בּוֹ.

And it also says (*Devarim* 33:5):

וְנֶאֱמַר

"And God is the King over Israel when they
are upright (that is, they accept the yoke
of His Kingdom)

וַיְהִי בִישֻׁרוּן מֶלֶךְ

at the gathering of the heads of the nation,
our elders and our judges

בְּהִתְאַסֵּף רָאשֵׁי עָם

and when all the tribes of Israel join to make
one group, with peace among them
(then Hashem is their King)."

יַחַד שִׁבְטֵי יִשְׂרָאֵל.

And in Your Holy Writings
(that were said with Divine Inspiration)

וּבְדִבְרֵי קָדְשְׁךָ

it is written (*Tehillim* 22:29):

כָּתוּב לֵאמֹר

"(At the time of the Redemption all
will recognize) that to God — the Master
of all — alone is the rule of the world

כִּי לַיהוה הַמְּלוּכָה

and He rules with a powerful hand
over all the nations."

וּמוֹשֵׁל בַּגּוֹיִם.

And it also says (*Tehillim* 93:1):

וְנֶאֱמַר

"(In the days of *Mashiach* they will say)
God — the Master of all — has reigned

יהוה מָלָךְ

and He will have clothed Himself with grandeur

גֵּאוּת לָבֵשׁ

(in the future) only the Master of all
will have donned grandeur

לָבֵשׁ יהוה

and then He will gird Himself with might
to show His power

עֹז הִתְאַזָּר

(then all will realize that with God's pride
and strength) He even set up the world
that it should not fall."

אַף תִּכּוֹן תֵּבֵל בַּל תִּמּוֹט.

And it also says (*Tehillim* 24:7-10):

וְנֶאֱמַר

"O gates of Zion and Jerusalem, lift up your
lintel (so that the *Shechinah* should enter)

שְׂאוּ שְׁעָרִים רָאשֵׁיכֶם

and the entrances of the [First] Temple
(whose place is established) forever,
should be lifted by others

וְהִנָּשְׂאוּ פִּתְחֵי עוֹלָם

and the King to Whom all honor belongs
should enter.

וְיָבוֹא מֶלֶךְ הַכָּבוֹד.

Who is this King to Whom all honor belongs
(and the gates should be opened because
of fear of Him)?

מִי זֶה מֶלֶךְ הַכָּבוֹד

(The answer is:) Master of all — the mighty
One — Who shows His strength in His actions

יהוה עִזּוּז וְגִבּוֹר

(and He is) the Master of all Who helps those
whom He loves to be victorious in battle.

יהוה גִּבּוֹר מִלְחָמָה.

O gates of Zion and Jerusalem
(in the future, at the time of the redemption)
lift up your lintel

שְׂאוּ שְׁעָרִים רָאשֵׁיכֶם

and the entrances of the [Third] Temple
(whose place is established) forever,
should lift themselves up

וּשְׂאוּ פִּתְחֵי עוֹלָם

and the King to whom all honor belongs
should enter.

וְיָבֹא מֶלֶךְ הַכָּבוֹד.

Who is this King to whom all honor belongs
(that the gates should open themselves
because of fear of Him)?

מִי הוּא זֶה מֶלֶךְ הַכָּבוֹד

(The answer is:) The Master of all, Who rules over all the Heavenly and earthly legions	יְהֹוָה צְבָאוֹת
He is the King to whom all honor belongs at all times forever.''	הוּא מֶלֶךְ הַכָּבוֹד סֶלָה.
And through Your messengers, the Prophets	**וְעַל יְדֵי** עֲבָדֶיךָ הַנְּבִיאִים
it is written (*Yeshayahu* 44:6):	כָּתוּב לֵאמֹר
"So says the Master of all	כֹּה אָמַר יְהֹוָה
Who is the King of Israel and Who will redeem them from the exile	מֶלֶךְ יִשְׂרָאֵל וְגֹאֲלוֹ
(Who is) the Master of all Who rules over all the Heavenly and earthly legions	יְהֹוָה צְבָאוֹת
(He says) I was the first (i.e., before the world was created)	אֲנִי רִאשׁוֹן
and I will be the last (i.e., after the world is destroyed)	וַאֲנִי אַחֲרוֹן
and (even now) there is no power other than Me.''	וּמִבַּלְעָדַי אֵין אֱלֹהִים.
And it also says (*Ovadiah* 1:21):	וְנֶאֱמַר
"And the saviors — *Mashiach* ben Yosef and *Mashiach*[10] — ben David will go up on Mount Zion	וְעָלוּ מוֹשִׁיעִים בְּהַר צִיּוֹן
to punish those that remain on the mountain of *Esav* for what they did to the Jews and then all nations will submit to the Kingdom of God — the Master of all.''	לִשְׁפֹּט אֶת הַר עֵשָׂו וְהָיְתָה לַיהֹוָה הַמְּלוּכָה.
And it also says (*Zechariah* 14:9):	וְנֶאֱמַר

---

10. This explanation is from *Rokeach;* see also *Ramban* (*Shemos* 17:9). The concept of two *Mashiachs* is based on the Talmud (*Succah* 52a). For an interesting explanation of the two periods of *Mashiach,* see *Chidushei HaGra* (*Berachos* 13a).

"And then (at the time of the redemption) the nations will realize that the Master of all is the ruler of the entire world

וְהָיָה יהוה לְמֶלֶךְ עַל כָּל הָאָרֶץ

on that day (the gentiles will leave their gods and realize that) the Master of all is one (and there is no other god)

בַּיּוֹם הַהוּא יִהְיֶה יהוה אֶחָד

and His Name will be mentioned by all (and no other god's name will be mentioned in the world)."

וּשְׁמוֹ אֶחָד.

And in Your Torah it is also written (*Devarim* 6:4):

וּבְתוֹרָתְךָ כָּתוּב לֵאמֹר

"Hear, understand and accept (the yoke of Heaven), Israel[11]

שְׁמַע יִשְׂרָאֵל

(that) the Master of all, the Master of all strength Who is able to do anything and Who takes care of us with Divine Providence,

יהוה אֱלֹהֵינוּ

He is the Master of all — the One and Only."

יהוה אֶחָד.

The Master of all strength, Who is able to do anything and Who takes care of us with Divine Providence, and the God Who took care of our Fathers with Divine Providence

אֱלֹהֵינוּ

וֵאלֹהֵי אֲבוֹתֵינוּ

demonstrate Your Kingship with the revelation of Your Divine Presence on the entire creation

מְלוֹךְ עַל כָּל הָעוֹלָם כֻּלּוֹ בִּכְבוֹדֶךָ

---

11. This three-part explanation of the word "*Shema*" is the view of many *Rishonim*, among them *Rashba* [*Teshuvos HaRashba* 5:55], R' David *Avudraham* and R' Menachem ben Aharon [*Tzeidah LaDerech* 1:1:33]. Other *Rishonim* cite only two of the three parts of this explanation. [I have not come across any *Rishon* who says it means only "hear." Indeed, the verse of "*Shema*" is called the *mitzvah* of **accepting** the yoke of Heaven (*Berachos* 13b).]

Chovos HaLevavos writes (in the introduction to the first *shaar* [section]) that the intention of the word "*Shema*" is **not** to "hear," but rather, to believe in one's heart and accept, as in (*Shemos* 24:7) "*na'aseh ve'nishma*" [i.e., we will do and we will accept all that Hashem commands us].

and display Your exaltedness on all the creations on earth through Your kindness	וְהִנָּשֵׂא עַל כָּל הָאָרֶץ בִּיקָרֶךָ
and reveal Your glorious might in judgment	וְהוֹפַע בַּהֲדַר גְּאוֹן עֻזֶּךָ
on all the inhabitants of Your earth.	עַל כָּל יוֹשְׁבֵי תֵבֵל אַרְצֶךָ
And (by Your bringing them in judgment) even every plant will know that You made it	וְיֵדַע כָּל פָּעוּל כִּי אַתָּה פְעַלְתּוֹ
and every living being (including animals) will understand that You created it	וְיָבִין כָּל יָצוּר כִּי אַתָּה יְצַרְתּוֹ
and every living person (even the wicked) will say	וְיֹאמַר כֹּל אֲשֶׁר נְשָׁמָה בְאַפּוֹ
the Master of all, Who takes care of Israel with Divine Providence, is the true King over all	יהוה אֱלֹהֵי יִשְׂרָאֵל מֶלֶךְ
and His Kingdom shall reign over everything.	וּמַלְכוּתוֹ בַּכֹּל מָשָׁלָה

ON SHABBOS ADD:	
The Master of all strength, Who is able to do anything and Who takes care of us with Divine Providence,	אֱלֹהֵינוּ
and the God Who took care of our Fathers with Divine Providence	וֵאלֹהֵי אֲבוֹתֵינוּ
let our rest be pleasant before You	רְצֵה בִמְנוּחָתֵנוּ

make us holy from Above so that we should do Your *mitzvos* properly	קַדְּשֵׁנוּ בְּמִצְוֹתֶיךָ
and grant us Divine assistance so that all of our occupation should be in Torah study	וְתֵן חֶלְקֵנוּ בְּתוֹרָתֶךָ
bestow upon us good in a way that we will be satisfied with it (and not pursue our physical desires)	שַׂבְּעֵנוּ מִטּוּבֶךָ
and cause us to rejoice through the salvation that You will bring us	וְשַׂמְּחֵנוּ בִּישׁוּעָתֶךָ

and give us as an inheritance
(the holiness that Shabbos inspires)

וְהַנְחִילֵנוּ

Master of all, the Master of all strength,
Who is able to do anything and
Who takes care of us with Divine Providence,

יהוה אֱלֹהֵינוּ

because of the love with which You loved us
(when You gave us Shabbos)

בְּאַהֲבָה

and because of the desire You have for us
(that You want us to bring sacrifices even on Shabbos)

וּבְרָצוֹן

[give us as an inheritance] the inspiration
of Shabbos, the day that You made holy,

שַׁבַּת קָדְשֶׁךָ

and (through this inspiration)
You should cause Israel to have
a complete rest on Shabbos

וְיָנְוּחוּ בוֹ יִשְׂרָאֵל

for they sanctify Your Name (by keeping Shabbos)

מְקַדְּשֵׁי שְׁמֶךָ

and (we ask that You) purify
our hearts so that we serve You
sincerely (without other motives)

וְטַהֵר לִבֵּנוּ לְעָבְדְּךָ בֶּאֱמֶת

for You, the Master of all strength
Who is able to do anything,
are truthful (and we should serve You in truth)

כִּי אַתָּה אֱלֹהִים אֱמֶת

and Your word — "and you will be for Me
a nation, and I will be for you a God"
(*Yirmiyahu* 11:4) — is true and will not change forever.

וּדְבָרְךָ אֱמֶת וְקַיָּם לָעַד

You are the Source of Blessing, Master of all,

בָּרוּךְ אַתָּה יהוה

the King over all the inhabitants of the earth

מֶלֶךְ עַל כָּל הָאָרֶץ

Who chose Israel and made them holier
(than the other nations)

מְקַדֵּשׁ יִשְׂרָאֵל

Who made the Shabbos holier (than the
other days — and gave it to us as a present)
and made Israel holier (than the other nations)

מְקַדֵּשׁ הַשַּׁבָּת וְיִשְׂרָאֵל

(and through Israel) He makes holy the day
of Rosh Hashanah (on which everyone
is remembered and judged).[12]

וְיוֹם הַזִּכָּרוֹן.

זכרונות

God Remembers All Actions[13] and Remembers His Covenant with the Forefathers for Us

On Rosh Hashanah you remember all the
actions that were done in the world[14]

אַתָּה זוֹכֵר מַעֲשֵׂה עוֹלָם

and You consider the judgment of all the
people that have lived (since Creation).[15]

וּפוֹקֵד כָּל יְצוּרֵי קֶדֶם

---

12. We should intend here to offer great thanks to God for having given us this day of
Rosh Hashanah, to enable us to earn for ourselves a favorable judgment (*Korban
Aharon*).

13. The *Gemara* (*Rosh Hashanah* 16a) says that we recite this *brachah* (*Zichronos*) in
order that our remembrance should come before God for the good. One can ask, therefore, how does this entire introduction concerning the order of the judgment fit in with
this objective? The answer must be that when one contemplates the all-encompassing
knowledge, scrutiny and judgment of God it will inspire him to begin bringing God more
into his daily life, thereby spurring him on to greater service of God. That will cause him
to be remembered for the good.

14. R' Moshe Chaim Luzzatto (*Yalkut Yedios HaEmes*, p. 261) writes that this paragraph
describes the order of the judgment, namely, scrutiny of the past, present and future.
Why is it that God views the past and future in order to judge the present?
   R' Chaim Friedlander (*Sifsei Chaim* vol. 1, p. 105) explains that the purpose of the
nation of Israel is to perfect the world and bring it to its fulfillment. The judgment on
Rosh Hashanah is to determine how much each individual has contributed to this task.
Therefore every one of a person's actions are judged as to whether they are a continu-
ation of the actions of our Forefathers (the past) and whether they are providing
another step towards the perfection of the world (the future). In other words, the
judgment is to determine the success of our role in helping the world reach the goal that
God has determined. This emphasizes the tremendous responsibility of each individual
to contribute to the purpose of Creation.

15. *Derech HaChaim* writes here that even those who have already died are included in
the judgment. *Sifsei Chaim* explains that one's actions often have an impact which
continues for several generations. For example, a teacher of students affects not only
the person who benefited directly, but also his descendants; and a writer of *sefarim* can
affect all the future generations who learn from his works. Conversely, someone who
causes others to abandon *mitzvah* observance has adversely affected not one individual,
but several generations. Therefore, they also come to judgment on Rosh Hashanah, to
receive reward for all the good deeds that they have generated, or additional punishment for the evil they have brought about during the past year.

Before You everything is revealed, even that which the person himself did not realize he did	לְפָנֶיךָ נִגְלוּ כָּל תַּעֲלוּמוֹת
and also the myriad actions that were purposely concealed since the days of Creation	וַהֲמוֹן נִסְתָּרוֹת שֶׁמִּבְּרֵאשִׁית
for there is no forgetting before Your Throne of Glory (since everything is written down and stored there)	כִּי אֵין שִׁכְחָה לִפְנֵי כִסֵּא כְבוֹדֶךָ
and it is impossible to hide anything from before Your eyes (for Your eyes see everything).	וְאֵין נִסְתָּר מִנֶּגֶד עֵינֶיךָ
You remember everything that happened (even with the land and plants, not just with people)	אַתָּה זוֹכֵר אֶת כָּל הַמִּפְעָל
and no creature (even one hidden today, like a baby in the womb) is hidden from Your knowledge.	וְגַם כָּל הַיְצוּר לֹא נִכְחָד מִמֶּךָ
Everything is revealed and known before You, even the future generations	הַכֹּל גָּלוּי וְיָדוּעַ לְפָנֶיךָ
Master of all, the Master of all strength Who is able to do anything and Who takes care of us with Divine Providence,	יהוה אֱלֹהֵינוּ
since You see and examine until the end of all generations	צוֹפֶה וּמַבִּיט עַד סוֹף כָּל הַדּוֹרוֹת
when You bring the people of the world to judgment on Rosh Hashanah by remembering their deeds	כִּי תָבִיא חֹק זִכָּרוֹן
to judge every body and soul	לְהִפָּקֵד כָּל רוּחַ וָנֶפֶשׁ
(and) You remember the many actions (of each person, without any confusion)	לְהִזָּכֵר מַעֲשִׂים רַבִּים

and (You remember) all the numerous actions of the myriad people without end.	וַהֲמוֹן בְּרִיּוֹת לְאֵין תַּכְלִית
From the beginning of the world (when you judged Adam) You made it known that You would judge on this day	מֵרֵאשִׁית כָּזֹאת הוֹדָעְתָּ
and even before the world was created, You revealed through Your actions[16] that there would be a judgment.	וּמִלְּפָנִים אוֹתָהּ גִּלִּיתָ
This day — Rosh Hashanah — is the day that Man (the purpose of Creation) was created	זֶה הַיּוֹם תְּחִלַּת מַעֲשֶׂיךָ
(therefore You set the Day of Judgment today) a remembrance of the merciful judgment of Adam on that first day;[17]	זִכָּרוֹן לְיוֹם רִאשׁוֹן
for it is a time for Israel to be considered with mercy	כִּי חֹק לְיִשְׂרָאֵל הוּא
for it is the day of judgment by the God of Israel.	מִשְׁפָּט לֵאלֹהֵי יַעֲקֹב.
And on the countries (which are judged first) it is proclaimed	וְעַל הַמְּדִינוֹת בּוֹ יֵאָמֵר
which is destined for the sword, and which for peace	אֵיזוֹ לַחֶרֶב וְאֵיזוֹ לַשָּׁלוֹם
which is destined for hunger, and which for satiety.	אֵיזוֹ לָרָעָב וְאֵיזוֹ לְשֹׂבַע

---

16. The Talmud (*Pesachim* 54a) reveals to us that God created seven things prior to creating the world, and they are: Torah, *teshuvah* (the concept of repentance), *Gan Eden* (the Garden of Eden, the place designated for reward), *Gehinnom* (hell, the place of retribution), the Throne of His Glory, the *Beis HaMikdash* (the Holy Temple), and the name of *Mashiach*. Since God created *Gan Eden* and *Gehinnom* before the world, it was already revealed then that there would be a judgment to determine the amount of reward or punishment.

17. The *Midrash* [*Pesikta d'Rav Kahana* (p. 150a)] says that God told Adam, "Just as you underwent judgment on this day and came out with mercy, so too, your children will enter judgment on this day and emerge with mercy." *Rokeach* writes that this is referring specifically to Israel.

And (then) the individuals will be judged

וּבְרִיּוֹת בּוֹ יִפָּקֵדוּ

to mention which will be destined for
life and which for death.

לְהַזְכִּירָם לְחַיִּים וְלַמָּוֶת

Who will be able to (escape and) not be
judged this day (and so too every year
on Rosh Hashanah);

מִי לֹא נִפְקָד כְּהַיּוֹם הַזֶּה

because (at the time of judgment)
the remembrance of every being
and his characteristics come before You

כִּי זֵכֶר כָּל הַיְצוּר לְפָנֶיךָ בָּא

(as well as) the actions of everyone as they
relate to their purpose in life (come before You)

מַעֲשֵׂה אִישׁ וּפְקֻדָּתוֹ

and (also one's small actions, such as)
the footsteps of a person (are judged,
to see if they were for good)

וַעֲלִילוֹת מִצְעֲדֵי גָבֶר

(and even) the thoughts of the person when he did
the action (whether his intention was good or not)

מַחְשְׁבוֹת אָדָם

and his schemes (come before You)

וְתַחְבּוּלוֹתָיו

and (also) the strength of one's good and evil
inclinations at the time of the action (are considered).

וְיִצְרֵי מַעַלְלֵי אִישׁ

Praiseworthy is a man who does not
forget You (but his thoughts are
constantly clinging to You)

אַשְׁרֵי אִישׁ שֶׁלֹּא יִשְׁכָּחֶךָ

and (praiseworthy is) a man
who truly puts his trust in You.

וּבֶן אָדָם יִתְאַמֶּץ בָּךְ.

For those who cling to You constantly,
no evil will ever befall them

כִּי דוֹרְשֶׁיךָ לְעוֹלָם לֹא יִכָּשֵׁלוּ

and those who trust in You
will not be embarrassed forever

וְלֹא יִכָּלְמוּ לָנֶצַח כָּל הַחוֹסִים בָּךְ

for the remembrance of all
their actions will come before You
(and their merits will avert embarrassment)

כִּי זֵכֶר כָּל הַמַּעֲשִׂים לְפָנֶיךָ בָּא

and You will search their actions to find a merit so they will be found righteous in judgment.	וְאַתָּה דוֹרֵשׁ מַעֲשֵׂה כֻלָּם
And also Noach (because of his stature in comparison to his generation) You remembered with love	וְגַם אֶת נֹחַ בְּאַהֲבָה זָכַרְתָּ
and You judged him to save him from the Flood and to have mercy on him to increase his offspring	וַתִּפְקְדֵהוּ בִּדְבַר יְשׁוּעָה וְרַחֲמִים
when You brought the waters of the Flood	בַּהֲבִיאֲךָ אֶת מֵי הַמַּבּוּל
to destroy all living beings	לְשַׁחֵת כָּל בָּשָׂר
because of their evil actions (of corruption and immorality).	מִפְּנֵי רֹעַ מַעַלְלֵיהֶם
Since Noach was considered righteous amongst them, his remembrance came before You favorably	עַל כֵּן זִכְרוֹנוֹ בָּא לְפָנֶיךָ
Master of all, the Master of all strength Who is able to do anything and Who takes care of us with Divine Providence,	יהוה אֱלֹהֵינוּ
to increase his offspring (referring to the nations of the world) like the dust of the earth	לְהַרְבּוֹת זַרְעוֹ כְּעַפְרוֹת תֵּבֵל
and his descendants (referring to Israel) like the sand on the seashore	וְצֶאֱצָאָיו כְּחוֹל הַיָּם
as it is written in Your Torah (*Bereishis* 8:1)[18]	כַּכָּתוּב בְּתוֹרָתֶךָ
"And the Master of all strength Who is able to do anything remembered Noach (because of his righteousness)	וַיִּזְכֹּר אֱלֹהִים אֶת נֹחַ

---

18. Here begin the ten verses of *Zichronos*. The *Yesod VeShoresh HaAvodah* writes that when saying these verses, one should be careful to say them slowly, with great concentration, enunciating each word precisely.

and (He remembered) all the wild animals
[including birds] (for they had not corrupted themselves)

וְאֵת כָּל הַחַיָּה

and all the animals that were
with Noach in the ark
(which had not corrupted themselves)

וְאֵת כָּל הַבְּהֵמָה אֲשֶׁר אִתּוֹ בַּתֵּבָה

and a spirit of comfort and pleasantness
passed before the Master of all strength
Who is able to do anything

וַיַּעֲבֵר אֱלֹהִים רוּחַ

concerning the earth (to act with it in mercy)

עַל הָאָרֶץ

and the waters subsided.''

וַיָּשֹׁכּוּ הַמָּיִם.

And it also says (*Shemos* 2:24):

וְנֶאֱמַר

"And the Master of all strength
Who is able to do anything heard
the cries of the children of Israel

וַיִּשְׁמַע אֱלֹהִים אֶת נַאֲקָתָם

and (through this) the Master of all
strength Who is able to do anything
remembered His covenant

וַיִּזְכֹּר אֱלֹהִים אֶת בְּרִיתוֹ

with Abraham, with Isaac,
and with Jacob (to be a God for
them and for their descendants).''

אֶת אַבְרָהָם אֶת יִצְחָק וְאֶת יַעֲקֹב.

And it also says (*Vayikra* 26:42):

וְנֶאֱמַר

"And I will remember with mercy
My covenant with Jacob
(to bring the redemption)

וְזָכַרְתִּי אֶת בְּרִיתִי יַעֲקוֹב

and (if Jacob alone is not worthy enough,
I will remember) also My covenant with Isaac

וְאַף אֶת בְּרִיתִי יִצְחָק

and (if both of them are not worthy
enough) I will also remember
my covenant with Abraham

וְאַף אֶת בְּרִיתִי אַבְרָהָם אֶזְכֹּר

and I will also remember the land of Israel with mercy
(that it should again be inhabited by the entire nation).''

וְהָאָרֶץ אֶזְכֹּר.

And in Your Holy Writings
(that were said with Divine Inspiration)

וּבְדִבְרֵי קָדְשְׁךָ

it is written (*Tehillim* 111:4):

כָּתוּב לֵאמֹר

"God established Shabbos, Festivals and other
mitzvos for Israel to remember His wonders
(when He took them out of Egypt)[19]

זֵכֶר עָשָׂה לְנִפְלְאֹתָיו

because the Master of all is gracious and merciful
(toward the Jewish people, and therefore made
reminders of His wonders so that they would
improve and deserve reward)."

חַנּוּן וְרַחוּם יהוה.

And it also says (*Tehillim* 111:5):

וְנֶאֱמַר

"God gave manna to those who feared Him
(when the Jews went through the desert
after leaving Egypt)

טֶרֶף נָתַן לִירֵאָיו

because He constantly remembered
His covenant (with the Fathers, to preserve
the nation of Israel)."

יִזְכֹּר לְעוֹלָם בְּרִיתוֹ.

And it also says (*Tehillim* 106:45):

וְנֶאֱמַר

"And God remembered for the nation of Israel
the covenant that He made with the Fathers

וַיִּזְכֹּר לָהֶם בְּרִיתוֹ

and He relented from bringing evil on Israel
according to His abundant kindness
(and not because of their actions)."

וַיִּנָּחֵם כְּרֹב חֲסָדָיו.

And through Your messengers,
the Prophets

וְעַל יְדֵי עֲבָדֶיךָ הַנְּבִיאִים

---

19. It is difficult to understand how this verse fits with the idea of this blessing, that God remembers our actions and the covenant He made with the Fathers.

  Sifsei Chaim explains that the wonders God performed were not a one-time occurrence, rather, they are the impetus for recurring wonders every year, at that time of year, to bring salvation to all generations. [Cf. *Radak* on this verse.] Therefore, it seems that mentioning these times that God set for remembrances is meant to arouse Him to do similar wonders for us.

it is written (*Yirmiyahu* 2:2):

כָּתוּב לֵאמֹר

"Go and call out this prophecy

הָלֹךְ וְקָרֵאתָ

in the ears of the inhabitants of Jerusalem,
saying:

בְּאָזְנֵי יְרוּשָׁלַיִם לֵאמֹר

So says the Master of all:

כֹּה אָמַר יהוה

'I remember for you the kindness that you
did with Me in your youth when you left Egypt

זָכַרְתִּי לָךְ חֶסֶד נְעוּרַיִךְ

and the love of your "wedding" at Mount Sinai
(where Israel was considered the bride
and God the groom)

אַהֲבַת כְּלוּלֹתָיִךְ

that you went after My messengers — Moses
and Aaron — into a desert (without provisions)

לֶכְתֵּךְ אַחֲרַי בַּמִּדְבָּר

in a land that was not sown
(and there was nothing to eat,
but nevertheless you followed Me there).' "

בְּאֶרֶץ לֹא זְרוּעָה.

And it also says (*Yechezkel* 16:60):

וְנֶאֱמַר

"And I will remember the covenant
(to be for you for a God) that I made
with you (children of Israel)

וְזָכַרְתִּי אֲנִי אֶת בְּרִיתִי אוֹתָךְ

in the days of your youth (at Mount Sinai)

בִּימֵי נְעוּרָיִךְ

and I will fulfill it for you
as an everlasting covenant."[20]

וַהֲקִימוֹתִי לָךְ בְּרִית עוֹלָם.

And it also says (*Yirmiyahu* 31:19):

וְנֶאֱמַר

"Is the nation of Israel (which is referred to as
Efraim) My precious son who has never sinned?

הֲבֵן יַקִּיר לִי אֶפְרַיִם

---

20. *Yesod VeShoresh HaAvodah* writes that here one should pray that God hasten to fulfill this everlasting covenant so that we should no longer be subjugated by the gentiles; He should do this for the sake of His great Name so that all will know that God alone is supreme over the entire world.

(And) is he like a desirable child whose
father delights in him (so much)

אִם יֶלֶד שַׁעֲשׁוּעִים

that any time that I (God) talk about him

כִּי מִדֵּי דַבְּרִי בּוֹ

I should continue to remember him
(for a long time, like a father who delights
in the mention of his son)?

זָכֹר אֶזְכְּרֶנּוּ עוֹד

But, since he (Israel) regrets his sins
and repents,[21] therefore My innards (so to speak)
are aroused to (have mercy on) him

עַל כֵּן הָמוּ מֵעַי לוֹ

and therefore I will certainly have mercy
on Him, so says the Master of all.''

רַחֵם אֲרַחֲמֶנּוּ נְאֻם יהוה.

The Master of all strength, Who is able to do anything
and Who takes care of us with Divine Providence,

אֱלֹהֵינוּ

and the God who took care of our Fathers
with Divine Providence,

וֵאלֹהֵי אֲבוֹתֵינוּ

remember us for good before
Your Throne of Glory

זָכְרֵנוּ בְּזִכָּרוֹן טוֹב לְפָנֶיךָ

and judge us with a judgment
of salvation and mercy

וּפָקְדֵנוּ בִּפְקֻדַּת יְשׁוּעָה וְרַחֲמִים

from (the special mercy that is in)
the uppermost heavens before the Throne of Glory

מִשְּׁמֵי שְׁמֵי קֶדֶם

and remember for us

וּזְכָר לָנוּ

---

21. This verse has been explained according to *Rashi* (both in *Yirmiyahu* as well as in
Siddur Otzar HaTefillos) and *Metzudas David,* among others. Although at first it may
appear that this verse's connotation is not a favorable remembrance of Israel, *Rashi*
says that this verse is really connected to the verses which precede it in *Yirmiyahu*
(31:17-18): ''I have indeed heard *Efraim* moaning, 'You have chastised me, and I have
become chastened, like an untrained calf; [please] inspire me to come back and and I will
return, for You, the Master of all, are my God. For after my repenting, I regretted; and
after being made to know, I slapped my thigh [in anguish]; I was outwardly ashamed
and inwardly humiliated, for I bore the disgrace of my youth.' '' It is after this that God
says, ''My love for *Efraim* is not because he is a precious son who has never sinned, but
rather because he has repented from his sins. Therefore My innards (so to speak) are
aroused to remember him to have mercy on him.''

Master of all, the Master of all strength, Who is able to do anything and Who takes care of us with Divine Providence,	יהוה אֱלֹהֵינוּ
(the merit of) the covenant of circumcision	אֶת הַבְּרִית
and (the merit of) the kindnesses that Abraham did	וְאֶת הַחֶסֶד
and (remember) the oath	וְאֶת הַשְּׁבוּעָה
that You swore to Abraham our father (that his descendants will never be annihilated)	אֲשֶׁר נִשְׁבַּעְתָּ לְאַבְרָהָם אָבִינוּ
on Mount Moriah (the site of the *Akeidah*)	בְּהַר הַמּוֹרִיָּה
and let it be seen before You (the remembrance of . . .)	וְתֵרָאֶה לְפָנֶיךָ
the *Akeidah* when Abraham our father bound Isaac, his son, (on this day, Rosh Hashanah)	עֲקֵדָה שֶׁעָקַד אַבְרָהָם אָבִינוּ אֶת יִצְחָק בְּנוֹ
on the (same) altar (that was used by Adam and others)	עַל גַּבֵּי הַמִּזְבֵּחַ
and he suppressed his (fatherly instincts to have) mercy (on his son)	וְכָבַשׁ רַחֲמָיו
to do Your desire with all his heart[22]	לַעֲשׂוֹת רְצוֹנְךָ בְּלֵבָב שָׁלֵם
so (measure for measure), Your mercy should suppress Your anger on us (resulting from our actions)	כֵּן יִכְבְּשׁוּ רַחֲמֶיךָ אֶת כַּעַסְךָ מֵעָלֵינוּ

---

22. The *Rashba* [*Teshuvos HaRashba* 5:55] gives a succinct portrayal of the test of the *Akeidah,* which emphasizes its uniqueness and places a great demand on us. Abraham was the epitome of kindness, and had longed for a child his entire life. He begot a child at the age of 100, a most perfect and superior child, and yet Abraham was willing to slaughter him with his own hand for the love of God.

It is the triumph that Abraham displayed in this phenomenal test that provides us with the merit to be inscribed for a good year. The *Chasam Sofer* writes that one should say the blessing of *Zichronos* in such a manner that he will resolve to emulate Abraham and Isaac's remarkable display of love of God, and through that we will merit a favorable remembrance before God.

and with Your great goodness
You should retract Your strong anger

וּבְטוּבְךָ הַגָּדוֹל יָשׁוּב חֲרוֹן אַפֶּךָ

from Your nation — Israel

מֵעַמֶּךָ

and from Your city — Jerusalem

וּמֵעִירְךָ

and from Your Heritage — the Temple

וּמִנַּחֲלָתֶךָ

and fulfill for us

וְקַיֶּם לָנוּ

Master of all, the Master of all strength
Who is able to do anything and
Who takes care of us with Divine Providence,

יהוה אֱלֹהֵינוּ

that which You promised us
in Your Torah

אֶת הַדָּבָר שֶׁהִבְטַחְתָּנוּ בְּתוֹרָתֶךָ

that Moshe wrote as a messenger
of Yours just as he heard from the
"mouth" of Your Glory

עַל יְדֵי מֹשֶׁה עַבְדֶּךָ מִפִּי כְבוֹדֶךָ

as it says (*Vayikra* 26:45):

כָּאָמוּר

(God promised saying:) "And I will remember
for them — Israel

וְזָכַרְתִּי לָהֶם

the covenant I made with the Tribes
(never to annihilate their descendants)

בְּרִית רִאשׁוֹנִים

when I took them out from
the land of Egypt

אֲשֶׁר הוֹצֵאתִי אֹתָם מֵאֶרֶץ מִצְרַיִם

before the eyes of the nations (who saw
all the wonders that I did for Israel)

לְעֵינֵי הַגּוֹיִם

(having taken them out) to serve Me and that
I — the Master of all strength Who is able to do
anything — will give them Divine Providence

לִהְיוֹת לָהֶם לֵאלֹהִים

I am the Master of all
(and am trusted to pay them reward)."

אֲנִי יהוה.

For You remember all those things
that are forgotten (by people)

כִּי זוֹכֵר כָּל הַנִּשְׁכָּחוֹת

(and) You have existed eternally
(even before the world was created)

אַתָּה הוּא מֵעוֹלָם

and there is no forgetfulness before
Your Throne of Glory (since everything
is written down and stored there)

וְאֵין שִׁכְחָה לִפְנֵי כִסֵּא כְבוֹדֶךָ

and (therefore we ask that [You remember])
Akeidas Yitzchak on our behalf — as his descendants

וַעֲקֵדַת יִצְחָק לְזַרְעוֹ

You should remember today
(the date of the Akeidah) with mercy.[23]

הַיּוֹם בְּרַחֲמִים תִּזְכּוֹר

You are the Source of Blessing, Master of all,

בָּרוּךְ אַתָּה יהוה

Who remembers the covenant
(that He made with Abraham to remember the Akeidah).

זוֹכֵר הַבְּרִית.

שופרות
Shofaros: Past, Present and Future[24]

You, God, revealed Yourself
(at the time of the giving of the Torah)

אַתָּה נִגְלֵיתָ

---

23. The Sages tell us [*Pesikta Rabbasi* (Ch. 40, p. 171b)] that *Akeidas Yitzchak* took place on Rosh Hashanah. [It is likely that the merit of the *Akeidah* is even more powerful on its anniversary, and that is why we make so many references to it, and ask to evoke its merit specifically on Rosh Hashanah.] The Sages tell us that after the *Akeidah*, Abraham requested of God, "When the children of Isaac are judged before You on this day, even if there are many accusations against them [please remember this]: Just as I was silent and I didn't answer You, ignoring any contradictions (i.e., You had previously said that my descendants will come through Isaac, yet now I was being asked to sacrifice him before he had any children), so too, You should ignore all the accusations [and forgive them]."

24. Although the Talmud does not state why we say this section, *Shofaros*, we might think it is simply because today is the day of blowing the *shofar*, and thus we talk about *shofar* blasts. However, we still must understand what this has to do with the revelation at Mount Sinai, which is the topic of the introduction to this section, and how that relates to the prayer of Rosh Hashanah.

Pirkei d'Rabbi Eliezer (end of Ch. 31) states that the two horns of the ram that Abraham brought instead of his son Isaac, after the test of the *Akeidah*, were used by God for special events. The left horn was blown at Mount Sinai, and the right one, which

in a cloud that showed Your Divine Presence

בַּעֲנַן כְּבוֹדֶךָ

to speak with Your holy nation (who, having purified themselves, had attained the level of angels).

עַל עַם קָדְשְׁךָ לְדַבֵּר עִמָּם

From Heaven You let them hear Your voice

מִן הַשָּׁמַיִם הִשְׁמַעְתָּם קוֹלֶךָ

and You showed Your Presence to them in a dark cloud which was clear at its center

וְנִגְלֵיתָ עֲלֵיהֶם בְּעַרְפַלֵּי טֹהַר

and the (entire) world, even the gentile kings, trembled before You

גַּם (כָּל) הָעוֹלָם כֻּלּוֹ חָל מִפָּנֶיךָ

and all of creation — even the mountains — shook from Your Presence

וּבְרִיּוֹת בְּרֵאשִׁית חָרְדוּ מִמֶּךָּ

when You, our King, revealed Yourself on Mount Sinai

בְּהִגָּלוֹתְךָ מַלְכֵּנוּ עַל הַר סִינַי

to teach to Your nation, Israel, Torah and *mitzvos*

לְלַמֵּד לְעַמְּךָ תּוֹרָה וּמִצְוֹת

and You made Israel hear the grandeur of Your voice

וַתַּשְׁמִיעֵם אֶת הוֹד קוֹלֶךָ

and Your Ten Commandments that emerged with fiery flames from Your "mouth."

וְדִבְּרוֹת קָדְשְׁךָ מִלַּהֲבוֹת אֵשׁ

---

was larger, will be blown in the future to gather in all the exiles (and it is that blast for which we pray at the end of this blessing: "Blow the *shofar* that is great etc."). Since, as we mentioned previously, the *Akeidah* took place on Rosh Hashanah, it emerges that the revelation at Sinai (as well as the future *shofar*-blowing) is related to the *Akeidah*, and thereby Rosh Hashanah, and that may be why we mention it here.

R' Chaim Friedlander (*Sifsei Chaim* pp. 121 and 321) explains that the spiritual power of the *shofar* causes the subjugation and abolishment of evil, and simultaneously the strengthening of good. This is accomplished in three stages: first, by the revelation at Mount Sinai (therefore we speak about the *shofar* at Mount Sinai, including the three verses from the Torah); second, by our blowing the *shofar* today (reflected in the three verses from the Writings — *Kesuvim*); and last, by the ultimate redemption when a great *shofar* will be blown (as described in the recitation of the three verses from the Prophets).

With thunder and lightning
You revealed Yourself to them
(at Mount Sinai)

בְּקֹלֹת וּבְרָקִים עֲלֵיהֶם נִגְלֵיתָ

and with the very powerful sound
of a *shofar* You showed them
the splendor of Your Presence

וּבְקוֹל שֹׁפָר עֲלֵיהֶם הוֹפָעְתָּ

as it is written in Your Torah (*Shemos* 19:16):[25]

כַּכָּתוּב בְּתוֹרָתֶךְ

"And it was on the third day (of separation
for purifying themselves — on the 6th of Sivan)

וַיְהִי בַיּוֹם הַשְּׁלִישִׁי

when it became morning (close to sunrise)

בִּהְיֹת הַבֹּקֶר

and there were sounds of thunder and lightning

וַיְהִי קֹלֹת וּבְרָקִים

and a thick cloud on Mount Sinai

וְעָנָן כָּבֵד עַל הָהָר

and a very powerful sound of the *shofar*
(greater than any *shofar* ever heard)

וְקֹל שֹׁפָר חָזָק מְאֹד

and all of Israel, who were in the camp
(opposite Mount Sinai), trembled."

וַיֶּחֱרַד כָּל הָעָם אֲשֶׁר בַּמַּחֲנֶה.

And it also says (*Shemos* 19:19):

וְנֶאֱמַר

"And the sound of the *shofar*
was growing increasingly stronger

וַיְהִי קוֹל הַשֹּׁפָר הוֹלֵךְ וְחָזֵק מְאֹד

Moshe spoke (the Ten Commandments)

מֹשֶׁה יְדַבֵּר

and the Master of all strength Who is able to do
anything helped his voice be heard by all of Israel."

וְהָאֱלֹהִים יַעֲנֶנּוּ בְקוֹל.

And it also says (*Shemos* 20:15):

וְנֶאֱמַר

"And the entire nation (men, women and children,
and even people who were previously blind)

וְכָל הָעָם

---

25. Here begin the three verses from the Torah. While saying them, one should yearn that he merit hearing God's voice and experiencing such a revelation, which will occur with the ultimate redemption, may it be soon and in our days (*Yesod VeShoresh HaAvodah*).

could see the words of the
commandments emerge from God's
'mouth,' and (also) the flames

רֹאִים אֶת הַקּוֹלֹת וְאֶת הַלַּפִּידְם

and [they saw] the sound
of the *shofar* and the mountain
that appeared full of smoke

וְאֶת קוֹל הַשֹּׁפָר וְאֶת הָהָר עָשֵׁן

and the nation saw (these things) and trembled

וַיַּרְא הָעָם וַיָּנֻעוּ

and (having been frightened) they stood from afar."

וַיַּעַמְדוּ מֵרָחֹק.

And in Your Holy Writings
(that were said with Divine Inspiration)

וּבְדִבְרֵי קָדְשְׁךָ

it is written (*Tehillim* 47:6):

כָּתוּב לֵאמֹר

"When Israel blows a *teruah* the Master
of all strength Who is able to do anything
is aroused to stand up from His Throne of Judgment

עָלָה אֱלֹהִים בִּתְרוּעָה

and with the merit of the sound of the *shofar*
the Master of all is aroused to sit on the
Throne of Mercy to judge the world."

יהוה בְּקוֹל שׁוֹפָר.

And it also says (*Tehillim* 98:6):

וְנֶאֱמַר

"With the (blowing of a) horn (which is
straight) and the sound of the *shofar*
(which is bent)

בַּחֲצֹצְרוֹת וְקוֹל שׁוֹפָר

they shall come to the *Beis HaMikdash*
to blow before the King, the Master of all."

הָרִיעוּ לִפְנֵי הַמֶּלֶךְ יהוה.

And it also says (*Tehillim* 81:4-5):

וְנֶאֱמַר

"Blow a *shofar* on Rosh Chodesh
(the first of the month of Tishrei)

תִּקְעוּ בַחֹדֶשׁ שׁוֹפָר

on the day that was set to be a festival
(Rosh Hashanah)

בַּכֶּסֶה לְיוֹם חַגֵּנוּ.

for it is a time for Israel to be considered with mercy,	כִּי חֹק לְיִשְׂרָאֵל הוּא
it is the day of judgment by the God of Jacob."	מִשְׁפָּט לֵאלֹהֵי יַעֲקֹב.
And it also says (*Tehillim* Ch. 150):	וְנֶאֱמַר
"All of you shall praise God.	הַלְלוּיָהּ
Praise the Almighty because of His revelation in the Temple (His holy place)	הַלְלוּ אֵל בְּקָדְשׁוֹ
praise Him for the great spheres in the heaven (like the sun) by which one can discern His strength.	הַלְלוּהוּ בִּרְקִיעַ עֻזּוֹ.
Praise Him for the wonders He constantly does for us	הַלְלוּהוּ בִּגְבוּרֹתָיו
praise Him for the great kindnesses that He does.	הַלְלוּהוּ כְּרֹב גֻּדְלוֹ.
Praise Him with the sound of a *shofar* (that calls people to come closer to Him),	הַלְלוּהוּ בְּתֵקַע שׁוֹפָר
praise Him with an instrument that has many strings, and with a harp (one that has a few strings).	הַלְלוּהוּ בְּנֵבֶל וְכִנּוֹר.
Praise Him with a small drum that is hit with the hand, and with a large drum that is beaten with a stick,	הַלְלוּהוּ בְּתֹף וּמָחוֹל
praise Him with a multi-toned instrument that makes many different sounds and with a flute.	הַלְלוּהוּ בְּמִנִּים וְעֻגָב.
Praise Him with cymbals that make a pleasant sound,	הַלְלוּהוּ בְּצִלְצְלֵי שָׁמַע
praise Him with cymbals that produce the sound of a *teruah*.	הַלְלוּהוּ בְּצִלְצְלֵי תְרוּעָה.
All living creatures shall praise God (for He created them)	כֹּל הַנְּשָׁמָה תְּהַלֵּל יָהּ
all of you shall praise God."	הַלְלוּיָהּ.

And through Your messengers, the Prophets	**וְעַל יְדֵי** עֲבָדֶיךָ הַנְּבִיאִים
it is written (*Yeshayahu* 18:3):[26]	כָּתוּב לֵאמֹר
"All those who dwell on earth (the living) and all those who reside in the ground (the dead)	כָּל יֹשְׁבֵי תֵבֵל וְשֹׁכְנֵי אָרֶץ
all of them will see when He makes a sign on the mountaintops (to gather the exiles)	כִּנְשֹׂא נֵס הָרִים תִּרְאוּ
and when He blows a *shofar* to revive the dead, all will hear."	וְכִתְקֹעַ שׁוֹפָר תִּשְׁמָעוּ.
And it also says (*Yeshayahu* 27:13):	וְנֶאֱמַר
"And it will be on that day of the redemption	וְהָיָה בַּיּוֹם הַהוּא
God will blow a great *shofar* that will symbolize our freedom (redemption)	יִתָּקַע בְּשׁוֹפָר גָּדוֹל
and the Ten Tribes that were lost from Israel in the land of *Ashur* (and never returned from their exile) will come	וּבָאוּ הָאֹבְדִים בְּאֶרֶץ אַשּׁוּר
and also the tribes of Yehudah and Binyamin that were exiled from Israel to Egypt (at the time of the destruction of the first Temple)	וְהַנִּדָּחִים בְּאֶרֶץ מִצְרָיִם
and all of them will bow down to the Master of all on the Temple Mount	וְהִשְׁתַּחֲווּ לַיהוה בְּהַר הַקֹּדֶשׁ
which is in Jerusalem."	בִּירוּשָׁלָיִם.

---

26. R' Hirtz Shatz (in his commentary here) points out that there are three *shofaros* that will be blown for different purposes at the time of the ultimate redemption: One will be to revive the dead (the first verse from the Prophets here); a second to gather in the exiles (the second verse from the Prophets); and a third to overthrow the angel of *Edom* [the enemy of Israel] (the third verse from the Prophets).

Yesod VeShoresh HaAvodah writes that when saying these verses we should pray that God act for the sake of His Name's honor, and blow these *shofaros* very soon, for then all the nations of the world will recognize God's greatness.

And it also says (*Zechariah* 9:14-15): וְנֶאֱמַר

"And the Master of all will reveal Himself
to fight for Israel against their enemies וַיהוה עֲלֵיהֶם יֵרָאֶה

and He will send His arrows like lightning
(that burns quickly) וְיָצָא כַבָּרָק חִצּוֹ

and the Master of all, Who is the Master
of all strengthand is able to do anything,
(will execute judgment on the enemies) [אֱלֹהִים – read] וַאדֹנָי יֱהֹוִה

(and) He will blow the *shofar* to terrify
the enemies in battle בַּשׁוֹפָר יִתְקָע

and He will go with a strong wind and blast
Edom (who come from the south of Israel). וְהָלַךְ בְּסַעֲרוֹת תֵּימָן.

The Master of all Who rules over all the
Heavenly and earthly legions
will protect Israel then." יהוה צְבָאוֹת יָגֵן עֲלֵיהֶם

So too, may You protect Your nation
Israel with Your complete peace. כֵּן תָּגֵן עַל עַמְּךָ יִשְׂרָאֵל בִּשְׁלוֹמֶךָ.

The Master of all strength,
Who is able to do anything and
Who takes care of us with Divine Providence, אֱלֹהֵינוּ

and the God who took care of our
Fathers with Divine Providence, וֵאלֹהֵי אֲבוֹתֵינוּ

blow the *shofar* that is great in significance
(because it will be one of the signs of the
ultimate Redemption) תְּקַע בְּשׁוֹפָר גָּדוֹל

to free us from our servitude to the nations of the world לְחֵרוּתֵנוּ

and raise a banner that the time has come to
gather all of our exiles throughout the world וְשָׂא נֵס לְקַבֵּץ גָּלְיוֹתֵנוּ

and bring close to You all the Jews who were exiled among the nations close to the land of Israel	וְקָרֵב פְּזוּרֵינוּ מִבֵּין הַגּוֹיִם
and also gather those of us who were scattered to distant places, even from the ends of the earth	וּנְפוּצוֹתֵינוּ כַּנֵּס מִיַּרְכְּתֵי אָרֶץ
and bring us to Your city Zion with the sound of joyous songs	וַהֲבִיאֵנוּ לְצִיּוֹן עִירְךָ בְּרִנָּה
and to Jerusalem, where the Temple is,	וְלִירוּשָׁלַיִם בֵּית מִקְדָּשְׁךָ
with ever-lasting joy.	בְּשִׂמְחַת עוֹלָם
There we will be able to do before You in the Temple	וְשָׁם נַעֲשֶׂה לְפָנֶיךָ
[our obligatory *korbanos*][27]	[אֶת קָרְבְּנוֹת חוֹבוֹתֵינוּ]
as commanded to us in Your Torah	כְּמִצְוָה עָלֵינוּ בְּתוֹרָתֶךָ
that Moshe wrote as a messenger of Yours, just as he heard from the "mouth" of Your Glory	עַל יְדֵי מֹשֶׁה עַבְדֶּךָ מִפִּי כְבוֹדֶךָ
as it is written (*Bamidbar* 10:10):	כָּאָמוּר
"And on your Shabbos (which gladdens the heart with an extra *neshamah* — soul)	וּבְיוֹם שִׂמְחַתְכֶם
and on the three Festivals (Pesach, Shavuos, and Succos)	וּבְמוֹעֲדֵיכֶם
and on your days of Rosh Chodesh	וּבְרָאשֵׁי חָדְשֵׁיכֶם
you shall blow a straight silver horn	וּתְקַעְתֶּם בַּחֲצֹצְרוֹת

---

27. *Siddur Avodas Yisrael* points out that this phrase is difficult, since the intention here is to lead up to the tenth verse of *Shofaros,* which describes the blowing of horns while bringing the *korbanos,* rather than to mention the actual sacrificing of the *korbanos.* Indeed, many older versions of the *machzor* omitted these three words. Most versions do contain these words, however, and their intent is likely that since the *shofar* -blowing was done at the time the *korbanos* were offered, we mention not only the *shofar blasts,* but the *korbanos* as well.

when bringing your communal *korban olah*

עַל עֹלֹתֵיכֶם

and on your communal *korban shelamim*

וְעַל זִבְחֵי שַׁלְמֵיכֶם

and through that you will have
a good remembrance

וְהָיוּ לָכֶם לְזִכָּרוֹן

before the Master of all strength, Who is able to do
anything and Who takes care of you with
Divine Providence,

לִפְנֵי אֱלֹהֵיכֶם

I am the Master of all, the Master of all strength
Who is able to do anything and Who takes care
of you with Divine Providence.''

אֲנִי יהוה אֱלֹהֵיכֶם

[And now, blow the *shofar* that will
herald the redemption] for You hear
the sound of our *shofar* (mercifully)

כִּי אַתָּה שׁוֹמֵעַ קוֹל שׁוֹפָר

and You listen to the sound of our *teruah*
(and prayers,[28] and thereby judge us favorably)

וּמַאֲזִין תְּרוּעָה

and there is no one else like You
(for You consider even the sound of
the *shofar* and have mercy on us).

וְאֵין דּוֹמֶה לָךְ

You are the Source of Blessing, Master of all,

בָּרוּךְ אַתָּה יהוה

Who hears the sound of the *teruah*
of His nation Israel

שׁוֹמֵעַ קוֹל תְּרוּעַת עַמּוֹ יִשְׂרָאֵל

(and thereby changes from dealing with us with
the attribute of judgment to dealing with us)
with the attribute of mercy.

בְּרַחֲמִים.

---

28. The *Rokeach* quotes a *Pesikta* [see *Pesikta Rabbasi* 185a and 198b] which notes that to a human king one must bring many presents, but God is appeased with words, as it says (*Hoshea* 14:3): ''Take words with you and return to God.'' The *Rokeach* explains this phrase of the prayers as meaning, God listens to our words and our *teruah* and judges us favorably. This seems to also be the intention of *Rashi* on the verse (*Tehillim* 89:16), ''Praiseworthy is the nation who knows the *teruah*.'' *Rashi* comments there, ''that they know how to appease their Creator on Rosh Hashanah with the *teruah* with which they recite *Malchiyos, Zichronos* and *Shofaros*.''

עבודה
Return of the Temple Service

Be pleased[29]	רְצֵה
Master of all,	יהוה
the Master of all strength, Who is able to do anything and Who takes care of us with Divine Providence,	אֱלֹהֵינוּ
with Your nation, Israel (because they are praying for the rebuilding of the Temple)	בְּעַמְּךָ יִשְׂרָאֵל
and with their prayer (for the rebuilding of the Temple)	וּבִתְפִלָּתָם
and return the service of the Temple	וְהָשֵׁב אֶת הָעֲבוֹדָה
(even) to the Holy of Holies.	לִדְבִיר בֵּיתֶךָ
And the fire-offerings that they will bring	וְאִשֵּׁי יִשְׂרָאֵל
and the prayer of Israel (which is now in place of the offerings)	וּתְפִלָּתָם
because of Your love for the Jews	בְּאַהֲבָה
accept with desire	תְקַבֵּל בְּרָצוֹן
and help us that it should always be desirable	וּתְהִי לְרָצוֹן תָּמִיד
the service (whether offerings or prayers) of Israel, Your nation.	עֲבוֹדַת יִשְׂרָאֵל עַמֶּךָ

---

29. Before reciting this blessing one should instill in his heart the love of all Jews, regardless of their origin or affiliation, for we ask here that God should be pleased with all of His nation Israel (*Darchei Chaim*). [The saintly Chofetz Chaim wrote (*Ahavas Yisrael*, Ch. 2) that we constantly pray for the rebuilding of the Temple, but we neglect to contemplate the cause of its destruction, which was hatred for an unjustifiable reason. Therefore if we want the Temple to be rebuilt we must first rectify this sin and love all Jews.]

And let us merit to see (the *Shechinah* – Divine Presence) with our own eyes (i.e., soon, in our days)	וְתֶחֱזֶינָה עֵינֵינוּ
when You return Your Presence to the Temple (even if it is) in mercy (and not through our merits).	בְּשׁוּבְךָ לְצִיּוֹן בְּרַחֲמִים
You are the Source of Blessing, Master of all,	בָּרוּךְ אַתָּה יהוה
Who will return His Divine Presence to the Temple.	הַמַּחֲזִיר שְׁכִינָתוֹ לְצִיּוֹן.

הוֹדָאָה
Thanking God[30]

We give thanks to You, acknowledging	**מוֹדִים** אֲנַחְנוּ לָךְ
that You are the Master of all	שָׁאַתָּה הוּא יהוה
the Master of all strength, Who is able to do anything and Who takes care of us with Divine Providence,	אֱלֹהֵינוּ
and the God Who took care of our Fathers with Divine Providence	וֵאלֹהֵי אֲבוֹתֵינוּ
(and that You will continue to take care of us) forever.	לְעוֹלָם וָעֶד
[You are] the Rock – Creator and Sustainer – of our lives	צוּר חַיֵּינוּ
[and You are] the Protector Who saves us from all troubles	מָגֵן יִשְׁעֵנוּ
You are the One [Who keeps us alive and saves us] in every generation.	אַתָּה הוּא לְדוֹר וָדוֹר

---

30. The *Beis Elokim* explains that the reason we bow at the beginning and end of this *brachah* is to show humility, recognizing our unworthiness for Hashem's special care, and realizing that our lives and all goodness come from Him.

We will always express our thanks to You	נוֹדֶה לְךָ
and we will tell Your praise to others	וּנְסַפֵּר תְּהִלָּתֶךָ
for our lives — each breath — that are given over into Your hand	עַל חַיֵּינוּ הַמְּסוּרִים בְּיָדֶךָ
and for our souls that are entrusted to You (while we sleep)	וְעַל נִשְׁמוֹתֵינוּ הַפְּקוּדוֹת לָךְ
and for the hidden miracles that You do for us every day	וְעַל נִסֶּיךָ שֶׁבְּכָל יוֹם עִמָּנוּ
and for Your wonders of "nature" (which You renew constantly)	וְעַל נִפְלְאוֹתֶיךָ
and for Your favors (that You do for us constantly)	וְטוֹבוֹתֶיךָ
that You do in all parts of the day	שֶׁבְּכָל עֵת
in the evening, morning, and afternoon.	עֶרֶב וָבֹקֶר וְצָהֳרָיִם
You are the ultimate Good One	הַטּוֹב
for Your mercy has never finished — for You withhold punishment from those deserving it	כִּי לֹא כָלוּ רַחֲמֶיךָ
and You are the ultimate Merciful One (Who not only withholds punishment, but ...)	וְהַמְרַחֵם
Whose kindness never ends — for You even give these undeserving people additional kindnesses —	כִּי לֹא תַמּוּ חֲסָדֶיךָ
we have always put our hope in You.	מֵעוֹלָם קִוִּינוּ לָךְ
And for all of these wonders and favors that You do for us constantly	וְעַל כֻּלָּם
[Your Name] should be praised with the recognition that You are the Source of all Blessing	יִתְבָּרַךְ

and may Your Name (which represents
Your acts) be exalted through the
recognition of Your greatness

וְיִתְרוֹמַם שִׁמְךָ

since You are our King
(Who takes care of us especially)
[and we desire that Your Name be praised and exalted]

מַלְכֵּנוּ

constantly, every day,

תָּמִיד

forever and ever.

לְעוֹלָם וָעֶד

**And inscribe for a good life
(i.e., life that will be good
for earning the World to Come)**

וּכְתוֹב לְחַיִּים טוֹבִים

all the children of Your covenant.

כָּל בְּנֵי בְרִיתֶךָ

And all the living (those who will come back to life
by the Revival of the Dead)

וְכֹל הַחַיִּים

will thank You constantly forever

יוֹדוּךָ סֶּלָה

and they will praise Your Name
(which comes from Your deeds)
truthfully, without any other motive

וִיהַלְלוּ אֶת שִׁמְךָ בֶּאֱמֶת

the Almighty

הָאֵל

Who saves us in all our troubles

יְשׁוּעָתֵנוּ

and Who helps us to succeed

וְעֶזְרָתֵנוּ

constantly, forever.

סֶלָה

You are the Source of Blessing, Master of all,

בָּרוּךְ אַתָּה יהוה

Whose Name is "The Good One"
(for You are the ultimate good)

הַטּוֹב שִׁמְךָ

and to You alone it is fitting to give thanks
(because You are the cause of all goodness).

וּלְךָ נָאֶה לְהוֹדוֹת.

שָׁלוֹם
Peace

Grant peace (which includes peace of mind, peace in one's house, peace between Jews, and peace in the country)	**שִׂים** שָׁלוֹם
(and grant what is) good for each person	טוֹבָה
and (grant) prosperity and success	וּבְרָכָה
(and) let us find favor in Your eyes and thereby find favor in the eyes of all who see us	חֵן
and grant our requests (even though we are not deserving)	וָחֶסֶד
and have mercy on us (not to punish us according to our wrongdoings)	וְרַחֲמִים
on those of us here (praying together)	עָלֵינוּ
and on all of Israel, Your nation.	וְעַל כָּל יִשְׂרָאֵל עַמֶּךָ
Since You are our Father, give us an abundance of goodness and success	בָּרְכֵנוּ אָבִינוּ
all of us like one (equally)	כֻּלָּנוּ כְּאֶחָד
with the "light of Your face" (which is a symbol of Your great love)	בְּאוֹר פָּנֶיךָ
because we already know from the Revelation at Sinai that with the "light of Your face" come great things:	כִּי בְאוֹר פָּנֶיךָ
You gave to us as a present (not because we were deserving),	נָתַתָּ לָּנוּ
Master of all,	יהוה
the Master of all strength, Who is able to do anything and Who takes care of us with Divine Providence,	אֱלֹהֵינוּ

the Torah that teaches us how to live | תּוֹרַת חַיִּים

and (through it) the love of doing kindness | וְאַהֲבַת חֶסֶד

and (You gave us with the Torah more opportunities for) reward in the World to Come (by fulfilling the many *mitzvos*) | וּצְדָקָה

and (as reward for keeping the Torah You give us also) an abundance of goodness and success (in this world) | וּבְרָכָה

and (in the merit of keeping the Torah You give us) special mercy | וְרַחֲמִים

and (as a reward for keeping the Torah You give us) a long, healthy life | וְחַיִּים

and (through the Torah we have) peace of body and mind (because all the ways of the Torah are peaceful). | וְשָׁלוֹם

And it should be good in Your eyes | וְטוֹב בְּעֵינֶיךָ

to give an abundance of goodness and success to Your nation, Israel | לְבָרֵךְ אֶת עַמְּךָ יִשְׂרָאֵל

in all parts of the day | בְּכָל עֵת

and in all hours of each part of the day | וּבְכָל שָׁעָה

with Your peace (which is a complete peace). | בִּשְׁלוֹמֶךָ

In the book of life | בְּסֵפֶר חַיִּים

of abundant goodness and success | בְּרָכָה

and peace between a man and his friend | וְשָׁלוֹם

and a good (ample and easy) livelihood | וּפַרְנָסָה טוֹבָה

may we be remembered | נִזָּכֵר

and may we be inscribed before You | וְנִכָּתֵב לְפָנֶיךָ

we (who are standing together praying) | אֲנַחְנוּ

and all of Your nation, Israel	וְכָל עַמְּךָ בֵּית יִשְׂרָאֵל
(let us be remembered and inscribed) for a truly good life (i.e., a life that will enable us to earn the World to Come)	לְחַיִּים טוֹבִים
and for peace within ourselves (that we should be satisfied with the materialistic things that we have).	וּלְשָׁלוֹם.

THERE ARE DIFFERENT CUSTOMS CONCERNING THE CONCLUSION OF THIS BLESSING AND EVERYONE SHOULD FOLLOW HIS CUSTOM. IF ONE DOES NOT KNOW HIS CUSTOM HE SHOULD RECITE THE VERSION ON THE RIGHT.

You are the Source of Blessing,	בָּרוּךְ אַתָּה	You are the Source of Blessing, Master of all,	בָּרוּךְ אַתָּה יהוה
Master of all,	יהוה	Who gives an abundance of goodness and success	הַמְבָרֵךְ
Who makes peace among all.	עוֹשֶׂה הַשָּׁלוֹם.	to His nation, Israel,	אֶת עַמּוֹ יִשְׂרָאֵל
		with peace.	בַּשָּׁלוֹם.

תחנונים
Personal Requests

The Master of all strength Who is able to do anything and Who takes care of me with Divine Providence,	אֱלֹהַי
help me to guard my tongue from speaking bad about others (lashon hara)	נְצוֹר לְשׁוֹנִי מֵרָע
and [help me to guard] my lips from speaking deceit or falsehood	וּשְׂפָתַי מִדַּבֵּר מִרְמָה
and help me so that my soul should be silent (and even in thought I should not get angry) at those who curse me	וְלִמְקַלְלַי נַפְשִׁי תִדּוֹם
and help me so that my soul should be like dust (very humble) before everyone (and not mind insults).	וְנַפְשִׁי כֶּעָפָר לַכֹּל תִּהְיֶה

Open up my heart so that it should be receptive and understand Your Torah	פְּתַח לִבִּי בְּתוֹרָתֶךָ
and help my soul eagerly pursue Your *mitzvos*.	וּבְמִצְוֹתֶיךָ תִּרְדּוֹף נַפְשִׁי
And all those who want to harm me (whether in mundane matters or spiritual matters, i.e., to cause me to sin)	וְכָל הַחוֹשְׁבִים עָלַי רָעָה
quickly annul their plan	מְהֵרָה הָפֵר עֲצָתָם
and ruin their thought (even before they make plans).	וְקַלְקֵל מַחֲשַׁבְתָּם
Act (take us out of exile) for the sake of Your Name, which is desecrated now among the gentiles	עֲשֵׂה לְמַעַן שְׁמֶךָ
act (take us out of exile) for the sake of Your right hand, which You have now withdrawn in our exile	עֲשֵׂה לְמַעַן יְמִינֶךָ
act (take us out of exile) for the sake of Your Holiness (so that all will know that You lead us with holiness)	עֲשֵׂה לְמַעַן קְדֻשָּׁתֶךָ
act (take us out of exile) for the sake of Your Torah (so the Torah can be studied properly and completely)	עֲשֵׂה לְמַעַן תּוֹרָתֶךָ
and in order that Your dear ones, Israel, should be released from all troubles	לְמַעַן יֵחָלְצוּן יְדִידֶיךָ
save them with (the wonders and miracles that are attributed to) Your right hand	הוֹשִׁיעָה יְמִינְךָ
and answer (even) me in this prayer.	וַעֲנֵנִי.
Let the words of my prayer be desirable to You[31]	יִהְיוּ לְרָצוֹן אִמְרֵי פִי

---

31. *Seder HaYom* (quoted also in *Mishnah Berurah* 122:8) writes that one should say this verse with great concentration, for it will help considerably that his prayers should not go unanswered.

and also the thoughts of my heart which I cannot express [should be desirable] before You,	וְהֶגְיוֹן לִבִּי לְפָנֶיךָ
Master of all,	יהוה
My Rock, on Whom I rely for all my requests	צוּרִי
and Who will be my Redeemer.	וְגֹאֲלִי.

ONE SHOULD BOW AND GO BACK THREE STEPS
LIKE A SERVANT DEPARTING FROM HIS MASTER

The One Who makes peace in Heaven (among the angels)	**עֹשֶׂה** [הַ]שָּׁלוֹם בִּמְרוֹמָיו
may He make peace (for those on earth, who are naturally quarrelsome)	הוּא יַעֲשֶׂה שָׁלוֹם
on those of us here (praying together)	עָלֵינוּ
and on all of Israel	וְעַל כָּל יִשְׂרָאֵל
and (you, the angels who escort me,) agree to my prayer, and say Amen!	וְאִמְרוּ אָמֵן.
May it be Your desire,	**יְהִי רָצוֹן** מִלְּפָנֶיךָ
Master of all,	יהוה
the Master of all strength, Who is able to do anything and Who takes care of us with Divine Providence,	אֱלֹהֵינוּ
and the God Who took care of our Fathers with Divine Providence,	וֵאלֹהֵי אֲבוֹתֵינוּ
that You should rebuild the Temple (so that we will be able to do the ultimate *avodah* — service to You)	שֶׁיִּבָּנֶה בֵּית הַמִּקְדָּשׁ
quickly and in our lifetime	בִּמְהֵרָה בְיָמֵינוּ
and help us so that all our toil should be in learning Your Torah.	וְתֵן חֶלְקֵנוּ בְּתוֹרָתֶךָ

And there, in the Temple, we will bring
offerings (the ultimate service) with reverence

וְשָׁם נַעֲבָדְךָ בְּיִרְאָה

as [they brought offerings and served in reverence]
in the earlier days (of Moshe)

כִּימֵי עוֹלָם

and as they did in the previous years
(of Shlomo *HaMelech*).

וּכְשָׁנִים קַדְמוֹנִיּוֹת.

And then, it will be pleasing to the Master of all

וְעָרְבָה לַיהוה

the offerings that will be brought
in the Temple (which is in the portion
of Yehudah in Jerusalem)

מִנְחַת יְהוּדָה וִירוּשָׁלָיִם

as [the offerings were pleasing]
in the earlier days (of Moshe)

כִּימֵי עוֹלָם

and as they were in the previous years
(of Shlomo *HaMelech*).

וּכְשָׁנִים קַדְמוֹנִיּוֹת.

Yom Kippur / The Day of Atonement

The Prayers of Yom Kippur

The main theme of Yom Kippur is *teshuvah,* repenting for our misdeeds and returning to God. *Rabbeinu Yonah* writes in his fundamental *sefer* on *teshuvah, Shaarei Teshuvah* (2:14 and 4:17), that although we are obligated to do *teshuvah* at all times, nevertheless, it is a special *mitzvah* to repent on Yom Kippur, as it says (*Vayikra* 16:30): "from all your sins before God you should cleanse yourselves." *Rambam (Hilchos Teshuvah* 2:7) writes, "Yom Kippur is a time to repent for all, both for the individual and the multitude, and it is the main time of forgiveness and atonement for Israel; therefore everyone is obligated to do *teshuvah* and confess on Yom Kippur."[1]

The *Midrash (Vayikra Rabbah* 10:5) cites a dispute concerning the annulment of a punishment which God has decreed on someone. The discussion centers on whether *tefillah* accomplishes half and *teshuvah* everything, or whether the opposite, that *tefillah* accomplishes everything and *teshuvah* does half. Therefore, writes the *Chida* (at the end of his commentary to *Sefer Chassidim*), if one prays **and** does *teshuvah* then according to both opinions he will accomplish everything.

That is really the essence of our Yom Kippur. We spend the entire day in the synagogue praying and confessing, which is the primary component of *teshuvah,* as the *Rokeach* (p. 36) writes. By doing this, we are exerting ourselves in all ways to ward off Divine retribution and merit a complete atonement.

However, we must know that saying the words alone does not suffice. The primary aspect of prayer is concentration, and that is why the Talmud (*Taanis* 2a) calls prayer "the service of the heart" (see the Introduction of *Pathway to Prayer — Shemoneh Esrei* for a full discussion of this). Especially on the day when all decrees will be sealed, one must exert oneself exceedingly to concentrate on the words of the prayers, and say them from the heart. As the *Mateh Efraim* (a primary halachic work concerning the High Holidays) so

---

1. Confession is mentioned by the *Rambam,* for the *Rambam* holds that confession is the crucial and completing stage of the *teshuvah* process. Merely reciting a list of sins is not considered repenting, rather it is like purifying oneself in a *mikveh* while holding something impure. Therefore one must first repent and then say the confession. (See *Kiryas Sefer* at the beginning of *Hilchos Teshuvah.*)

beautifully writes (619:15): "One should pray with an awareness of the One before Whom he stands, as well as the seriousness and holiness of the day, which aids in purifying a person from all his sins. Therefore, a person must purify himself and remove from his heart all other thoughts, and pray with his mind focused towards the One Who knows thoughts, and prepare himself to pray **with concentration of the heart."**

Shalmei Tzibbur (p. 314) writes a very inspiring thought: "The custom is that on Yom Kippur, both at night and by day, we say the sentence [immediately following the first verse of *Shema*] of *'Baruch Sheim Kevod Malchuso'* out loud [although throughout the year we say it silently. The reason is that] on this day we are comparable to angels [since we purify ourselves and do not eat or drink], therefore we may say this great praise [out loud] and they [the angels] will not condemn us. And thus, one who fears God will understand from this and take a lesson that he must make himself exceedingly holy, and strengthen himself in all of his blessings and prayers on this day, to say them with **tremendous concentration** and humility, more than on all other days, to truly be comparable to angels!"

Yesod VeShoresh HaAvodah (11:11) writes that one must pray with **great concentration,** and even if he feels weak because of the fast, he should gird himself with strength, thinking before the *amidah* (the silent prayer): "How many sins have I committed over the year, and how much have I angered my Creator, and this awesome day is the main time of forgiveness and atonement for all of my sins! Woe to me if I do not pray with concentration; how will I face the King Who forgives and pardons?"

Although many of the prayers of Yom Kippur are already familiar to us from Rosh Hashanah, the *Viduy* (Confession) is recited only on Yom Kippur. The *Viduy* requires great **preparation,** both to know what one is saying and in order to recognize the sin that one is confessing, for without thought the *Viduy* is meaningless. In fact, it is really worse than meaningless — it is a sin, as we say in the confession itself, "For the sins we have sinned before You with confession said just with our mouth." *Seder HaYom* (p. 47) writes: "The main element of the *Viduy* is that it is said **from his heart** and soul, not just with his mouth insincerely, for then his punishment will be greater, and it would have been better had he not said the *Viduy."*

The *Chofetz Chaim* wrote (in the Appendix of *Shem Olam*) that one should not just say the standard version of the Confession and then think that God should forgive this sin and that sin, but rather one should contemplate **beforehand** for what he is asking forgiveness, and commit himself not to return to do that foolish sin. After that he may come before God to ask forgiveness for this act, for the *mitzvah* of *Viduy* must, by law, follow his regret and recognition of sin and his resolve not to repeat it.

Therefore, one must ponder his sins before reciting the *Viduy,* and that includes realizing the severity of what one has done. To that end, this volume includes footnotes on many parts of the *Viduy* citing the severity of the sin as described by the Sages, *Rishonim* and *Acharonim.* It is advisable to learn these notes, as well, before saying the *Viduy,* so that one will have true regret, and thereby his confession will be sincere.

And let us conclude with the inspiring words of R' Yisrael Salanter, the father of the *mussar* movement (*Or Yisrael,* 7): "**Yom Kippur is exceedingly great,** a day of forgiveness and atonement! There is no greater holiday for Israel than Yom Kippur [as stated in *Taanis* 30b]! **There is nothing better than it,** if we would just make the proper preparations to correct our ways. For Yom Kippur atones, if one does *teshuvah;* that is, if he forsakes his sins. Even if one only accomplishes a fraction it is a great accomplishment; **there is nothing in the world that can compare to it.** We must attempt to make at least some commitment for the future on Yom Kippur!"

Maariv, Shacharis, and Minchah
for the Day of Atonement[1]

AT MINCHAH ADD:

When I call in the name of the Master of all

you should ascribe greatness to the Master
of all strength, Who is able to do anything
and Who takes care of us with Divine Providence.

כִּי שֵׁם יהוה אֶקְרָא
הָבוּ גֹדֶל לַאלֹהֵינוּ.

Master of all — in particular, My Master[2]

אֲדֹנָי

please open my lips (because I am afraid
and ashamed to open them)

שְׂפָתַי תִּפְתָּח

and [help me pray with concentration, so]
my mouth will [be able to] tell Your true praise.

וּפִי יַגִּיד תְּהִלָּתֶךָ.

אבות
Our God and the God of Our Fathers,
Who Created Everything, and Protected Abraham[3]

You are the source of blessing (an expression of praise)[5]

[4]**בָּרוּךְ** אַתָּה

Master of all (Who always was, is, and will be)

יהוה

---

1. R' Dovid Kronglas pointed out that although one's natural tendency might be to concentrate more on the prayers which are special to Yom Kippur, the truth is that the first *brachah* is the most crucial, for if one does not concentrate for every word of the first blessing he has not fulfilled his obligation to pray (unlike the other *brachos,* where lack of concentration does not invalidate the prayer). And therefore, especially on Yom Kippur when our lives lie in the balance, we have to exert ourselves to concentrate on the first *brachah* more than any other, for it is the main one. [See note 3.]

2. The *Mesillas Yesharim* (1707-1746)] (Ch. 19) writes that a person should think about three things when he comes to pray. It is possible that these three thoughts are hinted at in these three phrases that introduce the *Shemoneh Esrei:*
 (a) He is standing in front of Hashem — "Master of all";
 (b) the exaltedness of Hashem — "Open my lips because I am afraid";
 (c) the lowliness of man — "And help me tell Your true praise."

3. As noted above, one must be very careful to concentrate when saying this *brachah,* because otherwise he does not fulfill his obligation to pray. It is worthwhile noting that the *Mishnah Berurah* [the authoritative halachic work] (101:4) states that if one did not yet say ברוך אתה ה' at the end of this *brachah,* he may go back to אלהי אברהם and repeat from there with concentration, thereby rectifying his previous lack of concentration.

4. The *Beis Elokim* explains that we bow at the beginning and end of this *brachah* because it contains a summary of all the praises of Hashem and His all encompassing powers which signify His Oneness. Recognizing this, we bow down to Hashem in humility.

5. See Appendix concerning the reason for this translation, rather than the common translation "blessed."

the Master of all strength, Who is able to do anything and Who takes care of us with Divine Providence,	אֱלֹהֵינוּ
and the God Who took care of our Fathers with Divine Providence (and made a covenant with each of them)	וֵאלֹהֵי אֲבוֹתֵינוּ
the God Who made a covenant with our father Abraham (who excelled in kindness)	אֱלֹהֵי אַבְרָהָם
the God Who made a covenant with our father Isaac (who excelled in service of God)	אֱלֹהֵי יִצְחָק
and the God Who made a covenant with our father Jacob (who excelled in learning Torah)	וֵאלֹהֵי יַעֲקֹב
He is the Almighty (all power is His, especially in exercising the attribute of mercy)	הָאֵל
Who is the Great One (all greatness is His, especially in exercising the attribute of kindness)	הַגָּדוֹל
(and) He is the Strong One (all strength is His, especially in exercising the attribute of judgment)	הַגִּבּוֹר
and He alone deserves to be feared (because no being has the ability to do good or bad except Him)	וְהַנּוֹרָא
for He is the supreme God Who is the ultimate cause of everything	אֵל עֶלְיוֹן
Who always does kindnesses that are purely good	גּוֹמֵל חֲסָדִים טוֹבִים
and He recreates everything, constantly, every day	וְקוֹנֵה הַכֹּל
and every day He recalls for our benefit the kindnesses performed by the forefathers	וְזוֹכֵר חַסְדֵי אָבוֹת
and He constantly brings the Redeemer closer	וּמֵבִיא גּוֹאֵל

to the forefathers' children's children (even though the merit of the forefathers might already be used up)	לִבְנֵי בְנֵיהֶם
for the sake of His Name (which will be sanctified at the time of the Redemption)	לְמַעַן שְׁמוֹ
[and He will also bring the Redeemer] because of His great love for the Jewish people.	בְּאַהֲבָה
Remember us for life in this world (in order that we may earn the World to Come by doing mitzvos here)	**זָכְרֵנוּ לְחַיִּים**
King, Who desires life (and not death for a sinner, but rather that he should repent)[6]	**מֶלֶךְ חָפֵץ בַּחַיִּים**
and write us in the Book of the Righteous, for life	**וְכָתְבֵנוּ בְּסֵפֶר הַחַיִּים**
for Your sake, in order that we may serve You[7]	**לְמַעַנְךָ**
the Master of all strength, Who is able to do anything and is the One Who apportions life to all.	**אֱלֹהִים חַיִּים**
He is the King over all	מֶלֶךְ
Who is the Helper (to help one succeed)	עוֹזֵר
and the Savior (from trouble)	וּמוֹשִׁיעַ
and the Protector (to prevent trouble from coming).	וּמָגֵן
You are the Source of Blessing, Master of all,	בָּרוּךְ אַתָּה יהוה
the Protector of Abraham (and because of Abraham He continues His protection over us).	מָגֵן אַבְרָהָם.

---

6. R' Hirtz Shatz in his *Siddur* writes that when one says these words he should think that if he only repents he will live, and should resolve to do *teshuvah*.

7. R' Yechezkel Levenstein said that this word should alert us to the type of life we are requesting; that is, a life of service to Hashem, the kind of life that Hashem desires, and not merely a life of self-fulfillment and self-indulgence.

גבורות
The Mighty Acts of God and the Revival of the Dead[8]

You alone are eternally Strong	**אַתָּה** גִּבּוֹר לְעוֹלָם
Master of all	אֲדֹנָי
You even revive the dead (which shows the greatest strength, contradicting all laws of nature)	מְחַיֵּה מֵתִים אַתָּה
[and] You have an abundance of strength with which to save.	רַב לְהוֹשִׁיעַ
He provides all the living with their food and other needs in kindness (not because they are deserving)	מְכַלְכֵּל חַיִּים בְּחֶסֶד
He revives the dead with great mercy (searching for merits with which they would deserve revival)	מְחַיֵּה מֵתִים בְּרַחֲמִים רַבִּים
He supports those who are falling (whether physically, emotionally, or financially)	סוֹמֵךְ נוֹפְלִים
and He heals the sick from all types of illnesses (even when doctors have given up hope)	וְרוֹפֵא חוֹלִים
and He opens the bonds of those who are restricted (e.g., giving movement to our limbs when we awaken)	וּמַתִּיר אֲסוּרִים
and He will keep His promise to those sleeping in the dust (the dead), to revive them.	וּמְקַיֵּם אֱמוּנָתוֹ לִישֵׁנֵי עָפָר
Who is like You (who can do as many mighty deeds, which are infinite, even for one person)?	מִי כָמוֹךָ
— You, to Whom all mighty deeds belong! —	בַּעַל גְּבוּרוֹת

8. While reciting this *berachah* we should instill in ourselves perfect belief in the Revival of the Dead, one of the thirteen principles of faith outlined by the *Rambam* [Maimonides].

And who is comparable to You in even one of Your mighty deeds (which are of the highest quality)?

וּמִי דוֹמֶה לָךְ

You are the King over all

מֶלֶךְ

Who causes death and revival in many respects (such as sleep and awakening, poverty and wealth)

מֵמִית וּמְחַיֶּה

and, like the sprouting of a seed, You bring the Salvation (the Revival of the Dead).[9]

וּמַצְמִיחַ יְשׁוּעָה

Who is like You, who has as much mercy on his sons as You, the Merciful Father, have for us

מִי כָמוֹךָ אַב הָרַחֲמִים

(and) remembers His creatures, out of mercy, for life.

זוֹכֵר יְצוּרָיו לְחַיִּים בְּרַחֲמִים

And (from the mighty deeds that we mentioned) we see that You are surely trusted to revive the dead.

וְנֶאֱמָן אַתָּה לְהַחֲיוֹת מֵתִים

You are the Source of Blessing, Master of all,

בָּרוּךְ אַתָּה יהוה

the Reviver of all the dead (from Adam until the time of the Revival).[10]

מְחַיֵּה הַמֵּתִים.

---

9. This salvation refers to the Revival of the Dead, which is a major topic in this *brachah*. A similar expression is used in the Shabbos morning prayers where it says, "And no one is comparable to You, our **Savior,** for the Revival of the Dead [R' Yehudah ben Yakar].

This *brachah's* comparison of the Revival of the Dead to the sprouting of a seed (a comparison found also in *Kesubos* 111b) is explained beautifully by *Dover Shalom* (in *Siddur Otzar HaTefillos*), who says that death is not the end of a person; rather, it is like the burying of a seed, which decomposes in the earth to produce an even greater plant. In the same way, Hashem causes death in order to bring a person back to life in a more glorious form than he had been originally. The *Tiferes Yisrael* (*Or HaChaim* 2a) mentions another analogy to this: The caterpillar crawls around for a short time and then enshrouds itself in a cocoon, which is really like a grave, where it decomposes; but after a few weeks, out comes a creature with beautiful wings that can fly thousands of miles — a butterfly !

10. Even though many bodies have decomposed over thousands of years, and some have been burned and their dust has been scattered, and others have drowned at sea, Hashem with His great might will recognize and recompose the bodies and return to them their original souls (*Yesod VeShoresh HaAvodah*).

קְדוּשַׁת הַשֵּׁם
Return of the Glory of God's Kingdom (to Zion)[11]

You, Yourself, are holy (different and separate from everything)	**אַתָּה** קָדוֹשׁ
and Your Name (which comes from Your many acts) reveals holiness	וְשִׁמְךָ קָדוֹשׁ
and the holy ones − Israel −	וּקְדוֹשִׁים
(when *Mashiach* comes) will praise You every day, forever.	בְּכָל יוֹם יְהַלְלוּךָ סֶּלָה.
And then (in the time of *Mashiach*) [may it be speedily in our days]	[12]וּבְכֵן
[You shall] put Your fear (which will be a catalyst for repentance)	תֵּן פַּחְדְּךָ
Master of all	יהוה
the Master of all strength, Who is able to do anything and Who takes care of us with Divine Providence,	אֱלֹהֵינוּ

---

11. The *Aruch HaShulchan* (O.C. 582:10) notes, regarding the insertion of this prayer here, that the special prayers of Rosh Hashanah and Yom Kippur revolve around the glorification of the Name of God. This blessing ends with the words, "the King Who is holier than all else," which alludes to the future when God's Kingdom will be revealed to all. Thus the Sages added these paragraphs, beginning with "And then [You shall] put Your fear . . . ," which speak of the ultimate goal of Creation and the apex of our hopes − the Return of the Glory of God's Kingdom to Zion.

This may be the explanation of the *Midrash* (*Midrash Tehillim*, Ch. 102), "R' Yitzchak said that future generations who have no prophet, and no Kohen [to serve in the Temple], and no Temple to atone for them, still have one prayer left for them to pray on Rosh Hashanah and Yom Kippur which God will not despise [but will grant them atonement]." Which prayer is only said on both Rosh Hashanah and Yom Kippur? It is this prayer, pleading for the revelation of the Glory of God's Kingdom − and this prayer brings about atonement.

12. The *Avudraham* notes that the word וּבְכֵן, which is not commonly found in prayer, was chosen here to introduce these prayers to allude to the verse וּבְכֵן אָבוֹא אֶל הַמֶּלֶךְ, *And then I will come to the King* (*Esther* 4:16), so that we should realize that now is the time of judgment and we are coming before the King of Kings! The *Siddur Maggid Tzedek* expounds on this and explains that just as the end of that verse states that Esther was coming unlawfully to King Achashveirosh, so too, we have to consider ourselves unfit to stand in front of the King of the world, and thereby come very humbly.

on all Your works (which refers to the Jewish people)	עַל כָּל מַעֲשֶׂיךָ
and (put) Your dread	וְאֵימָתְךָ
on all that You have created (which refers to the gentiles)	עַל כָּל מַה שֶׁבָּרֵאתָ
and then all the Jews will fear You	וְיִירָאוּךָ כָּל הַמַּעֲשִׂים
and all the nations of the world will bow down to You in subjugation	וְיִשְׁתַּחֲווּ לְפָנֶיךָ כָּל הַבְּרוּאִים
and all of mankind will make one group	וְיֵעָשׂוּ כֻלָּם אֲגֻדָּה אַחַת
to do Your will with a complete heart (submitting all their tendencies to Divine service).	לַעֲשׂוֹת רְצוֹנְךָ בְּלֵבָב שָׁלֵם
As we already know (Your power from the Exodus from Egypt)	כְּמוֹ שֶׁיָּדַעְנוּ
Master of all	יהוה
the Master of all strength, Who is able to do anything and Who takes care of us with Divine Providence,	אֱלֹהֵינוּ
(where You revealed) that dominion is Yours	שֶׁהַשָּׁלְטָן לְפָנֶיךָ
and strength (in the constant running of the world) is in Your (left) hand	עֹז בְּיָדְךָ
and might (to do miracles) is in Your right hand	וּגְבוּרָה בִּימִינֶךָ
and (when You again reveal this in the time of *Mashiach*) Your Name will be revered on all the nations of the world.	וְשִׁמְךָ נוֹרָא עַל כָּל מַה שֶׁבָּרֵאתָ.
And, then, Master of all, give honor to Your nation, Israel	**וּבְכֵן** תֵּן כָּבוֹד יהוה לְעַמֶּךָ
(and cause everyone to) praise those who fear You	תְּהִלָּה לִירֵאֶיךָ
and (give) to those who cling to You the good for which they rely on You	וְתִקְוָה [טוֹבָה] לְדוֹרְשֶׁיךָ

and (give) to those who yearn
for Your salvation, the ability to
praise You as they desire (without fear)

וּפִתְחוֹן פֶּה לַמְיַחֲלִים לָךְ

(and then when they no longer fear anyone) there
will be an inner joy in the land of Israel
(with the ingathering of the exiles)

שִׂמְחָה לְאַרְצֶךְ

and there will be open joy in Your city, Jerusalem,
(where the glory of the Divine Presence will be felt most)

וְשָׂשׂוֹן לְעִירֶךְ

and then the kingdom of the family of
David Your servant will sprout forth
(with the coming of *Mashiach*)

וּצְמִיחַת קֶרֶן לְדָוִד עַבְדֶּךְ

and the influence of the
son of Yishai (father of David)
Your appointed one (*Mashiach*) will spread

וַעֲרִיכַת נֵר לְבֶן יִשַׁי מְשִׁיחֶךָ

(and we ask that this should happen)
speedily in our days (so that we should
witness the return of the honor of God).

בִּמְהֵרָה בְיָמֵינוּ.

And then (when *Mashiach* has come)

וּבְכֵן

the righteous will see (that the glory
of God has returned) and they will have inner joy

צַדִּיקִים יִרְאוּ וְיִשְׂמָחוּ

and the upright ones (who do everything
just for the sake of Heaven) will be
inspired to dance from joy

וִישָׁרִים יַעֲלֹזוּ

and the pious (who do more than
they are required to do by the Torah)
will raise their voices in jubilant song

וַחֲסִידִים בְּרִנָּה יָגִילוּ

and all those who do injustice and iniquity
will close their mouths

וְעוֹלָתָה תִּקְפָּץ פִּיהָ

and all evil will vanish like smoke

וְכָל הָרִשְׁעָה כֻּלָּהּ כֶּעָשָׁן תִּכְלֶה

when you remove evil
kingdoms from the earth.

כִּי תַעֲבִיר מֶמְשֶׁלֶת זָדוֹן מִן הָאָרֶץ.

And (then it will be apparent) that You
alone, the Master of all, are the only King

וְתִמְלוֹךְ אַתָּה יהוה לְבַדֶּךָ

on all Your works (the Jews and the other nations)

עַל כָּל מַעֲשֶׂיךָ

(and Your rule will be especially
evident) in the Temple, the place
of the manifestation of the Divine Presence,

בְּהַר צִיּוֹן מִשְׁכַּן כְּבוֹדֶךָ

and in Jerusalem which is designated
as Your holy city

וּבִירוּשָׁלַיִם עִיר קָדְשֶׁךָ

as it is written in Your holy words
(*Tehillim* 146:10):

כַּכָּתוּב בְּדִבְרֵי קָדְשֶׁךָ

"God will reign forever

יִמְלֹךְ יהוה לְעוֹלָם

(that is,) the Master of all strength
and the One able to do anything,
Who dwells particularly in Zion (the Temple)

אֱלֹהַיִךְ צִיּוֹן

(He will reign) for all generations

לְדֹר וָדֹר

(therefore, Israel) praise God."

הַלְלוּיָהּ.

You are holy (different and separate from everything)

קָדוֹשׁ אַתָּה

and Your Name (which is evident from

וְנוֹרָא שְׁמֶךָ

Your many acts) causes awe
and there is no other power except You

וְאֵין אֱלוֹהַ מִבַּלְעָדֶיךָ

as it is written (*Yeshayahu* 5:16):[13]

כַּכָּתוּב

"And the Master of all, Who is the ruler over
all the Heavenly and earthly legions, will be exalted

וַיִּגְבַּהּ יהוה צְבָאוֹת

---

13. The fact that this verse is quoted after the previous three lines, indicates that it is a
biblical support for these three concepts. It appears that the phrase "and the Almighty,
who is holy" parallels "You are holy"; that which it says "And the Master of all . . . when
He does judgment on all [he will be exalted]" refers to "and Your Name causes awe"; and
that which the verse says "Who is the ruler over all the Heavenly and earthly legions"
corresponds to "and there is no other power except You."

when He does judgment on all	בְּמִשְׁפָּט
and the Almighty, Who is holy (different and separate from everything),	וְהָאֵל הַקָּדוֹשׁ
will become more holy in our eyes through the kindness He does with us.''	נִקְדַּשׁ בִּצְדָקָה
You are the Source of Blessing, Master of all	בָּרוּךְ אַתָּה יהוה
the King, Who is holier than all else.	**הַמֶּלֶךְ הַקָּדוֹשׁ.**

קְדוּשַׁת הַיוֹם
The Holiness of the Day — Atoning of Our Sins

You chose us (the Nation of Israel) from all nations (when You took us out of Egypt)	**אַתָּה** בְחַרְתָּנוּ מִכָּל הָעַמִּים
You showed Your love for us (by giving us the Torah)	אָהַבְתָּ אוֹתָנוּ
and You showed that You desired us (by giving us the special protection of the Clouds of Glory even though we had sinned with the Golden Calf)	וְרָצִיתָ בָּנוּ
and You elevated us from all languages (by giving us the holy language — Hebrew — which is spoken in Heaven)[14]	וְרוֹמַמְתָּנוּ מִכָּל הַלְּשׁוֹנוֹת

---

14. One may suggest that this second group of phrases is highlighting the special qualities of the three major Festivals (*Yamim Tovim*), as well as the Days of Awe, as follows: Just as in *Tehillim* (114:1) we find the double expression "When Israel went out from Egypt, the House of Jacob from a nation that speaks a foreign language," so too here we find a similar double expression, "You chose us from all nations" and "You elevated us from all languages," implying that God took us out of Egypt (alluding to Pesach) not only in a physical sense, but also spiritually, represented by *lashon hakodesh*, the holy tongue, which conveys the morals and conduct of the Torah (see *Moreh Nevuchim* 3:8). Following this, "You made us holy by giving us the *mitzvos*" expands upon what was stated previously, "You showed your love for us," since the Torah that God gave us (alluding to Shavuos) is not simply a book of knowledge, but rather teaches us how to act in a way that imbues us with holiness. "And Your Name . . . You have called on us" develops the earlier phrase "and You showed that You desired us," for God not only showed that He desired us by protecting us with the Clouds of

and You made us holy by giving us the *mitzvos* which permeate us with holiness

וְקִדַּשְׁתָּנוּ בְּמִצְוֹתֶיךָ

and You have brought us close, our King, to Your service

וְקֵרַבְתָּנוּ מַלְכֵּנוּ לַעֲבוֹדָתֶךָ

and Your Name which is great (as we see from Your acts)

וְשִׁמְךָ הַגָּדוֹל

and holy (as we see from Your directing the world with a mastery beyond our comprehension)

וְהַקָּדוֹשׁ

You have called on us — for we are called the Nation of God.

עָלֵינוּ קָרָאתָ.

And the Master of all, the Master of all strength, Who is able to do anything and Who takes care of us with Divine Providence, gave us

וַתִּתֶּן לָנוּ יהוה אֱלֹהֵינוּ

with love (because of His love for us)[15]

בְּאַהֲבָה

ON SHABBOS ADD:

[with love You gave us] this Shabbos day [which is called a great gift]

אֶת יוֹם הַשַּׁבָּת הַזֶּה

(whose primary purpose is) for holiness and rest and ...

... וְ לִקְדֻשָּׁה וְלִמְנוּחָה

---

this Day of Atonement[16]

אֶת יוֹם הַכִּפּוּרִים הַזֶּה

(whose primary purpose is) to forgive the punishment of the sin

לִמְחִילָה

Glory (alluding to Succos), but He also attached His Great and Holy Name to us to signify our uniqueness. We also mention "and You have brought us close, **our King,** to Your service," which represents the Days of Awe, connoting that these special days are meant to bring us closer to the service of God.

15. The reference of this word depends on whether it is Shabbos. On a weekday the obvious reference is to the love with which God gave us the day of Yom Kippur. However, on Shabbos when we add "the Shabbos day" before mentioning Yom Kippur, the reference is to the love with which God gave us Shabbos, and the second "with love" refers to Yom Kippur, which is mentioned in the same phrase (R' Avraham Pam).

16. "There was great joy before God that He gave Yom Kippur to Israel *with great love.* Furthermore, when He forgives the sins of Israel there is no sadness in His 'heart,' rather He rejoices with great happiness" (*Tanna d'Vei Eliyahu,* Ch. 1).

and to forgive the actual sin	וְלִסְלִיחָה
and to atone completely (to such an extent that it is as if we had never sinned)	וּלְכַפָּרָה
and in that way pardon all of our sins	וְלִמְחָל בּוֹ אֶת כָּל עֲוֹנוֹתֵינוּ

ON SHABBOS SAY:

with love (because of Your love for us)]	בְּאַהֲבָה
a day on which we are called and gather to sanctify ourselves in prayer	מִקְרָא קֹדֶשׁ
(and) it is a day that is a remembrance of our going out of Egypt.[17]	זֵכֶר לִיצִיאַת מִצְרָיִם.
The Master of all strength, Who is able to do anything and Who takes care of us with Divine Providence,	אֱלֹהֵינוּ
and the God Who took care of our Fathers with Divine Providence	וֵאלֹהֵי אֲבוֹתֵינוּ
may our remembrance and consideration go up	יַעֲלֶה
and come	וְיָבֹא
and reach	וְיַגִּיעַ
and be seen in a good way	וְיֵרָאֶה
and be accepted with desire	וְיֵרָצֶה
and be heard well	וְיִשָּׁמַע
and be considered	וְיִפָּקֵד

17. *Sifsei Chaim* explains that on Yom Kippur we were forgiven for the sin of the Golden Calf. This atonement was considered a purification from the impurities of Egypt that the Jews had absorbed during their enslavement there, and which they eventually took out with them when they left. Therefore this day represents a spiritual exodus from Eygpt (i.e. from Egyptian influence).

and be remembered forever

וְיִזָּכֵר

our remembrance (i.e., our special relationship with You)

זִכְרוֹנֵנוּ

and Your special consideration to do good for us

וּפִקְדוֹנֵנוּ

and the remembrance of the covenants
You made with our Fathers

וְזִכְרוֹן אֲבוֹתֵינוּ

and the remembrance of
the promise to bring *Mashiach,*
a descendant of David Your servant,

וְזִכְרוֹן מָשִׁיחַ בֶּן דָּוִד עַבְדֶּךָ

and the remembrance
of Jerusalem, the city of
Your Holiness, which is now in ruins

וְזִכְרוֹן יְרוּשָׁלַיִם עִיר קָדְשֶׁךָ

and the remembrance of Your nation,
the House of Israel, which is now in exile

וְזִכְרוֹן כָּל עַמְּךָ בֵּית יִשְׂרָאֵל

(may all of these remembrances) come before You

לְפָנֶיךָ

for salvation (for all of Israel)

לִפְלֵיטָה

for good (for all of Israel)

לְטוֹבָה

to find favor in Your eyes and in everyone's eyes

לְחֵן

and to grant us our requests (even
though we are not deserving)

וּלְחֶסֶד

and for mercy (not punishing us
according to our wrongdoings)

וּלְרַחֲמִים

and for life (for all of Israel)

לְחַיִּים

and for peace (for all of Israel)

וּלְשָׁלוֹם

on this Day of Atonement.

בְּיוֹם הַכִּפּוּרִים הַזֶּה

Remember us,

זָכְרֵנוּ

Master of all

יהוה

the Master of all strength, Who is able to do
anything and Who takes care of us with Divine Providence,

אֱלֹהֵינוּ

on this day of Yom Kippur
to give everyone whatever is good for him

בּוֹ לְטוֹבָה

and consider us on this day
for prosperity and success

וּפָקְדֵנוּ בוֹ לִבְרָכָה

and save us on this day (of judgment)
so that we will merit life.

וְהוֹשִׁיעֵנוּ בוֹ לְחַיִּים

And with Your previous promise to
save us and to have mercy on us

וּבִדְבַר יְשׁוּעָה וְרַחֲמִים

have mercy on us because You are our Creator,
and favor us (with salvation)

חוּס וְחָנֵּנוּ

and have mercy on us because
of our lowly nature and save us,
even though we are undeserving

וְרַחֵם עָלֵינוּ וְהוֹשִׁיעֵנוּ

because our eyes are looking to You in hope

כִּי אֵלֶיךָ עֵינֵינוּ

because You are the Almighty King over all

כִּי אֵל מֶלֶךְ

and You are gracious and merciful
(even to the undeserving).

חַנּוּן וְרַחוּם אָתָּה.

The Master of all strength, Who is able to do
anything and Who takes care of us with Divine Providence,

אֱלֹהֵינוּ

and the God who took care of our
Fathers with Divine Providence

וֵאלֹהֵי אֲבוֹתֵינוּ

forgive our sins

מְחַל לַעֲוֹנוֹתֵינוּ

ON WEEKDAYS SAY:

on this Day of Atonement.

בְּיוֹם הַכִּפּוּרִים הַזֶּה

ON SHABBOS SAY:

on this Shabbos and
on this Day of Atonement.

בְּיוֹם הַשַּׁבָּת הַזֶּה וּבְיוֹם הַכִּפּוּרִים הַזֶּה

Blot out [our sins]	מְחֵה
and remove entirely (leaving no vestige of)	וְהַעֲבֵר
our sins that were committed with intent	פְּשָׁעֵינוּ
and our sins that were committed without intention	וְחַטֹּאתֵינוּ
[wipe them out] from before Your eyes	מִנֶּגֶד עֵינֶיךָ
as it says (*Yeshayahu* 43:25):	כָּאָמוּר
"I forgave the generation of the Exodus their sins and I forgive in every generation your intentional sins	אָנֹכִי אָנֹכִי הוּא מֹחֶה פְשָׁעֶיךָ
for My sake (so that My Name should not be profaned among the nations if I destroy you)	לְמַעֲנִי
and what you have done unwillfully, I will not even remember (there will be no vestige of it)."	וְחַטֹּאתֶיךָ לֹא אֶזְכֹּר.
And it is also written (*Yeshayahu* 44:22):	וְנֶאֱמַר
"I have always blotted out what you have done intentionally like a wind dissipates a thick cloud (leaving some remnant)	מָחִיתִי כָעָב פְּשָׁעֶיךָ
and like a thin cloud gets scattered (without leaving any trace) so I have erased your unintentional sins	וְכֶעָנָן חַטֹּאתֶיךָ
therefore, return to Me in repentance for I will redeem you."	שׁוּבָה אֵלַי כִּי גְאַלְתִּיךָ.
And it is also written (*Vayikra* 16:30):	וְנֶאֱמַר
"For on this day of Yom Kippur	כִּי בַיּוֹם הַזֶּה
God will forgive you (for your sins) as if they never were	יְכַפֵּר עֲלֵיכֶם

in order to purify your souls
(from the tendency to repeat the sins)

לְטַהֵר אֶתְכֶם

(but) from all your sins

מִכֹּל חַטֹּאתֵיכֶם

it is incumbent upon you to cleanse yourselves
(with repentance)[18] before the Master of all.''

לִפְנֵי יהוה תִּטְהָרוּ.

ON SHABBOS ADD:

The Master of all strength, Who is able to do
anything and Who takes care of us with Divine Providence,

אֱלֹהֵינוּ

and the God who took care of our Fathers
with Divine Providence

וֵאלֹהֵי אֲבוֹתֵינוּ

let our rest be pleasant before You

רְצֵה בִמְנוּחָתֵנוּ

---

make us holy from Above so that
we should do Your *mitzvos* properly

קַדְּשֵׁנוּ בְּמִצְוֹתֶיךָ

and give us Divine assistance
that all of our occupation should be
in Torah study

וְתֵן חֶלְקֵנוּ בְּתוֹרָתֶךָ

grant us good in a way that we will be
satisfied with what we have
(and not run after our desires)

שַׂבְּעֵנוּ מִטּוּבֶךָ

and cause us to rejoice through
the salvation that You will bring us

וְשַׂמְּחֵנוּ בִּישׁוּעָתֶךָ

ON SHABBOS ADD:

and give us as an inheritance
(the holiness that Shabbos inspires)

וְהַנְחִילֵנוּ

Master of all, the Master of all strength,
Who is able to do anything and Who takes
care of us with Divine Providence,

יהוה אֱלֹהֵינוּ

because of the love that You loved us
(when You gave us Shabbos)

בְּאַהֲבָה

---

18. Although it is a *mitzvah* all year long to do *teshuvah* (repentance), there is a specific
commandment to repent on Yom Kippur, as it says, ''It is incumbent upon you to cleanse
yourselves before the Master of all.'' This cleansing refers to repentance and correcting
our actions (*Rabbeinu Yonah, Shaarei Teshuvah* 2:14 and 4:17).

and because of the desire You have for us (that You want us to bring sacrifices even on Shabbos)

וּבִרְצוֹן

[give us as an inheritance] the inspiration of Shabbos, the day that You made holy,

שַׁבַּת קָדְשֶׁךָ

MINCHAH   SHACHARIS   MAARIV

and (through this inspiration) You should cause Israel to have a complete rest on Shabbos

וְיָנוּחוּ בָה / בוֹ / בָם יִשְׂרָאֵל

for they sanctify Your Name (by keeping Shabbos).

מְקַדְּשֵׁי שְׁמֶךָ

And (we ask that You) purify our hearts that we should serve You sincerely (without other motives)

וְטַהֵר לִבֵּנוּ לְעָבְדְּךָ בֶּאֱמֶת

[do all this] because You are the Forgiver of Israel constantly

כִּי אַתָּה סָלְחָן לְיִשְׂרָאֵל

and You are the Pardoner of Israel — who go in the straight path[19] —

וּמָחֳלָן לְשִׁבְטֵי יְשֻׁרוּן

in every generation

בְּכָל דּוֹר וָדוֹר

and except for You

וּמִבַּלְעָדֶיךָ

we have no other king who will completely pardon and forgive us

אֵין לָנוּ מֶלֶךְ מוֹחֵל וְסוֹלֵחַ

(— only You).

(אֶלָּא אָתָּה)

You are the Source of Blessing, Master of all,

בָּרוּךְ אַתָּה יהוה

---

19. The term *"Shivtei Yeshurun"* [lit. the tribes of Jeshurun], referring to Israel who follow the path that is *yashar,* upright, is very uncommon in prayer. The *Meshech Chochmah* (*Vayikra* 16:30) and the *Baruch She'amar* both offer the same explanation: There are two general categories of sins, those that are between man and God and those that are primarily between man and his fellow man. The root, or paradigm, of all sins against God is the sin of the Golden Calf, whereas the root or paradigm of all sins against man is the selling of Joseph as a slave by his brothers. *Shivtei Yeshurun* refers to the sons of Jacob, and it is to the type of sin between man and man that this phrase refers. Therefore, the blessing means: *You are the Forgiver of Israel* concerning sins between man and God, and *You are the Pardoner of Israel* concerning sins between man and man. Once one has been granted forgiveness by the one against whom he has sinned, then God forgives him as well.

Who completely pardons and forgives the sins of the individual	מֶלֶךְ מוֹחֵל וְסוֹלֵחַ לַעֲווֹנוֹתֵינוּ
and (through that completely forgives the sins) of the entirety of the house of His nation, Israel	וְלַעֲווֹנוֹת עַמּוֹ בֵּית יִשְׂרָאֵל
and (You) remove our iniquities each and every year,[20]	וּמַעֲבִיר אַשְׁמוֹתֵינוּ בְּכָל שָׁנָה וְשָׁנָה
the King over all the inhabitants of the earth	מֶלֶךְ עַל כָּל הָאָרֶץ

ON WEEKDAYS SAY:

Who chose Israel and made them holier (than the other nations)	מְקַדֵּשׁ יִשְׂרָאֵל

ON SHABBOS SAY:

Who made the Shabbos holier (than the other days — and gave it to us as a present) and made Israel holier (than the other nations)	מְקַדֵּשׁ הַשַּׁבָּת וְיִשְׂרָאֵל

(and through Israel) He makes holy the Day of Atonement (to forgive our sins on it).	וְיוֹם הַכִּפּוּרִים.

עבודה
Return of the Temple Service

Be pleased[21]	רְצֵה
Master of all,	יהוה

---

20. One should feel a tremendous gratitude towards the Almighty for the gift of Yom Kippur, the day on which He forgives our sins, if we repent. Were the sins of the world to keep piling up year after year, the measure would soon be full and the world would be condemned to destruction. But after the sin of the Golden Calf was forgiven, this day was established for forgiveness, and aids in the repentance process; and that is what is meant by "Yom Kippur atones" (*Yoma* 86a) [based on *Sefer HaChinuch, Mitzvah* 185].

21. Before reciting this blessing one should instill in his heart the love of all Jews, regardless of their origin or affiliation, for we ask here that God be pleased with all of His nation Israel (*Darchei Chaim*). [The saintly Chofetz Chaim wrote (*Ahavas Yisrael,* Ch. 2) that we constantly pray for the rebuilding of the Temple, but we neglect to contemplate the cause of its destruction, which was hatred for an unjustifiable reason. Therefore if we want the Temple to be rebuilt we must first rectify this sin and love all Jews.]

the Master of all strength, Who is able to do anything and Who takes care of us with Divine Providence,	אֱלֹהֵינוּ
with Your nation, Israel (because they are praying for the rebuilding of the Temple)	בְּעַמְּךָ יִשְׂרָאֵל
and with their prayer (for the rebuilding of the Temple)[22]	וּבִתְפִלָּתָם
and return the service of the Temple	וְהָשֵׁב אֶת הָעֲבוֹדָה
(even) to the Holy of Holies.	לִדְבִיר בֵּיתֶךָ
And the fire-offerings that they will bring	וְאִשֵּׁי יִשְׂרָאֵל
and the prayer of Israel (which is now in place of the offerings)	וּתְפִלָּתָם
because of Your love for the Jews	בְּאַהֲבָה
accept with desire	תְקַבֵּל בְּרָצוֹן
and help us that it should always be desirable	וּתְהִי לְרָצוֹן תָּמִיד
the service (whether offerings or prayers) of Israel, Your nation.	עֲבוֹדַת יִשְׂרָאֵל עַמֶּךָ
And let us merit to see (the *Shechinah* – Divine Presence) with our own eyes (i.e., soon, in our days)	וְתֶחֱזֶינָה עֵינֵינוּ
when You return Your Presence to the Temple (even if it is) in mercy (and not through our merits).	בְּשׁוּבְךָ לְצִיּוֹן בְּרַחֲמִים
You are the Source of Blessing, Master of all,	בָּרוּךְ אַתָּה יהוה
Who will return His Divine Presence to the Temple.	הַמַּחֲזִיר שְׁכִינָתוֹ לְצִיּוֹן.

---

22. Since Jews pray in every *Shemoneh Esrei* for the rebuilding of the Temple (and not only for material things, as is the way of the world), God should accept and answer our prayers (R' Yehudah ben Yakar).

הוֹדָאָה
Thanking God[23]

We give thanks to You, acknowledging	**מוֹדִים** אֲנַחְנוּ לָךְ
that You are the Master of all	שָׁאַתָּה הוּא יהוה
the Master of all strength, Who is able to do anything and Who takes care of us with Divine Providence,	אֱלֹהֵינוּ
and the God Who took care of our Fathers with Divine Providence	וֵאלֹהֵי אֲבוֹתֵינוּ
(and that You will continue to take care of us) forever.	לְעוֹלָם וָעֶד
[You are] the Rock — Creator and Sustainer — of our lives	צוּר חַיֵּינוּ
[and You are] the Protector Who saves us from all troubles	מָגֵן יִשְׁעֵנוּ
You are the One [Who keeps us alive and saves us] in every generation.	אַתָּה הוּא לְדוֹר וָדוֹר
We will always express our thanks to You	נוֹדֶה לְּךָ
and we will tell Your praise to others	וּנְסַפֵּר תְּהִלָּתֶךָ
for our lives — each breath — that are given over into Your hand	עַל חַיֵּינוּ הַמְּסוּרִים בְּיָדֶךָ
and for our souls that are entrusted to You (while we sleep)[24]	וְעַל נִשְׁמוֹתֵינוּ הַפְּקוּדוֹת לָךְ
and for the hidden miracles that You do for us every day[25]	וְעַל נִסֶּיךָ שֶׁבְּכָל יוֹם עִמָּנוּ

23. The *Beis Elokim* explains that the reason we bow at the beginning and end of this *brachah* is to show humility, recognizing our unworthiness for Hashem's special care, and realizing that our lives and all goodness come from Him.

24. The *Midrash* (*Tehillim* 25) tells us that every night a person gives over his weary soul to God, and He returns it each morning renewed. It is concerning this that we say the *brachah* of "*Elokai Neshamah*" each morning.

25. Rabbeinu Bachai writes in his introduction to *Parshas Ki Sisa*, **"There is no individual in *Klal Yisrael* for whom hidden miracles don't happen *every day*!"**

and for Your wonders of "nature" (which You renew constantly)[26]	וְעַל נִפְלְאוֹתֶיךָ
and for Your favors (that You do for us constantly)	וְטוֹבוֹתֶיךָ
that You do in all parts of the day	שֶׁבְּכָל עֵת
in the evening, morning, and afternoon.	עֶרֶב וָבֹקֶר וְצָהֳרָיִם
You are the ultimate Good One	הַטּוֹב
for Your mercy has never finished – for You withhold punishment from those deserving it	כִּי לֹא כָלוּ רַחֲמֶיךָ
and You are the ultimate Merciful One (Who not only withholds punishment, but ...)	וְהַמְרַחֵם
Whose kindness never ends – for You even give these undeserving people additional kindnesses –	כִּי לֹא תַמּוּ חֲסָדֶיךָ
we have always put our hope in You.	מֵעוֹלָם קִוִּינוּ לָךְ
And for all of these wonders and favors that You do for us constantly	וְעַל כֻּלָּם

---

26. The wonders of nature that have been revealed by men so far are much too numerous for anyone to think of. But if one thinks about one of the myriad wonders while saying this prayer, it would make the words so much more meaningful. The *Chovos HaLevavos* (*Shaar HaBechinah,* Ch. 5) writes that the wonders in one's own body are the closest to him and are the ones he should investigate.

To cite just one example: We all know that the thing that life needs most, and constantly, is oxygen. We are, however, quite unaware of what we do with the oxygen once we have it. Many people think that one inhales the oxygen into a balloon-like organ, called a lung, and then exhales it. Really, the lungs are not at all like a balloon, but rather like a sponge with over 300 **million** tiny air sacs, called alveoli, that if flattened out would cover about 600 square feet (about the size of half a tennis-court)! All in the area of your ribcage!

Each of these alveoli is surrounded by a network of tiny blood vessels, called capillaries. The blood passes through these capillaries single file – in about a *second* – and a remarkable thing happens. Simultaneously, oxygen passes through the thin membrane walls of the alveoli and gets absorbed by the blood vessels around it to circulate throughout the body, and at the same time the blood vessels diffuse their cargo of carbon dioxide into the alveoli to be exhaled! Therefore, what we breathed in is not the same as what we breathe out, rather a miraculous chemical exchange has taken place, all automatically, in the span of a second! And this takes place 16 times a minute – more while you're exercising – over 8 million times a year!!

No wonder that the Sages exhort us (*Bereishis Rabbah* 14:9) that for each and every breath one takes, he must praise the Creator. The more one understands the wonder of this most vital function of the body, greater, and more heartfelt, his praise will be (from *Designer World* [by R' Avrohom Katz], Ch. 9).

[Your Name] should be praised with the recognition that You are the Source of all Blessing	יִתְבָּרַךְ
and may Your Name (which represents Your acts) be exalted through the recognition of Your greatness	וְיִתְרוֹמַם שִׁמְךָ
since You are our King (Who takes care of us especially) [and we desire that Your Name be praised and exalted]	מַלְכֵּנוּ
constantly, every day,	תָּמִיד
forever and ever.	לְעוֹלָם וָעֶד
And inscribe for a good life (i.e., life that will be good for earning the World to Come)	**וּכְתוֹב לְחַיִּים טוֹבִים**
all the children of Your covenant.	**כָּל בְּנֵי בְרִיתֶךָ**
And all the living (those who will come back to life by the Revival of the Dead)	וְכֹל הַחַיִּים
will thank You constantly forever	יוֹדוּךָ סֶּלָה
and they will praise Your Name (which comes from Your deeds) truthfully, without any other motive	וִיהַלְלוּ אֶת שִׁמְךָ בֶּאֱמֶת
the Almighty	הָאֵל
Who saves us in all our troubles	יְשׁוּעָתֵנוּ
and Who helps us to succeed	וְעֶזְרָתֵנוּ
constantly, forever.	סֶלָה
You are the Source of Blessing, Master of all,	בָּרוּךְ אַתָּה יהוה
Whose Name is "The Good One" (for You are the ultimate good)	הַטּוֹב שִׁמְךָ
and to You alone it is fitting to give thanks (because You are the cause of all goodness).	וּלְךָ נָאֶה לְהוֹדוֹת.

שָׁלוֹם
Peace[27]

FOR MAARIV AND MINCHAH THE FOLLOWING IS SAID
(FOR SHACHARIS SAY שִׂים שָׁלוֹם BELOW):

שָׁלוֹם רָב

An abundant peace (which includes many forms of peace: of mind, in one's house, between Jews, in the country)

עַל יִשְׂרָאֵל עַמְּךָ תָּשִׂים לְעוֹלָם

may You place upon Israel, Your nation, forever

כִּי אַתָּה הוּא מֶלֶךְ

for You are the King over all

אָדוֹן לְכָל הַשָּׁלוֹם.

(and) the Master of all forms of peace (You can make peace in any situation).

CONTINUE AT וְטוֹב בְּעֵינֶיךָ ON PAGE 118

FOR SHACHARIS THE FOLLOWING IS SAID:

שִׂים שָׁלוֹם

Grant peace (which includes peace of mind, peace in one's house, peace between Jews, and peace in the country)

טוֹבָה

(and grant what is) good for each person

וּבְרָכָה

and (grant) prosperity and success

חֵן

(and) let us find favor in Your eyes and thereby find favor in the eyes of all who see us

וָחֶסֶד

and grant our requests (even though we are not deserving)

וְרַחֲמִים

and have mercy on us (not to punish us according to our wrongdoings)

עָלֵינוּ

on those of us here (praying together)

---

27. The last *Mishnah* states that God found no adequate vehicle for Israel's blessing other than peace. The Sages tell us (*Vayikra Rabbah* 9:9) that peace is so great that it comes at the end of all prayers. As the *Seder HaYom* writes, ''Peace encompasses everything and through peace we will merit everything.'' Therefore, one should concentrate espeacially on this all-encompassing final *brachah*.

and on all of Israel, Your nation.	וְעַל כָּל יִשְׂרָאֵל עַמֶּךְ
Since You are our Father, give us an abundance of goodness and success	בָּרְכֵנוּ אָבִינוּ
all of us like one (equally)	כֻּלָּנוּ כְּאֶחָד
with the "light of Your face" (which is a symbol of Your great love)	בְּאוֹר פָּנֶיךָ
because we already know from the Revelation at Sinai that with the "light of Your face" come great things:	כִּי בְאוֹר פָּנֶיךָ
You gave to us as a present (not because we were deserving),	נָתַתָּ לָּנוּ
Master of all,	יהוה
the Master of all strength, Who is able to do anything and Who takes care of us with Divine Providence,	אֱלֹהֵינוּ
the Torah that teaches us how to live	תּוֹרַת חַיִּים
and (through it) the love of doing kindness	וְאַהֲבַת חֶסֶד
and (You gave us with the Torah more opportunities for) reward in the World to Come (by fulfilling the many *mitzvos*)	וּצְדָקָה
and (as reward for keeping the Torah You give us also) an abundance of goodness and success (in this world)	וּבְרָכָה
and (in the merit of keeping the Torah You give us) special mercy	וְרַחֲמִים
and (as a reward for keeping the Torah You give us) a long, healthy life	וְחַיִּים
and (through the Torah we have) peace of body and mind (because all the ways of the Torah are peaceful).	וְשָׁלוֹם

CONTINUE HERE FOR ALL PRAYERS:

And it should be good in Your eyes	וְטוֹב בְּעֵינֶיךָ
to give an abundance of goodness and success to Your nation, Israel	לְבָרֵךְ אֶת עַמְּךָ יִשְׂרָאֵל

in all parts of the day	בְּכָל עֵת
and in all hours of each part of the day	וּבְכָל שָׁעָה
with Your peace (which is a complete peace).	בִּשְׁלוֹמֶךָ

In the book of life — בְּסֵפֶר חַיִּים

of abundant goodness and success — בְּרָכָה

and peace between a man and his friend· — וְשָׁלוֹם

and a good (ample and easy) livelihood — וּפַרְנָסָה טוֹבָה

may we be remembered — נִזָּכֵר

and may we be inscribed before You — וְנִכָּתֵב לְפָנֶיךָ

we (who are standing together praying) — אֲנַחְנוּ

and all of Your nation, Israel — וְכָל עַמְּךָ בֵּית יִשְׂרָאֵל

**(let us be remembered and inscribed)
for a truly good life (i.e., a life that will
enable us to earn the World to Come)** — לְחַיִּים טוֹבִים

**and for peace within ourselves
(that we should be satisfied with
the materialistic things that we have).** — וּלְשָׁלוֹם.

THERE ARE DIFFERENT CUSTOMS CONCERNING THE CONCLUSION OF THIS BLESSING;
AND EVERYONE SHOULD FOLLOW HIS CUSTOM. IF ONE DOES NOT KNOW HIS CUSTOM
HE SHOULD RECITE THE VERSION ON THE RIGHT.

You are the Source of Blessing,	בָּרוּךְ אַתָּה	You are the Source of Blessing, Master of all,	בָּרוּךְ אַתָּה יהוה
Master of all,	יהוה	Who gives an abundance of goodness and success	הַמְבָרֵךְ
Who makes peace among all.	עוֹשֶׂה הַשָּׁלוֹם.	to His nation, Israel,	אֶת עַמּוֹ יִשְׂרָאֵל
		with peace.	בַּשָּׁלוֹם.

וִידּוּי – Confession[28]

The Master of all strength, Who is able to do anything
and Who takes care of us with Divine Providence,

אֱלֹהֵינוּ

and the God who took care
of our Fathers with Divine Providence

וֵאלֹהֵי אֲבוֹתֵינוּ

let our prayers come before
Your Throne of Glory

תָּבֹא לְפָנֶיךָ תְּפִלָּתֵנוּ

and do not ignore that which
we say with humility before You

וְאַל תִּתְעַלַּם מִתְּחִנָּתֵנוּ

for we are not so brazen and stubborn
[to claim that we are righteous][29]

שֶׁאֵין אֲנַחְנוּ עַזֵּי פָנִים וּקְשֵׁי עֹרֶף

---

28. *Siddur Rokeach* says that *Viduy* (Confession) must be said with concentration, with a broken heart and with great sorrow; the penitent must admit what he has done and resolve to leave his bad ways. If one says it in this way, then perhaps he can hope that the Merciful One Whose Hand is open will have mercy on him.

Yesod VeShoresh HaAvodah writes that before saying the *Viduy* one should have in mind that he is fulfilling a positive biblical commandment, as it says (*Bamidbar* 5:7), "and they should confess the sins that they have done." He writes further that **the main part of the *Viduy* is** the absolute and complete regret for having committed the sin and the acceptance to make fences to prevent oneself from succumbing to the sin again, for anyone who has sense will admit that confession that is not accompanied by repentance shows great *chutzpah* and brazenness.

According to *Seder HaYom* it is of paramount importance that the *Viduy* be said from the heart, not merely lip-service, for insincere *Viduy* increases one's sins, since he seems to think he is fooling the One Who knows all.

R' Chaim David Azulai [known as the *Chida*] writes that the essence of the *Viduy* is for the person to realize that he has absolutely sinned, and not seek excuses.

[I have cited examples of common sins that are included in each confession in parentheses, attempting to avoid repetition, although many sins could fall under two or more categories.]

29. R' Leib Chasman [*Or Yahel* (vol. 3 p. 317)] offers a remarkable rebuke concerning our *Viduy*: If we plumb the recesses of the average person's heart and listen to what he is really saying, we will see that he actually feels that he is righteous and has not sinned. And the proof for that is the *Viduy* itself !

We all know how difficult it is for a person to ask forgiveness of another person, to say, "I have wronged you." People go to great lengths to avoid this, even when they know that they are wrong. If so, how is it so easy for us to let flow a river of confessions, as if it is a song? There is no greater proof that we really do not at all feel we have sinned. If so, one should ask himself whether or not he is brazen (in this confession).

Therefore, while saying the *Viduy,* we have to stop and realize that we are discussing our sins, and are not offering a praise or song to God. When we realize this, then our hearts will be humbled by the recognition that we are very poor in merits, and we will beseech God for undeserved mercy, and that will be our greatest source of merit.

to say before You,

לוֹמַר לְפָנֶיךָ

Master of all, the Master of all strength, Who is able to do anything and Who takes care of us with Divine Providence,

יהוה אֱלֹהֵינוּ

and the God who took care
of our Fathers with Divine Providence,

וֵאלֹהֵי אֲבוֹתֵינוּ

that we are righteous and have not sinned [we are not so brazen to say that]

צַדִּיקִים אֲנַחְנוּ וְלֹא חָטָאנוּ

but really we [and our forefathers] have sinned.[30]

אֲבָל אֲנַחְנוּ [וַאֲבוֹתֵינוּ] חָטָאנוּ.

We have sinned so much that we deserve to be destroyed.

אָשַׁמְנוּ[31]

We have been ungrateful for the good God has done for us (and have even responded to His goodness with evil).[32]

בָּגַדְנוּ

We have stolen (this includes borrowing without permission, fooling someone ["stealing his mind"] and disturbing someone's sleep).[33]

גָּזַלְנוּ

---

30. *Midrash Tanchuma* (*Chukas* 19) states that if one admits that he has sinned, God is immediately appeased. It also states there (*Balak* 10) that the destroying angel has no right to touch anyone who admits that he has sinned. Therefore, we start the *Viduy* with this general confession of "we have sinned" (R' Yehudah ben Yakar).

31. The *Viduy* follows the order of the twenty-two letters of the Hebrew alphabet (*alef-beis*) to signify that we have sinned against the Torah which was written with these letters. One should not limit the confession to this prescribed list, but should add any sin one knows he has committed. Remarkably, there are common sins which are not explicit in the standard *Viduy* (such as: violating Shabbos, eating without saying the proper blessing beforehand, and men wasting time from learning Torah, among others) and one should add them in their proper places. (The proper formula in Hebrew can be found in the *Viduy HaChida*. If one does not understand it in Hebrew he can confess in any language he understands, because the main part of the *Viduy* is the sincerity of the verbal confession.)

It should also be noted that no matter how severe the punishment is for a sin — even if one is liable to lose his portion in the World to Come — *teshuvah* helps, for there is nothing that stands before *teshuvah*. Even if one denied God his entire life and did *teshuvah* at the end of his life, he has a portion in the World to Come (*Rambam, Hilchos Teshuvah* 3:14).

32. The Sages (*Mishnas R' Eliezer*) exhort us that God punishes ingratitude severely because it is tantamount to denying the existence of God. To the contrary, one should have such a degree of appreciation for God's myriad kindnesses to him since his birth that he is deterred from ever sinning (*Totzaos Chaim,* para. 190).

33. The Sages (*Koheles Rabbah* 1:13) tell us that in a mound of sins, the sin of theft brings indictment first. Furthermore, there is no act in the world that prevents one's prayers from being heard in Heaven more than robbery (*Yesod VeShoresh HaAvodah* 10:2).

We have spoken disgracefully about others
(this includes slander).[34]

דִּבַּֽרְנוּ דֹּֽפִי

We have caused perversion (this includes causing
others to sin or preventing others from doing *mitzvos*).[35]

הֶעֱוִֽינוּ

And we have judged the righteous
as if they were evil (and not favorably).[36]

וְהִרְשַֽׁעְנוּ

We have sinned intentionally.

זַֽדְנוּ

We have taken things away from others against
their will (even if we have paid them more than it was worth).

חָמַֽסְנוּ

We have added one lie onto another
in order to reinforce it.[37]

טָפַֽלְנוּ שֶֽׁקֶר

We have given advice that was bad for the
one who sought our advice.

יָעַֽצְנוּ רָע

---

34. *Chovos HaLevavos* (6:6) writes that one should speak positively to people, judge them favorably, and not speak about their shortcomings.

35. The *Rambam* (*Hilchos Teshuvah* 4:1) lists twenty-four sins that prevent a person from doing *teshuvah* (repentance); four of them are so great that God does not assist him to repent. Among those listed is one who causes the masses to sin, and included in that is one who prevents the masses from doing a *mitzvah* (see there for the rest).

36. The *Talmud* (*Shabbos* 97a) states that one who suspects an innocent person is stricken with bodily punishment. But (ibid. 127b) if one judges others favorably, then God will judge him favorably.

The *Chofetz Chaim* wrote (*Shemiras HaLashon* 2:4) that if a person accustoms himself to looking at others in an accusatory manner and speaking bad about them, then the angels will speak bad about him. Therefore, a person must realize that the way he judges others sets up the type of judgment he will have in Heaven.

According to *halachah, Rabbeinu Yonah* (*Shaarei Teshuvah* 3:218) writes, if the person in question is a God-fearing person, one is obligated to judge him favorably even if it appears more than likely to be a sin. And if the person in question is an *average* person, who usually avoids sin, and there is an equal doubt, then there is a positive command (*Vayikra* 19:15), "with righteousness you shall judge your fellow." If it appears more than likely to be a sin, it is still very proper to leave it as a doubt in one's mind, and not judge him as guilty.

37. The Talmud (*Sotah* 42a) enumerates four groups of people that will not greet the Divine Presence in the World to Come: scoffers, flatterers, liars and slanderers. The *Sefer HaChinuch* (*Mitzvah* 74) writes that lying is abominable to all; one who lies incurs Divine wrath because "God's seal is truth" (*Shabbos* 55a). Therefore the Torah warns us (*Shemos* 23:7), "Distance yourself from falsehood"; the expression to "distance yourself" does not appear in any other prohibition in the Torah, and shows how despicable falsehood is to God.

We have not kept our promises (including those
that we have made to God to better our ways).[38]

פִּזַבְנוּ

We have scoffed at people, at words of Torah,
and at important things and actions (included
in this is wasting time with idle chatter).[39]

לַצְנוּ

We have known God and yet rebelled against Him
(the worst of all sins).

מָרַדְנוּ

We have angered God with our sins.

נִאַצְנוּ

We have turned our hearts away from the service of God.

סָרַרְנוּ

We have sinned only to fulfill our desires.

עָוִינוּ

We have sinned because we denied God's existence.

פָּשַׁעְנוּ

We have caused others pain.

צָרַרְנוּ

We have been stubborn and have not accepted
rebuke; we have not viewed personal hardships
as a message to improve our ways.[40]

קִשִּׁינוּ עֹרֶף

We have done actions that make us considered
wicked (like raising our hand to hit someone).

רָשַׁעְנוּ

---

38. God takes no pleasure in those who make many promises and do not fulfill them,
thinking that their good intentions are what counts. It is better not to make a promise
than to make one and not keep it. So too, it is better to resolve to improve in one small
way, rather than to accept to do something major and not fulfill it (*Ramban, Devarim*
23:23).

39. Scoffers are one of the four groups of people who do not merit greeting the Divine
Presence in the World to Come (see above note 37). In addition, the Talmud (*Avodah
Zarah* 18b) says regarding anyone who scoffs: Punishment befalls him, his food will be
diminished, he brings destruction to the world, and he falls into *gehinnom* (hell). The
Sages tell us (*Shir HaShirim Rabbah,* Ch. 1 3:2) that for every *word* of scoffing that
enters into one's heart, correspondingly, a word of Torah is lost.

There are many different forms of scoffing. The *Mishnah* (*Avos* 3:3) states that if two
men are sitting together and there are no words of Torah said between them, it is
considered a session of scoffers. *Rabbeinu Yonah* (*Shaarei Teshuvah* 3:177) writes that
the Sages would warn their students not to scoff even casually because of the great
danger of this trait.

40. *Sefer Chareidim* (21:26) notes that in the Torah (*Devarim* 10:16) there is a positive
commandment to love rebuke and the one who gives it, as well as a negative commandment (ibid.) not to be stubborn in accepting the rebuke.

We have corrupted ourselves with sins that are tantamount to immorality[41] and idolatry.[42]

שִׁחַתְנוּ

We have done acts that are abominable in the eyes of God (like actual immorality and idolatry).

תִּעַבְנוּ

We have strayed from the straight path of service to God.

תָּעִינוּ

We have done deceitful acts.[43]

תִּעְתָּעְנוּ.

We have turned away from fulfilling Your positive commandments

סַרְנוּ מִמִּצְוֹתֶיךָ

and from not fulfilling the good and pleasant positive commandments that You obligate us towards others

וּמִמִשְׁפָּטֶיךָ הַטּוֹבִים

and we have not gained by refraining from doing Your *mitzvos* (for we have lost much more than we have gained)

וְלֹא שָׁוָה לָנוּ

and You are righteous (justified) in all the punishments that You have brought on us[44]

וְאַתָּה צַדִּיק עַל כָּל הַבָּא עָלֵינוּ

because You have judged us truthfully

כִּי אֱמֶת עָשִׂיתָ

but we have been increasingly wicked.

וַאֲנַחְנוּ הִרְשָׁעְנוּ.

---

41. This includes all improper conduct with the opposite gender, as well as wasting one's own seed.

42. This includes haughtiness, anger and refraining from giving charity, all of which the Sages compare to idolatry.

43. The Talmud (*Sanhedrin* 92a) says that anyone who switches his words in deceit is like an idol worshiper. It says concerning Jacob that he was afraid that his father would perceive him as מְתַעְתֵּעַ, *deceiver* (*Bereishis* 27:12) [the same expression used for idolatry]. This is included in the four groups that do not merit greeting the Divine Presence in the World to Come (see above note 37) [*Rabbeinu Yonah, Shaarei Teshuvah* 3:180]. Concerning deceit in action, it says (*Mishlei* 11:1), "Deceitful scales are an abomination to God."

44. *Siddur Maggid Tzedek* says that one should say this phrase very humbly and sincerely, fully accepting God's judgment. He then quotes a *Midrash* (*Pesikta Rabbasi*, Ch. 35) which tells us that God says to the heavenly angels, "Come and see the righteousness of My children! Although I have brought upon them many retributions in every generation, yet they have not rebelled; rather, they call themselves wicked and they call Me righteous . . ." The *Kitzur Shelah* adds that we should say these words with joy, accepting God's punishments happily, recognizing that they are truly for our good, to atone our sins in order that we enter the World to Come purified.

What can we say before Your Throne
of Glory to justify ourselves

מַה נֹּאמַר לְפָנֶיךָ

(to You) Who sits high in the Heavens
(and Whose eyes gaze over the entire world)

יוֹשֵׁב מָרוֹם

and what can we confess of our sins
before You

וּמַה נְּסַפֵּר לְפָנֶיךָ

Who sits in the heavens (and knows all)

שׁוֹכֵן שְׁחָקִים

for all things, both those that are hidden
from people and those that are revealed,

הֲלֹא כָּל הַנִּסְתָּרוֹת וְהַנִּגְלוֹת

You already know.

אַתָּה יוֹדֵעַ.

You know the secrets of the universe

אַתָּה יוֹדֵעַ רָזֵי עוֹלָם

and all the actions people have tried to conceal.

וְתַעֲלוּמוֹת סִתְרֵי כָּל חָי

You search out all the
inner thoughts of a person

אַתָּה חֹפֵשׂ כָּל חַדְרֵי בָטֶן

and examine one's motives
and intentions (to determine
if the actions were premeditated, done with joy, etc.).

וּבֹחֵן כְּלָיוֹת וָלֵב

There is no thought that is hidden from You

אֵין (כָּל) דָּבָר נֶעְלָם מִמֶּךָ

and there is no action that escapes Your eyes.

וְאֵין נִסְתָּר מִנֶּגֶד עֵינֶיךָ.

And so [with this recognition],
we ask that it be a favorable time
to let our prayers come before You

וּבְכֵן יְהִי רָצוֹן מִלְּפָנֶיךָ

Master of all, the Master of all strength,
Who is able to do anything and Who takes
care of us with Divine Providence,

יהוה אֱלֹהֵינוּ

and the God who took care of
our Fathers with Divine Providence

וֵאלֹהֵי אֲבוֹתֵינוּ

that You forgive us for
the sins themselves that we
transgressed unintentionally

שֶׁתִּסְלַח לָנוּ עַל כָּל חַטֹאתֵינוּ

and You pardon us the insult to Your Honor
that we caused with our willful sins

וְתִמְחָל לָנוּ עַל כָּל עֲוֹנוֹתֵינוּ

and You atone (entirely
wipe out any trace) for our sins
that we did even rebelliously.

וּתְכַפֶּר לָנוּ עַל כָּל פְּשָׁעֵינוּ.

ONE SHOULD STRIKE THE LEFT SIDE OF THE CHEST (WHERE THE HEART IS)
WITH THE RIGHT FIST WHEN SAYING שֶׁחָטָאנוּ ("WE HAVE SINNED").
BY THE LAST GROUP (STARTING "AND FOR THE SINS FOR WHICH WE ARE OBLIGATED")
ONE SHOULD STRIKE THE CHEST WHEN SAYING שֶׁאָנוּ חַיָּבִים
("FOR WHICH WE ARE OBLIGATED") [MEKOR CHAIM, KITZUR HALACHOS, CH. 607].

[Forgive, pardon and atone] for the sins
we have sinned before You
(Whose Honor fills the earth)

עַל חֵטְא שֶׁחָטָאנוּ לְפָנֶיךָ

with coercion (when we were not permitted to submit[45])

בְּאֹנֶס

and those we have done willingly (with desire).

וּבְרָצוֹן.

And for the sins we havesinned before You

וְעַל חֵטְא שֶׁחָטָאנוּ לְפָנֶיךָ

with a hardened heart (this includes refraining from
giving charity, or any form of cruelty).[46]

בְּאִמּוּץ הַלֵּב.

For the sins we have sinned before You

עַל חֵטְא שֶׁחָטָאנוּ לְפָנֶיךָ

without thought (we have done things
without putting our minds to them,
including *mitzvos* not done expressly to serve God).

בִּבְלִי דָעַת.

---

45. This includes when one is coerced, even with the threat of death, to commit idolatry, immorality or murder. Likewise it includes an act which will cause a desecration of the Name of God, such as when there is a decree to uproot Judaism, in which case one may not transgress even the smallest Rabbinic decree.

The *Yaavetz* wrote that even in a case where one is coerced to do a sin to which he is permitted to submit, the act still requires forgiveness, for he should have prayed not to be put into such a predicament (as we pray every morning, "do not bring us . . . unto a difficult test").

46. In the verse (*Devarim* 15:7), "You should not harden your heart and you should not close your hand," the Torah admonishes us to eradicate the trait of cruelty from within ourselves; and we should implant in ourselves the traits of goodness, namely, true mercy and kindness (*Rabbeinu Yonah, Shaarei Teshuvah* 3:36).

And for the sins we have sinned before You	וְעַל חֵטְא שֶׁחָטָאנוּ לְפָנֶיךָ
with speech lacking proper contemplation (like making vows or promising to do something that we subsequently regret).	בְּבִטּוּי שְׂפָתָיִם.
For the sins we have sinned before You	עַל חֵטְא שֶׁחָטָאנוּ לְפָנֶיךָ
whether in a public place (without any sense of shame) or in seclusion (ignoring the omnipresence of God).[47]	בַּגָּלוּי וּבַסָּתֶר.
And for the sins we have sinned before You	וְעַל חֵטְא שֶׁחָטָאנוּ לְפָנֶיךָ
with immorality.[48]	בְּגִלּוּי עֲרָיוֹת.
For the sins we have sinned before You	עַל חֵטְא שֶׁחָטָאנוּ לְפָנֶיךָ
by speaking too much (which inevitably causes sins) and all sins of the mouth (including expressing a grudge).[49]	בְּדִבּוּר פֶּה.

---

47. In one way committing a sin overtly is worse, because it shows an open disregard for God, concerning which the Torah writes (*Bamidbar* 15:30-31), ''A person who acts highhandedly . . . that person will surely be cut off, his sin is upon him.'' This refers to someone who does something in public that everyone knows is a sin (*Rabbeinu Yonah, Shaarei Teshuvah* 3:143).

In another sense, committing a sin privately is worse, since it shows that one cares more about what people see than what God sees. The *Talmud* (*Bava Kamma* 79b) writes that the reason the Torah punished the thief who steals at night (covertly) more than one who robs in broad daylight, is that the daytime robber equates people with God (not caring what either sees), whereas a nighttime thief is more afraid of people than he is of God, and therefore he deserves a greater punishment.

48. This includes: forbidden sexual relationships (which is one of the three cardinal sins for which one is required to give up his life rather than transgress); any physical contact with the other gender that is not permitted by Jewish law; any violations of the laws of *niddah;* gazing at women (see *Mishnah Berurah* 75:7); and speaking excessively with a woman (see *Avos* 1:5).

49. *Rabbeinu Yonah* (*Shaarei Teshuvah* 3:63) points out that we can get an idea of how severe sins of the mouth are by contemplating that the punishment for cursing one's parents is greater than the punishment for hitting them! The *Vilna Gaon* (in his famous letter to his wife) wrote, ''The sins of the tongue are greater than anything . . . for the punishment of a terrible part of *gehinnom* (hell) called *kaf hakela* is just for the sin of idle talk, and for every speech one is 'flung' from one end of the world to the other, and that is only for extra words. But for forbidden speech, such as *lashon hara* (gossip) or *leitzanus* (scoffing), false oaths and vows, and arguments and curses, especially in a synagogue and on Shabbos or the Festivals one must go to an exceedingly deep pit, and it is impossible to imagine the great tribulations one must suffer for just one word!''

An amazing account of what happens in the Next World is printed in the introduction to *Kochvei Or* (vol. II, p. 21). R' Yitzchak Blazer (more commonly known as *R' Itzele*

And for the sins we have sinned before You

וְעַל חֵטְא שֶׁחָטָאנוּ לְפָנֶיךָ

by purposely sinning against our friend
or causing him damage, while deceitfully
claiming that it was unintentional.

בְּדַעַת וּבְמִרְמָה.

For the sins we have sinned before You

עַל חֵטְא שֶׁחָטָאנוּ לְפָנֶיךָ

with forbidden thoughts (like those of
idolatry or atheism, lustful thoughts
or obsession with money).[50]

בְּהַרְהוֹר הַלֵּב.

And for the sins we have sinned before You

וְעַל חֵטְא שֶׁחָטָאנוּ לְפָנֶיךָ

by causing our friend pain with hurtful
words or financial dishonesty.[51]

בְּהוֹנָאַת רֵעַ.

For the sins we have sinned before You

עַל חֵטְא שֶׁחָטָאנוּ לְפָנֶיךָ

with confession said only with our mouth, and not with
sincere regret, nor commitment not to sin again.[52]

בְּוִדּוּי פֶּה.

And for the sins we have sinned before You

וְעַל חֵטְא שֶׁחָטָאנוּ לְפָנֶיךָ

for having gathered for the purpose of lustfulness.

בִּוְעִידַת זְנוּת.

Peterburger) died in Jerusalem on 11 Av, 5667 (July 22, 1907). On the following Shabbos (July 27) he appeared in a dream to his dear friend R' Chaim Berlin, who asked him how he had fared in his judgment in that world. R' Itzele answered that the judgment in Heaven is very stringent — so much so, that no one in this world can imagine it at all, **and there is an especially great strictness concerning forbidden words!** [What makes this statement even more amazing is the fact that every year during the forty days from Rosh Chodesh Elul until after Yom Kippur it was R' Itzele's practice not to speak at all (except for learning and praying), and still he bemoaned the severe judgment for forbidden words.]

50. The *Gemara* (*Yoma* 29a) says that thoughts of doing a sin are worse than the sin, because they preoccupy the person. And the *Rambam* (*Hilchos Teshuvah* 4:5) writes that being constantly occupied with bad thoughts prevents one from doing *teshuvah*.

51. The *Talmud* (*Bava Metzia* 58b) says that paining someone with words (i.e. insulting or embarrassing him) is worse than hurting him financially (i.e. cheating him). Furthermore, if one embarrasses his friend in public it is tantamount to murdering him (ibid.) and he has no share in the World to Come (ibid. 59a). [See *Shaarei Teshuvah* 3:141.]

52. *Or Yahel* (vol. 3, p. 248) writes, "How foolish are people who say many long confessions while their hearts are not with them. They do not realize that not only do they not appease God by saying such confessions, but they add another sin to their account, as we say in this stanza. And how disgraceful it is that this line of the confession they also say only with their mouths!"

For the sins we have sinned before You

עַל חֵטְא שֶׁחָטָאנוּ לְפָנֶיךָ

whether with intention and knowledge of the sin, or without intention or knowledge of the sin.[53]

בְּזָדוֹן וּבִשְׁגָגָה.

And for the sins we have sinned before You

וְעַל חֵטְא שֶׁחָטָאנוּ לְפָנֶיךָ

by not giving honor, or even disgracing, our parents, teachers and rabbis.[54]

בְּזִלְזוּל הוֹרִים וּמוֹרִים.

For the sins we have sinned before You

עַל חֵטְא שֶׁחָטָאנוּ לְפָנֶיךָ

by forcing our friends, whether physically or otherwise, to do our will.

בְּחֹזֶק יָד.

And for the sins we have sinned before You

וְעַל חֵטְא שֶׁחָטָאנוּ לְפָנֶיךָ

by causing a desecration to the honor of God (by not thinking adequately before any action about its repercussions).[55]

בְּחִלּוּל הַשֵּׁם.

---

53. *Kochvei Or* [*R' Itzele Peterburger* (Ch. 3)] quotes the *Ramban* (*Vayikra* 1:9) who writes that when a person brings a sacrifice for having sinned to God with his body and soul, he should realize that it is fitting that his blood be spilled and his body burned — were it not for the kindness of God, Who accepted an animal in his stead. On this R' Itzele comments, how frightening it is that even for committing a sin *unintentionally* [which is the reason for a *korban chatas*] it is fitting that he should die; if so, how much greater is the punishment for one who commits a sin intentionally, for there is certainly no comparison between one who errs unintentionally and the terrible act of sinning intentionally. R' Itzele goes on to describe the tremendous gap between our perception and the true magnitude of an unintentional sin; nowadays, one who commits a sin unintentionally does not even feel that he needs to ask for forgiveness, but in truth, his misdeed is so terrible that, as the *Ramban* says, he deserves death! However, as noted above, note 31, *teshuvah* atones for all sins.

54. The *Talmud* (*Sanhedrin* 99b) defines an *apikores* as one who disgraces a Torah scholar. It is clear from the *Gemara* (ibid.), as well as from *Rambam* (*Hilchos Talmud Torah* 6:11), that one who disgraces a Torah scholar [and does not ask forgiveness from him] has no share in the World to Come! (See *Moadim U'Zemanim* vol. 2, Ch. 191, note 2 concerning the severity of this prohibition even on Purim.) The *Iyun Tefillah* writes that disgracing one's parents and teachers is the "grandfather" of all sins!

Included in the obligation of honor is the requirement to stand up fully when one's father, mother, Torah teacher or rabbi walks within seven feet of him, even if he is learning Torah at that time (see *Yorah Deah* 240:7, 242:30 and 244:1 and 11).

55. This is the most severe of all sins, for as the *Gemara* (*Yoma* 86a) says, unlike other sins, the transgression of *chillul Hashem* (the desecration of the Name of God) is not fully atoned for until death, even though one has done repentance, observed Yom Kippur, and been punished by retribution. However, *Rabbeinu Yonah* (*Shaarei Teshuvah* 1:47 and 4:16) writes two ways in which one can be forgiven in this world even for this terrible sin: (1) by increasing his actions to sanctify the Name of God, and by

For the sins we have sinned before You

עַל חֵטְא שֶׁחָטָאנוּ לְפָנֶיךָ

with idle talk (which shows everyone how foolish he is, wasting his time with meaningless chatter).[56]

בְּטִפְשׁוּת פֶּה.

And for the sins we have sinned before You

וְעַל חֵטְא שֶׁחָטָאנוּ לְפָנֶיךָ

with impure lips (i.e. talking obscene language or about indecent things).[57]

בְּטֻמְאַת שְׂפָתָיִם.

For the sins we have sinned before You

עַל חֵטְא שֶׁחָטָאנוּ לְפָנֶיךָ

by inciting our evil inclination.[58]

בְּיֵצֶר הָרָע.

---

supporting and strengthening truth (i.e., service of God), corresponding to the amount of desecration he caused; (2) by constantly thinking about Torah and exerting himself in its study. These are wonderful opportunities of hope for anyone who has transgressed this sin.

Rambam (Hilchos Yesodei HaTorah, end of Ch. 5) writes that one form of desecration of God is when a person whom people expect to act in an elevated manner, does not act that way. That is considered a chillul Hashem. Alei Shur (vol. 1, p. 49) writes that whenever a yeshivah student leaves the yeshivah building, he should immediately be on guard that his actions not cause chillul Hashem.

56. It is appropriate to quote here a selection from the saintly Chofetz Chaim (Shemiras HaLashon vol. 2, Ch. 6): "A person whose life is dear to him should be careful not to waste it, yet we see nowadays that people are not prudent concerning this. Let us explain: If it were possible for a person to give away part of his life to his friend, nevertheless no one would do so, even to give away a month or a week — and rightfully so, since there is nothing more precious than time; the limited amount of time that God granted a man in His kindness is meant for him to earn for himself eternal reward. However, people who are not careful in their speech knowingly and willingly squander a lot of time each day, sometimes even several hours. At least an hour each day goes to waste . . . and if he calculates he will find that in an entire year he has wasted **over 350 hours** [more than two week's worth of time in one year]. Certainly he has not gained any reward in the World to Come for these words, and not even any pleasure in this world. All that he has achieved by this is to create a void of a great deal of Torah [namely, all that he could have learned in that time]! Is there a greater foolishness than this?"

57. The Gemara (Shabbos 33a) states that because of the sin of obscene language, many calamities and harsh decrees come upon Israel, and young people die. Furthermore, regarding anyone who defiles his mouth with such speech, even if it was decreed that he should have a good life, it will change to bad, and (not only that but) he will descend to the depths of gehinnom.

The reason for the severity of this sin is that one who defiles his mouth with obscene language has left the ways of shame and modesty, which are the recognized character traits of the Jewish people (Rabbeinu Yonah, Shaarei Teshuvah 3:229).

58. The Talmud (Sanhedrin 107a) says that a person should never put himself into a situation of nisayon, a test [with his yetzer hara]. Included in this is viewing immodest pictures, reading articles that portray immodesty, or, certainly, viewing other media with such content.

The Sages have however advised how to save oneself from the evil inclination. The

And for the sins we have sinned before You

וְעַל חֵטְא שֶׁחָטָאנוּ לְפָנֶיךָ

by harming others in ways
that they know or in ways they don't know
(like slandering him behind his back).

בְּיוֹדְעִים וּבְלֹא יוֹדְעִים.

And for all the sins that we have mentioned

וְעַל כֻּלָּם

[You,] the God Who abundantly forgives, [please]

אֱלוֹהַּ סְלִיחוֹת

forgive us for the sins themselves

סְלַח לָנוּ

pardon us for the insult caused to Your Honor by our sins

מְחַל לָנוּ

(and) atone for us our sins as if they had never occurred.

כַּפֶּר לָנוּ.

For the sins we have sinned before You

עַל חֵטְא שֶׁחָטָאנוּ לְפָנֶיךָ

by giving or taking a bribe.[59]

בְּכַפַּת שֹׁחַד.

And for the sins we have sinned before You

וְעַל חֵטְא שֶׁחָטָאנוּ לְפָנֶיךָ

by denying what was (i.e., plain lying)
and by not keeping our promises.[60]

בְּכַחַשׁ וּבְכָזָב.

For the sins we have sinned before You

עַל חֵטְא שֶׁחָטָאנוּ לְפָנֶיךָ

Gemara (*Berachos* 5a) states that one should always stir up his *yetzer tov* (good inclination) to overcome his evil inclination, and, if he did not succeed with that alone, he should learn Torah. If that also does not stop the *yetzer hara,* then he should read *Shema* [which contains the declaration of the oneness of God], and if he still cannot overcome his evil urge, he should remind himself of the day of death. [See *Lev Eliyahu* vol. 3, p. 174 for a beautiful interpretation of this *Gemara.*]

It is also important to realize that when one has the opportunity to sin, but refrains from doing so because God forbade it, there is no *mitzvah* greater than that (*Rashi, Kiddushin* 39b), and he draws onto himself a light of holiness greater than anyone can imagine (*Karyana D'Igarta* vol. 1, p. 22).

59. The *Rambam* (*Hilchos Sanhedrin* 23:2) writes that just as the one who receives the bribe violates a negative commandment (*Shemos* 23:8), ''Do not accept a bribe,'' so too the giver violates the command of ''you shall not place a stumbling block before the blind'' (*Vayikra* 19:14). The *Gemara* (*Kesubos* 105a) further states that even a very wise man who takes a bribe will not die before he has a ''blindness of heart'' (i.e., he will become foolish).

60. See above, notes 37 and 38.

by speaking or accepting disparaging words about someone else, even if true.[61]

בִּלְשׁוֹן הָרָע.

And for the sins we have sinned before You

וְעַל חֵטְא שֶׁחָטָאנוּ לְפָנֶיךָ

by scoffing at people, words of Torah, and at important things and actions.[62]

בְּלָצוֹן.

For the sins we have sinned before You

עַל חֵטְא שֶׁחָטָאנוּ לְפָנֶיךָ

by dealing in business dishonestly (e.g. deception or faulty measures).[63]

בְּמַשָּׂא וּבְמַתָּן.

And for the sins we have sinned before You

וְעַל חֵטְא שֶׁחָטָאנוּ לְפָנֶיךָ

by eating and drinking (this includes eating non-kosher foods or foods that had insects; or eating without a blessing).[64]

בְּמַאֲכָל וּבְמִשְׁתֶּה.

For the sins we have sinned before You

עַל חֵטְא שֶׁחָטָאנוּ לְפָנֶיךָ

---

61. The *Talmud* (*Sotah* 42a) says that four groups of people do not merit to greet the Divine Presence in the World to Come; one of those is slanderers. The Sages tell us (*Yerushalmi Pe'ah* 1:1) that there are four sins for which God exacts judgment in this world, and even more so in the World to Come, and they are: idolatry, immorality, and murder; and slander is equal to them all. [See also *Rambam* (*Hilchos Dei'os* 7:3).] Because of the prevalence of this sin, an entire work was written on this subject by the saintly R' Yisrael Meir HaKohen called *Chofetz Chaim,* the name by which he became known.

62. See above, note 39.

63. The first question one is asked when he appears before the Heavenly Tribunal for judgment after death is, "Did you deal honestly in business?" (*Shabbos* 31a). Since the Sages have revealed this to us, this question should remain foremost in our minds while we are still in this world so that we will have a positive answer when the time comes.

64. The *Yesod VeShoresh HaAvodah* writes (1:10) that a person should realize how many blessings on food he said without concentration, for if one says a blessing without concentration God does not consider it a blessing, and logically we should not be able to tolerate this as a blessing.

There is an amazing story written in *Sefer Chasidim* (Ch. 46) [quoted also in *Chayei Adam* (5:26)]: There was a man who died and came to one of his relatives in a dream, more than twelve months after he had died, and revealed that every day he was being punished for not saying *hamotzi* [the blessing before eating bread], and the blessing on fruits, and *bircas hamazon* [the blessing after a meal] **with concentration!** "But," asked the relative, "isn't the judgment in *gehinnom,* even for the wicked, only twelve months?" [*Mishnah* in *Eduyos* (2:10)]. The deceased man answered, "I am not punished now with punishments as harsh as in the first twelve months!"

From this story we learn the importance of reciting *brachos* with proper concentration, and training our children from their youth in this matter.

by taking or paying interest (this includes verbal interest, or paying more for credit).[65]	בְּנֶשֶׁךְ וּבְמַרְבִּית.
And for the sins we have sinned before You	וְעַל חֵטְא שֶׁחָטָאנוּ לְפָנֶיךָ
(by walking) with an outstretched neck (in a haughty manner; includes any act of overt haughtiness).[66]	בִּנְטִיַּת גָּרוֹן.
For the sins we have sinned before You	עַל חֵטְא שֶׁחָטָאנוּ לְפָנֶיךָ
with a wink or motion of the eye (which is sometimes enough to harm others or entice them to sin).	בְּשִׂקּוּר עָיִן.
And for the sins we have sinned before You	וְעַל חֵטְא שֶׁחָטָאנוּ לְפָנֶיךָ
by saying words without concentration (like praying, saying blessings, or answering *Amen* without thinking).[67]	בְּשִׂיחַ שִׂפְתוֹתֵינוּ.

---

65. The *Gemara* (*Bava Metzia* 62a) says that the lender, borrower, guarantor and witnesses are all guilty of transgressing the command (*Vayikra* 25:36), "Do not take from him interest" [see *Rashi* ibid., that נשך and תרבית are synonymous (*Bava Metzia* 60b); the Torah wrote both so that all those who are involved in paying interest are in violation of two commandments. (The text of this confession obviously mirrors the expression in the Torah.)]

The punishment for transgressing this command is shocking; the Sages (*Shemos Rabbah* 31:6) state that one who lives on interest will not live in the World to Come. [See also *Rabbeinu Yonah* (*Shaarei Teshuvah* 3:25) who says that he will not arise by the Resurrection of the Dead, based on a verse in *Yechezkel* (18:13).]

Siach Yitzchak warns that anyone who wants to save himself from the many intricate violations concerning usury (especially a businessman) has no alternative but to learn the laws of interest thoroughly in the *Shulchan Aruch* (*Yoreh Deah* Chs. 159-177). [However, recently an excellent work has been published in English, *The Laws of Ribbis* (Mesorah Publications, 1995), which is written in a very practical and understandable way, and is highly recommended.]

66. It says in *Mishlei* (16:5), "Every haughty heart is the abomination of God." Haughtiness is an abomination even if it remains in the heart, all the more so if one displays it (*Orchos Tzaddikim*, Ch. 1). Because a haughty person is an abomination of God, he does not receive Divine assistance, and will be overcome by his evil inclination (*Shaarei Teshuvah* 1:27). The *Gemara* (*Sotah* 4b) teaches that haughtiness is likened to idolatry, denying the existence of God, and immorality. *Rabbeinu Yonah* (*Shaarei Teshuvah* 3:34) writes that haughtiness is one of the most severe sins which ruin and destroy the soul.

67. Concerning the severity of not praying with concentration, see Introduction to *Pathway to Prayer — Shemoneh Esrei*. Let it suffice to cite one quote here: *Sefer Chareidim* writes (p. 60), "The *Smak* counts *tefillah* as a *mitzvah* that depends on the heart, and if one does not concentrate when praying he has not fulfilled his requirement, and his punishment is very great ... *Yeshayahu HaNavi* (Isaiah the Prophet) said, 'Since this nation has approached [Me], it has honored Me with its mouth and its lips,

For the sins we have sinned before You

עַל חֵטְא שֶׁחָטָאנוּ לְפָנֶיךָ

by looking down at people because of our haughtiness.

בְּעֵינַיִם רָמוֹת.

And for the sins we have sinned before You

וְעַל חֵטְא שֶׁחָטָאנוּ לְפָנֶיךָ

by being brazen towards our rabbis or towards anyone greater than us.[68]

בְּעַזּוּת מֵצַח.

And for all the sins that we have mentioned

וְעַל כֻּלָּם

[You,] the God Who abundantly forgives, [please]

אֱלוֹהַּ סְלִיחוֹת

forgive us for the sins themselves

סְלַח לָנוּ

pardon us for the insult caused to Your Honor by our sins

מְחַל לָנוּ

(and) atone for us our sins as if they had never occurred.

כַּפֶּר לָנוּ.

For the sins we have sinned before You

עַל חֵטְא שֶׁחָטָאנוּ לְפָנֶיךָ

by throwing off the yoke of Heaven or even the yoke of one *mitzvah* (like the yoke of learning Torah).[69]

בִּפְרִיקַת עֹל.

---

but its heart it has distanced from Me . . . Therefore, I will continue to bring evil upon this nation . . .' (21:13-14). This reproof is referring to the Jews praying without concentration." See also above, note 52.

Concerning saying *Amen* with concentration, the *Rama* (O.C. 124:8) discusses the requirement to know which blessing one is affirming. See also *Chayei Adam* (5:1) concerning being meticulous to say the Name of God with concentration, and a frightening story pertaining to it.

68. The *Gemara* (*Taanis* 7b) says that it is permitted to call anyone who is brazen a "*rasha*" (wicked). *Orchos Tzaddikim* writes (Ch. 4) that it is easy for a brazen person to transgress any sin in the Torah, and concerning him it says (*Avos* 5:20), "a brazen-faced person is bound for *gehinnom*." A brazen person is also lacking one of the primary characteristics of a Jew, as the *Gemara* (*Yevamos* 79a) says, "These are the signs of a Jew: They are merciful, shame-faced [the opposite of this characteristic], and benevolent."

69. Virtually everyone is guilty of throwing off the yoke of Torah, for anyone who wastes time with meaningless pursuits when he could be learning, is guilty of throwing off this yoke (*Siach Yitzchak*). *Rabbeinu Yonah* (*Shaarei Teshuvah* 3:169) writes, describing those who "forsake God": "They are people who do not bear the yoke of fear of Heaven, fulfilling *mitzvos* by rote, and when they succumb to sin, they do not sigh or worry about their sin."

And for the sins we have sinned before You

וְעַל חֵטְא שֶׁחָטָאנוּ לְפָנֶיךָ

by perversion of judgment
(including questioning the justice of God).[70]

בִּפְלִילוּת.

For the sins we have sinned before You

עַל חֵטְא שֶׁחָטָאנוּ לְפָנֶיךָ

by entrapping a friend (even if no harm resulted).

בִּצְדִיַּת רֵעַ.

And for the sins we have sinned before You

וְעַל חֵטְא שֶׁחָטָאנוּ לְפָנֶיךָ

with a begrudging eye, feeling unhappy
when things go well for others (this also refers
to one who does not want to do good for others).

בְּצָרוּת עָיִן.

For the sins we have sinned before You

עַל חֵטְא שֶׁחָטָאנוּ לְפָנֶיךָ

by acting light-headedly (without fear of Heaven)
while doing *mitzvos* or in holy places (like a synagogue).[71]

בְּקַלּוּת רֹאשׁ.

And for the sins we have sinned before You

וְעַל חֵטְא שֶׁחָטָאנוּ לְפָנֶיךָ

---

70. The *Chofetz Chaim* (in his commentary on Torah to *Shemos* 33:13) gives a powerful parable to help us with any questions concerning Divine Providence, including the age-old question [first asked by *Moshe Rabbeinu,* as mentioned in *Berachos* (7a)] of why sometimes good people suffer, and sometimes bad people prosper.

It can be compared to a guest who came for a Shabbos to a synagogue and saw the *gabbai* calling people up to the Torah. Afterwards, the guest criticized the *gabbai,* saying, "Why did you call up the Kohen and the Levi from the south side of the synagogue? Wasn't there a more honorable Kohen and Levi on the east side of the synagogue?" He complained about all the *aliyos* in a similar vein.

One wise man retorted, "You have been in this synagogue for just one Shabbos, and you want to understand the order of the *aliyos*? If you would be here several weeks, then you would understand that the order of the *gabbai* is correct! Last week the *gabbai* called up the Kohen and Levi from the east side of the synagogue, and therefore this week he called up those from the south side. The same with all the *aliyos;* he skipped over those who recently had *aliyos,* and called up the others."

So too, says the *Chofetz Chaim,* a person comes to this world for just a short while, and yet he wants to know the answers to all the questions! Were he here for a few hundred years, then he would see why some people are poor and others rich. The poor man was actually rich [in his previous *gilgul* (transmigration of the soul)] and the rich man was poor [in his previous *gilgul*] and they both did not succeed in their tests, and because of that their lots were switched. But man, whose life is short, is like the one-Shabbos guest, and cannot possibly know all this. Therefore, we cannot question the ways of God. Rather, we should trust in God and believe that everything He does is correct.

71. Laughter and light-headedness bring a man to licentiousness (*Avos* 3:13). See *Mesillas Yesharim* (Ch. 5), which states that laughter and light-headedness remove one's heart from straight thoughts and gradually remove the fear of God from him.

by having been stubborn, not accepting rebuke or not looking at personal hardships as a message to improve our ways.[72]

בְּקַשְׁיוּת עֹרֶף.

For the sins we have sinned before You

עַל חֵטְא שֶׁחָטָאנוּ לְפָנֶיךָ

with feet running to do evil.[73]

בְּרִיצַת רַגְלַיִם לְהָרַע.

And for the sins we have sinned before You

וְעַל חֵטְא שֶׁחָטָאנוּ לְפָנֶיךָ

by tale-bearing (i.e., going from one to another relating information which causes ill will between people) or accepting the tale.[74]

בִּרְכִילוּת.

For the sins we have sinned before You

עַל חֵטְא שֶׁחָטָאנוּ לְפָנֶיךָ

by swearing falsely or in vain.[75]

בִּשְׁבוּעַת שָׁוְא

And for the sins we have sinned before You

וְעַל חֵטְא שֶׁחָטָאנוּ לְפָנֶיךָ

by hating other Jews without a valid reason.[76]

בְּשִׂנְאַת חִנָּם.

---

72. See above, note 40.

73. *Dover Shalom* writes that outside of the actual sin, God takes into account the way the sin was done, for example, whether it was done happily or sadly, anxiously or with hesitation. [This concept is hinted at before the עַל חֵטְא list; it says that God is בּוֹחֵן כְּלָיוֹת וָלֵב, He examines one's motives and intentions (to determine if the actions were premeditated, done with joy, etc.).]

74. The *Rambam* (*Hilchos Dei'os* 7:1-2) writes that tale-bearing causes the death of many Jews and destroys the world. See above, note 61, because *rechilus* (tale-bearing) is included in *lashon hora* (gossip), as *Rabbeinu Yonah* (*Shaarei Teshuvah* 3:222) writes.

75. It is written (*Shemos* 20:7), "You should not take the Name of God, your God, in vain, for God will not absolve anyone who takes His Name in vain." The *Gemara* (*Shevuos* 39a) comments on the harsh punishment stated in this verse, that concerning all other sins God will absolve the sinner, but here God will not absolve him. The *Gemara* continues that this is not the only difference between the punishment for a false oath and other sins, for with all other sins the retribution comes only upon him, but for this sin the retribution comes on him, his family and the entire world; and for other sins God sometimes delays the punishment, but for this sin he is punished immediately. The reason for this severity, explains *Rabbeinu Yonah* (*Shaarei Teshuvah* 3:45), is that one who swears falsely desecrates the Name of God, and the punishment for desecration of God's Name is greater than for all other sins (see above, note 55). See also *Midrash Tanchuma* (*Matos* 1), which notes that one who acts treacherously regarding oaths denies the existence of God [in whose Name he said the oath].

76. The *Gemara* (*Yoma* 9a) tells us that the First Temple was destroyed because of the sins of idolatry, immorality and murder, whereas the Second Temple was destroyed because of *sinas chinam* (unjustified hatred), to teach that *sinas chinam* is equal to the

For the sins we have sinned before You

עַל חֵטְא שֶׁחָטָאנוּ לְפָנֶיךָ

by not acting properly with money that was
entrusted to us (such as in a partnership,
or a loan that was not repaid on time).

בִּתְשׂוּמֶת יָד.

And for the sins we have sinned before You

וְעַל חֵטְא שֶׁחָטָאנוּ לְפָנֶיךָ

with a confusion of heart.[77]

בִּתִמְהוֹן לֵבָב.

And for all the sins that we have mentioned

וְעַל כֻּלָּם

[You,] the God Who abundantly forgives, [please]

אֱלוֹהַּ סְלִיחוֹת

forgive us for the sins themselves

סְלַח לָנוּ

pardon us for the insult caused to Your Honor by our sins

מְחַל לָנוּ

(and) atone for us our sins as if they had never occurred.

כַּפֶּר לָנוּ.

---

three cardinal sins. Who was greater, the people of the period of the First Temple or the people from the time of the Second Temple? The *Gemara* replies that the answer can be found by looking at the Temple Mount, which means (as *Rashi* explains) that the First Temple was rebuilt [after just seventy years] but the Second Temple has still not returned to us [and it was destroyed in 68 c.e.]! Thus we see that unjust hatred is even worse than the three cardinal sins (*R' Simchah Zissel Ziv, Chochmah U'Mussar* vol. 1, p. 191).

Many people mistakenly think that *sinas chinam* means baseless hatred, hating someone for nothing (and thereby they justify their hatred with reasons, like jealousy, different ideals, or revenge, because then it has a basis). But this is **not** the real meaning of *sinas chinam*. No sane person hates someone else for nothing! If a Jew, dressed like you, comes from a different city, someone who you have never known, is it possible that you would simply hate him? Of course not! No normal person hates someone for absolutely nothing. Obviously the destruction of the Second Temple was not brought about by some insane people, who hated others for nothing.

The real meaning of *sinas chinam* is explained by *Rashi* (*Shabbos* 32b): "*Sinas chinam* is when you did **not** see someone do a sin [in a situation (see *Pesachim* 113b)] where it would be **permitted** to hate him for it, and you hate him [anyway]." In other words, *sinas chinam* is any hatred for a fellow Jew other than a rebellious sinner (or the specific case in the Gemara in *Pesachim*). Thus, almost all hatred between Jews is really *sinas chinam* — unjustified hatred — the sin that caused the destruction of the Temple, and which has prolonged our exile for almost 2,000 years!

77. After all the other sins, we confess about a heart that does not feel what is right and what is wrong, and that is the biggest sin [for one is obligated to learn and know] (*R' Simchah Zissel Ziv, Chochmah U'Mussar* vol. 2, p. 352).

And for the sins for which
we are obligated to bring

וְעַל חֲטָאִים שֶׁאָנוּ חַיָּבִים עֲלֵיהֶם

a *korban olah* (e.g., for transgressing
a positive command, like *Tefillin*,[78] or
standing up fully for someone over seventy).[79]

עוֹלָה.

And for the sins for which
we are obligated to bring

וְעַל חֲטָאִים שֶׁאָנוּ חַיָּבִים עֲלֵיהֶם

a *korban chatas* (for committing a sin unintentionally,
that had it been done intentionally would be punished
by *kares*, e.g., desecrating Shabbos).[80]

חַטָּאת.

And for the sins for which
we are obligated to bring

וְעַל חֲטָאִים שֶׁאָנוּ חַיָּבִים עֲלֵיהֶם

a *korban oleh veyored* [that varies according to
the wealth of the sinner] (e.g., for unintentionally
entering the Temple when impure).

קָרְבָּן עוֹלֶה וְיוֹרֵד.

And for the sins for which
we are obligated to bring

וְעַל חֲטָאִים שֶׁאָנוּ חַיָּבִים עֲלֵיהֶם

---

78. This includes wearing *Tefillin* whose parchments are not kosher [which one can verify by having them checked by a *sofer* (scribe)] or whose straps are not completely black (see *Orach Chaim* 33:3).

79. This is a positive commandment, as it says (*Vayikra* 19:32), "In the presence of an old person you shall rise." *Shulchan Aruch* (*Yoreh Deah* 244:1) writes that one must stand up fully for any Jewish man [or woman] over 70, as long as he is not a *rasha* (a wicked person according to the Torah). The *Pele Yo'eitz* writes that many people are negligent in this particular *mitzvah,* and they are thereby causing themselves to lose a great benefit, for in the merit of keeping this *mitzvah* one gains fear of Heaven, as it states at the end of that verse, "and you **will** fear from your God" [lit. "and you should fear your God," which can also be translated "and you will"]. Is there a greater reward than that?

80. The *Mishnah Berurah* in his introduction to the laws of Shabbos, quoting the *Yaaros Devash,* writes, "It is totally impossible to be saved from violating Shabbos if one does not learn the laws of Shabbos very well." There are laws for which one is liable to be stoned which people are unaware of (e.g., sorting out mixed toys or assorted pieces of cake to put away; or putting a little water or saliva on a stained garment to clean it). There are excellent works today that make learning the laws of Shabbos much easier. [Of those, the all-encompassing *Shemiras Shabbos Kehilchasah* is highly recommended, as well as the more specific works, *The Shabbos Kitchen* and *The Shabbos Home.*]

a *korban asham* for a certain sin
(e.g., swearing falsely about someone else's
money in his hand) or possible sin.[81]

אָשָׁם וַדַּאי וְתָלוּי.

And for the sins
for which we incur

וְעַל חֲטָאִים שֶׁאָנוּ חַיָּבִים עֲלֵיהֶם

lashes for rebellion (e.g., for violating
a Rabbinic prohibition or refusing to do
a positive commandment).

מַכַּת מַרְדּוּת.

And for the sins
for which we incur

וְעַל חֲטָאִים שֶׁאָנוּ חַיָּבִים עֲלֵיהֶם

forty lashes (for one who transgresses
a biblical prohibition, e.g., rounding off
the corners of a man's head[82]).

מַלְקוּת אַרְבָּעִים.

And for the sins
for which we are obligated

וְעַל חֲטָאִים שֶׁאָנוּ חַיָּבִים עֲלֵיהֶם

to die young at the hands of the
Heavenly Court (e.g., one who renders
a decision in front of his rabbi; or emits semen in vain).

מִיתָה בִּידֵי שָׁמָיִם.

And for the sins
for which we are obligated

וְעַל חֲטָאִים שֶׁאָנוּ חַיָּבִים עֲלֵיהֶם

to be cut off from the World to Come
and die childless (e.g., one who intentionally
cohabits with a *niddah,* or eats on Yom Kippur).

כָּרֵת וַעֲרִירִי.

---

81. This applies to a questionable transgression where — had one really violated it — the sinner would be required to bring a sin-offering, e.g., if someone violated Shabbos between sunset and nightfall (when we are in doubt as to whether it is actually Shabbos).

82. The *Mishnah Berurah* (*Beur Halachah,* Ch. 251:2) goes out of his way to warn people not to neglect this Torah prohibition. Quoting the *Shulchan Aruch* (*Yoreh Deah* 181:9), he describes what the prohibition is: the limit of the corner (*pe'ah*) that one must leave is from opposite the hair of his forehead until below the ear (*Chasam Sofer, Responsa Orach Chaim* 154 also quotes this as the *halachah*). The entire width of that area is included in the prohibition, and one may not remove that hair entirely in any way (even with scissors). [See *Be'er Moshe,* Resp. Vol. I 62:9.]

And for the sins
for which we incur

וְעַל חֲטָאִים שֶׁאָנוּ חַיָּבִים עֲלֵיהֶם

one of the four types of death
administered by *beis din* (a Jewish court of law):[83]

אַרְבַּע מִיתוֹת בֵּית דִּין —

stoning (e.g., for desecrating Shabbos intentionally
or for homosexual relations)

סְקִילָה

burning (e.g., for relations with a woman and her daughter)

שְׂרֵפָה

beheading (e.g., for murder)

הֶרֶג

and strangling (e.g., for hitting one's parents
or having relations with a married woman).

וְחֶנֶק

[And we ask forgiveness] for not doing
one of the 248 positive commandments

עַל מִצְוַת עֲשֵׂה

and for any of the 365 negative
commandments that we have violated

וְעַל מִצְוַת לֹא תַעֲשֶׂה

whether it was one that could be
corrected by doing a positive act
(like returning an object he stole)

בֵּין שֶׁיֵּשׁ בָּהּ קוּם עֲשֵׂה

or whether it was of those that
do not have a positive act to rectify it
(like most transgressions, e.g., immorality).

וּבֵין שֶׁאֵין בָּהּ קוּם עֲשֵׂה

[We ask forgiveness for both]
the sins that are revealed to us

אֶת הַגְּלוּיִם לָנוּ

and those that are not revealed to us.

וְאֶת שֶׁאֵינָם גְּלוּיִם לָנוּ

Those that are revealed to us

אֶת הַגְּלוּיִם לָנוּ

---

83. The *Talmud* (*Kesubos* 30a) says that from the time the Temple was destroyed, *beis din* no longer has the authority to administer capital punishment. Nevertheless, God punishes a person with a death similar to the one he deserved from *beis din*. For example: One who is liable to be stoned might fall off a roof (part of the stoning process was to push the guilty person off a two-story high cliff); one who is liable to be burned might fall into a fire; one who is liable to be beheaded might be killed by a bandit; and one who is liable to be strangled might die by drowning or suffocating.

we have already said before You (in our confession)	כְּבָר אֲמַרְנוּם לְפָנֶיךָ
and we have confessed them to You;	וְהוֹדִינוּ לְךָ עֲלֵיהֶם
and those that are not revealed to us	וְאֶת שֶׁאֵינָם גְּלוּיִם לָנוּ
they are still revealed and known to You, Who knows all [and we ask forgiveness for them, too]	לְפָנֶיךָ הֵם גְּלוּיִם וִידוּעִים
as it says (Devarim 29:28):	כַּדָּבָר שֶׁנֶּאֱמַר
"The sins that are hidden from the one who did them (i.e., he did them unintentionally and unknowingly)	הַנִּסְתָּרֹת
are for the Master of all, the Master of all strength, Who is able to do anything and Who takes care of us with Divine Providence (to atone for us),	לַיהוה אֱלֹהֵינוּ
but the sins that are revealed	וְהַנִּגְלֹת
are for us and our children forever to repent for them to achieve atonement	לָנוּ וּלְבָנֵינוּ עַד עוֹלָם
(and) to keep all of these words of the Torah (i.e., all the mitzvos)."	לַעֲשׂוֹת אֶת כָּל דִּבְרֵי הַתּוֹרָה הַזֹּאת.
[So, please forgive us] because You are the Forgiver of Israel constantly	כִּי אַתָּה סָלְחָן לְיִשְׂרָאֵל
and You are the Pardoner of Israel — who go in the straight path —	וּמָחֲלָן לְשִׁבְטֵי יְשֻׁרוּן
in every generation	בְּכָל דּוֹר וָדוֹר
and except for You,	וּמִבַּלְעָדֶיךָ
we have no other king who will completely pardon and forgive us	אֵין לָנוּ מֶלֶךְ מוֹחֵל וְסוֹלֵחַ
(— only You).	(אֶלָּא אָתָּה).

The Master of all strength, Who is able
to do anything and Who takes care of me with Divine Providence,

אֱלֹהַי

before I was formed
I was not worthy to be created

עַד שֶׁלֹּא נוֹצַרְתִּי אֵינִי כְדַאי

and now that I have been formed

וְעַכְשָׁו שֶׁנּוֹצַרְתִּי

it is as if I was never formed (for the
world has not gained by my existence).

כְּאִלּוּ לֹא נוֹצַרְתִּי

I am like dust while I am still alive
(for I do not have sufficient good deeds)

עָפָר אֲנִי בְּחַיָּי

and I will surely be so in my death
(when I will no longer be able to perform *mitzvos*).

קַל וָחֹמֶר בְּמִיתָתִי

(Therefore) I stand before You

הֲרֵי אֲנִי לְפָנֶיךָ

like a vessel full of
embarrassment and shame.

כִּכְלִי מָלֵא בוּשָׁה וּכְלִמָּה.

May it be a time of favor before
Your Throne of Glory

יְהִי רָצוֹן מִלְּפָנֶיךָ

Master of all, the Master of all strength,
Who is able to do anything and Who takes care
of me with Divine Providence,

יהוה אֱלֹהַי

and the God who took care
of my Fathers with Divine Providence

וֵאלֹהֵי אֲבוֹתַי

that You help me so that I should not
sin anymore (by removing the causes of sin
and daily preoccupations)

שֶׁלֹּא אֶחֱטָא עוֹד

and that which I have already sinned before You

וּמַה שֶּׁחָטָאתִי לְפָנֶיךָ

cleanse with Your great mercy

מָרֵק בְּרַחֲמֶיךָ הָרַבִּים

but not through

אֲבָל לֹא עַל יְדֵי

terrible suffering or difficult illnesses
(rather through minor pains).

יִסּוּרִים וָחֳלָיִם רָעִים.

תַּחֲנוּנִים
Personal Requests[84]

אֱלֹהַי

The Master of all strength, Who is able to do anything and Who takes care of me with Divine Providence,

נְצוֹר לְשׁוֹנִי מֵרָע

help me to guard my tongue from speaking bad about others (*lashon hara*)

וּשְׂפָתַי מִדַּבֵּר מִרְמָה

and [help me to guard] my lips from speaking deceit or falsehood

וְלִמְקַלְלַי נַפְשִׁי תִדּוֹם

and help me so that my soul should be silent (and even in thought I should not get angry) at those who curse me

וְנַפְשִׁי כֶּעָפָר לַכֹּל תִּהְיֶה

and help me so that my soul should be like dust (very humble) before everyone (and not mind insults).

פְּתַח לִבִּי בְּתוֹרָתֶךְ

Open up my heart so that it should be receptive and understand Your Torah

וּבְמִצְוֹתֶיךָ תִּרְדּוֹף נַפְשִׁי

and help my soul eagerly pursue Your *mitzvos*

וְכָל הַחוֹשְׁבִים עָלַי רָעָה

and all those who want to harm me (whether in mundane matters or spiritual matters, i.e., to cause me to sin)

מְהֵרָה הָפֵר עֲצָתָם

quickly annul their plan

וְקַלְקֵל מַחֲשַׁבְתָּם

and ruin their thought (even before they make plans).

עֲשֵׂה לְמַעַן שְׁמֶךְ

Act (take us out of exile) for the sake of Your Name, which is desecrated now among the gentiles[85]

---

84. Although this paragraph is designated for personal requests, it is questionable whether one should make any personal requests on Yom Kippur. R' Chaim Palagi (*Mo'ed L'Chol Chai*, 13:15) quotes *Zohar* (*Tikkunei Zohar, Tikkun vav*) which indicates that one should not ask for personal things on Yom Kippur, but should rather be interested only in the honor of God. (See a similar thought concerning Rosh Hashanah in *Rosh Hashanah Maariv*, note 25.)

85. The *Tur* (*Orach Chaim*, Ch. 122) wrote that anyone who is careful to say these four phrases (starting with this one) will merit to greet the Divine Presence. At the end of our prayers we reiterate that which is most important to us — the honor of God — and therefore we ask God to take us out of exile for His sake, so that the whole world will see His glory. One who says this sincerely will merit greeting the Divine Presence.

act (take us out of exile) for the sake of Your right
hand,[86] which You have now withdrawn in our exile

עֲשֵׂה לְמַעַן יְמִינֶךְ

act (take us out of exile) for the sake of Your Holiness
(so that all will know that You lead us with holiness)

עֲשֵׂה לְמַעַן קְדֻשָּׁתֶךְ

act (take us out of exile) for the sake of Your Torah
(so the Torah can be studied properly and completely)

עֲשֵׂה לְמַעַן תּוֹרָתֶךְ

and in order that Your dear ones, Israel,
should be released from all troubles

לְמַעַן יֵחָלְצוּן יְדִידֶיךָ

save them with (the wonders and miracles that
are attributed to) Your right hand

הוֹשִׁיעָה יְמִינְךָ

and answer (even) me in this prayer.

וַעֲנֵנִי.

Let the words of my prayer be desirable to You[87]

יִהְיוּ לְרָצוֹן אִמְרֵי פִי

and also the thoughts of my heart which
I cannot express [should be desirable] before You,

וְהֶגְיוֹן לִבִּי לְפָנֶיךָ

Master of all,

יהוה

My Rock, on Whom I rely for all my requests

צוּרִי

and Who will be my Redeemer.

וְגֹאֲלִי.

ONE SHOULD BOW AND GO BACK THREE STEPS
LIKE A SERVANT DEPARTING FROM HIS MASTER

The One Who makes peace in Heaven
(among the angels)

עֹשֶׂה [הַ]שָּׁלוֹם בִּמְרוֹמָיו

May He make peace (for those on earth,
who are naturally quarrelsome)

הוּא יַעֲשֶׂה שָׁלוֹם

on those of us here (praying together)

עָלֵינוּ

and on all of Israel

וְעַל כָּל יִשְׂרָאֵל

and (you, the angels who escort me,)
agree to my prayer, and say Amen!

וְאִמְרוּ אָמֵן.

---

86. The "right hand" of God symbolizes His redeeming power (*The World of Prayer*).

87. *Seder HaYom* writes that one should say this verse with great concentration, for it
will help considerably that his prayers should not go unanswered (quoted also in *Mishnah Berurah* 122:8).

May it be Your desire,	**יְהִי רָצוֹן** מִלְּפָנֶיךָ
Master of all,	יהוה
the Master of all strength, Who is able to do anything and Who takes care of us with Divine Providence,	אֱלֹהֵינוּ
and the God Who took care of our Fathers with Divine Providence,	וֵאלֹהֵי אֲבוֹתֵינוּ
that You should rebuild the Temple (so that we will be able to do the ultimate *avodah* — service to You)	שֶׁיִּבָּנֶה בֵּית הַמִּקְדָּשׁ
quickly and in our lifetime	בִּמְהֵרָה בְיָמֵינוּ
and help us so that all our toil should be in learning Your Torah.	וְתֵן חֶלְקֵנוּ בְּתוֹרָתֶךָ
And there, in the Temple, we will bring offerings (the ultimate service) with reverence	וְשָׁם נַעֲבָדְךָ בְּיִרְאָה
as [they brought offerings and served in reverence] in the earlier days (of Moshe)	כִּימֵי עוֹלָם
and as they did in the previous years (of Shlomo *HaMelech*).	וּכְשָׁנִים קַדְמוֹנִיּוֹת.
And then, it will be pleasing to the Master of all	וְעָרְבָה לַיהוה
the offerings that will be brought in the Temple (which is in the portion of Yehudah in Jerusalem)	מִנְחַת יְהוּדָה וִירוּשָׁלָיִם
as [the offerings were pleasing] in the earlier days (of Moshe)	כִּימֵי עוֹלָם
and as they were in the previous years (of Shlomo *HaMelech*).	וּכְשָׁנִים קַדְמוֹנִיּוֹת.

Mussaf for the Day of Atonement

When I call in the name of the Master of all	**כִּי** שֵׁם יהוה אֶקְרָא
you should ascribe greatness to the Master of all strength, Who is able to do anything and Who takes care of us with Divine Providence.	הָבוּ גֹדֶל לֵאלֹהֵינוּ.
Master of all — in particular, My Master	אֲדֹנָי
please open my lips (because I am afraid and ashamed to open them)	שְׂפָתַי תִּפְתָּח
and [help me pray with concentration, so] my mouth will [be able to] tell Your true praise.	וּפִי יַגִּיד תְּהִלָּתֶךָ.

אבות

Our God and the God of Our Fathers, Who Created Everything, and Protected Abraham[1]

You are the source of blessing (an expression of praise)	**בָּרוּךְ** אַתָּה
Master of all (Who always was, is, and will be)	יהוה
the Master of all strength, Who is able to do anything and Who takes care of us with Divine Providence,	אֱלֹהֵינוּ
and the God Who took care of our Fathers with Divine Providence (and made a covenant with each of them)	וֵאלֹהֵי אֲבוֹתֵינוּ
the God Who made a covenant with our father Abraham (who excelled in kindness)	אֱלֹהֵי אַבְרָהָם

---

1. One must be very careful to concentrate when saying this *brachah*, because otherwise he does not fulfill his obligation to pray. In the time of the *Gemara* one would have had to repeat the *Shemoneh Esrei* if he had not concentrated. Nowadays, however, when we are not sure that the second time will yield the proper concentration either, we do not repeat the *Shemoneh Esrei*; therefore one has to be exceedingly careful to concentrate for the first *brachah* or there is no remedy to rectify his prayer. [Nevertheless, if one did not concentrate for the first *brachah* he should still finish the prayer (*Kehillos Yaakov, Brachos,* Ch. 26).]

the God Who made a covenant with our father Isaac (who excelled in service of God)	אֱלֹהֵי יִצְחָק
and the God Who made a covenant with our father Jacob (who excelled in learning Torah)	וֵאלֹהֵי יַעֲקֹב
He is the Almighty (all power is His, especially in exercising the attribute of mercy)	הָאֵל
Who is the Great One (all greatness is His, especially in exercising the attribute of kindness)	הַגָּדוֹל
(and) He is the Strong One (all strength is His, especially in exercising the attribute of judgment)	הַגִּבּוֹר
and He alone deserves to be feared (because no being has the ability to do good or bad except Him)	וְהַנּוֹרָא
for He is the supreme God Who is the ultimate cause of everything	אֵל עֶלְיוֹן
Who always does kindnesses that are purely good	גּוֹמֵל חֲסָדִים טוֹבִים
and He recreates everything, constantly, every day	וְקוֹנֵה הַכֹּל
and every day He recalls for our benefit the kindnesses performed by the forefathers	וְזוֹכֵר חַסְדֵי אָבוֹת
and He constantly brings the Redeemer closer	וּמֵבִיא גוֹאֵל
to the forefathers' children's children (even though the merit of the forefathers might already be used up)	לִבְנֵי בְנֵיהֶם
for the sake of His Name (which will be sanctified at the time of the Redemption)	לְמַעַן שְׁמוֹ
[and He will also bring the Redeemer] because of His great love for the Jewish people.	בְּאַהֲבָה
Remember us for life in this world (in order that we may earn the World to Come by doing *mitzvos* here)	**זָכְרֵנוּ לְחַיִּים**

King, Who desires life
(and not death for a sinner,
but rather that he should repent)

מֶלֶךְ חָפֵץ בַּחַיִּים

and write us in the
Book of the Righteous, for life

וְכָתְבֵנוּ בְּסֵפֶר הַחַיִּים

for Your sake, in order that we may serve You[2]

לְמַעַנְךָ

the Master of all strength,
Who is able to do anything and is the One
Who apportions life to all.

אֱלֹהִים חַיִּים

He is the King over all

מֶלֶךְ

Who is the Helper (to help one succeed)

עוֹזֵר

and the Savior (from trouble)

וּמוֹשִׁיעַ

and the Protector (to prevent trouble from coming).

וּמָגֵן

You are the Source of Blessing, Master of all,

בָּרוּךְ אַתָּה יהוה

the Protector of Abraham (and because of Abraham
He continues His protection over us).

מָגֵן אַבְרָהָם.

גבורות

The Mighty Acts of God and the Revival of the Dead

You alone are eternally Strong

אַתָּה גִּבּוֹר לְעוֹלָם

Master of all

אֲדֹנָי

You even revive the dead (which shows the
greatest strength, contradicting all laws of nature)

מְחַיֵּה מֵתִים אַתָּה

[and] You have an abundance of
strength with which to save.

רַב לְהוֹשִׁיעַ

---

2. R' Hirtz Shatz in his *Siddur* writes that when one says these words he should think
that if he only repents he will live, and should resolve to do *teshuvah*.

He provides all the living with their food
and other needs in kindness
(not because they are deserving)

מְכַלְכֵּל חַיִּים בְּחֶסֶד

He revives the dead with great
mercy (searching for merits with
which they would deserve revival)

מְחַיֶּה מֵתִים בְּרַחֲמִים רַבִּים

He supports those who are falling
(whether physically, emotionally, or financially)

סוֹמֵךְ נוֹפְלִים

and He heals the sick from all types of illnesses
(even when doctors have given up hope)

וְרוֹפֵא חוֹלִים

and He opens the bonds of those who are restricted
(e.g., giving movement to our limbs when we awaken)

וּמַתִּיר אֲסוּרִים

and He will keep His promise
to those sleeping in the dust (the dead),
to revive them.

וּמְקַיֵּם אֱמוּנָתוֹ לִישֵׁנֵי עָפָר

Who is like You (who can do as many mighty deeds,
which are infinite, even for one person)?

מִי כָמוֹךָ

— You, to Whom all mighty deeds belong! —

בַּעַל גְּבוּרוֹת

And who is comparable to You in even one of Your
mighty deeds (which are of the highest quality)?

וּמִי דּוֹמֶה לָּךְ

You are the King over all

מֶלֶךְ

Who causes death and revival in many respects
(such as sleep and awakening, poverty and wealth)

מֵמִית וּמְחַיֶּה

and, like the sprouting of a seed, You bring the
Salvation (the Revival of the Dead).

וּמַצְמִיחַ יְשׁוּעָה

**Who is like You, who has as
much mercy on his sons as You,
the Merciful Father, have for us**

מִי כָמוֹךָ אַב הָרַחֲמִים

**(and) remembers His
creatures, out of mercy, for life.**

זוֹכֵר יְצוּרָיו לְחַיִּים בְּרַחֲמִים

And (from the mighty deeds that we
mentioned) we see that You are surely
trusted to revive the dead.

וְנֶאֱמָן אַתָּה לְהַחֲיוֹת מֵתִים

You are the Source of Blessing, Master of all,

בָּרוּךְ אַתָּה יהוה

the Reviver of all the dead (from Adam
until the time of the Revival).[3]

מְחַיֵּה הַמֵּתִים.

קדושת השם
Return of the Glory of God's Kingdom (to Zion)

You, Yourself, are holy (different and
separate from everything)

אַתָּה קָדוֹשׁ

and Your Name (which comes from
Your many acts) reveals holiness

וְשִׁמְךָ קָדוֹשׁ

and the holy ones — Israel —

וּקְדוֹשִׁים

(when *Mashiach* comes) will praise You
every day, forever.

בְּכָל יוֹם יְהַלְלוּךָ סֶּלָה.

And then (in the time of *Mashiach*)
[may it be speedily in our days]

וּבְכֵן

[You shall] put Your fear (which will be a catalyst for repentance)

תֵּן פַּחְדְּךָ

Master of all

יהוה

the Master of all strength, Who is able to do anything
and Who takes care of us with Divine Providence,

אֱלֹהֵינוּ

on all Your works (which refers to the Jewish people)

עַל כָּל מַעֲשֶׂיךָ

and (put) Your dread

וְאֵימָתְךָ

---

3. Even though many bodies have decomposed over thousands of years, and some have
been burned and their dust has been scattered, and others have drowned at sea,
Hashem with His great might will recognize and recompose the bodies and return to
them their original souls (*Yesod VeShoresh HaAvodah*).

on all that You have created
(which refers to the gentiles).

עַל כָּל מַה שֶׁבָּרֶאתָ

And then all the Jews will fear You

וְיִירָאוּדְ כָּל הַמַּעֲשִׂים

And all the nations of the world will
bow down to You in subjugation

וְיִשְׁתַּחֲווּ לְפָנֶיךָ כָּל הַבְּרוּאִים

and all of mankind will make one group

וְיֵעָשׂוּ כֻלָּם אֲגֻדָּה אֶחָת

to do Your will with a
complete heart (submitting all
their tendencies to Divine service).

לַעֲשׂוֹת רְצוֹנְךָ בְּלֵבָב שָׁלֵם

As we already know (Your power from the
Exodus from Egypt)

כְּמוֹ שֶׁיָּדַעְנוּ

Master of all

יהוה

the Master of all strength, Who is able to do anything
and Who takes care of us with Divine Providence,

אֱלֹהֵינוּ

(where You revealed) that dominion is Yours

שֶׁהַשָּׁלְטָן לְפָנֶיךָ

and strength (in the constant running of the world)
is in Your (left) hand

עֹז בְּיָדְךָ

and might (to do miracles) is in Your right hand

וּגְבוּרָה בִּימִינֶךָ

and (when You again reveal this in the time
of *Mashiach*) Your Name will be revered

וְשִׁמְךָ נוֹרָא

on all the nations of the world.

עַל כָּל מַה שֶׁבָּרֶאתָ.

And, then, Master of all, give honor
to Your nation, Israel

וּבְכֵן תֵּן כָּבוֹד יהוה לְעַמֶּךָ

(and cause everyone to) praise those who fear You

תְּהִלָּה לִירֵאֶיךָ

and (give) to those who cling to You
the good for which they rely on You

וְתִקְוָה [טוֹבָה] לְדוֹרְשֶׁיךָ

and (give) to those who yearn
for Your salvation, the ability to
praise You as they desire (without fear)

וּפִתְחוֹן פֶּה לַמְיַחֲלִים לָךְ

(and then when they no longer fear anyone) there
will be an inner joy in the land of Israel
(with the ingathering of the exiles)

שִׂמְחָה לְאַרְצֶךְ

and there will be open joy in Your city, Jerusalem,
(where the glory of the Divine Presence will be felt most)

וְשָׂשׂוֹן לְעִירֶךְ

and then the kingdom of the family of
David Your servant will sprout forth
(with the coming of *Mashiach*)

וּצְמִיחַת קֶרֶן לְדָוִד עַבְדֶּךָ

and the influence of the
son of Yishai (father of David)
Your appointed one (*Mashiach*) will spread

וַעֲרִיכַת נֵר לְבֶן יִשַׁי מְשִׁיחֶךָ

(and we ask that this should happen)
speedily in our days (so that we should
witness the return of the honor of God).

בִּמְהֵרָה בְיָמֵינוּ.

And then (when *Mashiach* has come)

וּבְכֵן

the righteous will see (that the glory
of God has returned) and they will have inner joy

צַדִּיקִים יִרְאוּ וְיִשְׂמָחוּ

and the upright ones (who do everything
just for the sake of Heaven) will be
inspired to dance from joy

וִישָׁרִים יַעֲלֹזוּ

and the pious (who do more than
they are required to do by the Torah)
will raise their voices in jubilant song

וַחֲסִידִים בְּרִנָּה יָגִילוּ

and all those who do injustice and iniquity
will close their mouths

וְעוֹלָתָה תִּקְפָּץ פִּיהָ

and all evil will vanish like smoke

וְכָל הָרִשְׁעָה כֻּלָּהּ כֶּעָשָׁן תִּכְלֶה

when you remove evil kingdoms from the earth.	כִּי תַעֲבִיר מֶמְשֶׁלֶת זָדוֹן מִן הָאָרֶץ.
And (then it will be apparent) that You alone, the Master of all, are the only King	**וְתִמְלוֹךְ** אַתָּה יהוה לְבַדֶּךָ
on all Your works (the Jews and the other nations)	עַל כָּל מַעֲשֶׂיךָ
(and Your rule will be especially evident) in the Temple, the place of the manifestation of the Divine Presence,	בְּהַר צִיּוֹן מִשְׁכַּן כְּבוֹדֶךָ
and in Jerusalem which is designated as Your holy city	וּבִירוּשָׁלַיִם עִיר קָדְשֶׁךָ
as it is written in Your holy words (*Tehillim* 146:10):	כַּכָּתוּב בְּדִבְרֵי קָדְשֶׁךָ
"God will reign forever	יִמְלֹךְ יהוה לְעוֹלָם
(that is,) the Master of all strength and the One able to do anything, Who dwells particularly in Zion (the Temple)	אֱלֹהַיִךְ צִיּוֹן
(He will reign) for all generations	לְדֹר וָדֹר
(therefore, Israel) praise God."	הַלְלוּיָהּ.
You are holy (different and separate from everything)	**קָדוֹשׁ** אַתָּה
and Your Name (which is evident from Your many acts) causes awe	וְנוֹרָא שְׁמֶךָ
and there is no other power except You	וְאֵין אֱלוֹהַּ מִבַּלְעָדֶיךָ
as it is written (*Yeshayahu* 5:16):	כַּכָּתוּב
"And the Master of all, Who is the ruler over all the Heavenly and earthly legions, will be exalted	וַיִּגְבַּהּ יהוה צְבָאוֹת

when He does judgment on all	בַּמִּשְׁפָּט
and the Almighty, Who is holy (different and separate from everything),	וְהָאֵל הַקָּדוֹשׁ
will become more holy in our eyes through the kindness He does with us.''	נִקְדַּשׁ בִּצְדָקָה
You are the Source of Blessing, Master of all	בָּרוּךְ אַתָּה יהוה
the King, Who is holier than all else.	**הַמֶּלֶךְ הַקָּדוֹשׁ.**

קְדוּשַׁת הַיּוֹם
The Holiness of the Day
Atoning of Our Sins

You chose us (the Nation of Israel) from all nations (when You took us out of Egypt)	**אַתָּה** בְחַרְתָּנוּ מִכָּל הָעַמִּים
You showed Your love for us (by giving us the Torah)	אָהַבְתָּ אוֹתָנוּ
and You showed that You desired us (by giving us the special protection of the Clouds of Glory even though we had sinned with the Golden Calf)	וְרָצִיתָ בָּנוּ
and You elevated us from all languages (by giving us the holy language — Hebrew — which is spoken in Heaven)	וְרוֹמַמְתָּנוּ מִכָּל הַלְּשׁוֹנוֹת
and You made us holy by giving us the *mitzvos* which permeate us with holiness	וְקִדַּשְׁתָּנוּ בְּמִצְוֹתֶיךָ
and You have brought us close, our King, to Your service	וְקֵרַבְתָּנוּ מַלְכֵּנוּ לַעֲבוֹדָתֶךָ
and Your Name which is great (as we see from Your acts)	וְשִׁמְךָ הַגָּדוֹל

and holy (as we see from Your directing the world with a mastery beyond our comprehension)

וְהַקָּדוֹשׁ

You have called on us — for we are called the Nation of God.

עָלֵינוּ קָרֶאתָ.

And the Master of all, the Master of all strength, Who is able to do anything and Who takes care of us with Divine Providence, gave us

וַתִּתֶּן לָנוּ יהוה אֱלֹהֵינוּ

with love (because of His love for us)

בְּאַהֲבָה

ON SHABBOS ADD:

[with love You gave us] this Shabbos day [which is called a great gift]

אֶת יוֹם הַשַּׁבָּת הַזֶּה

(whose primary purpose is) for holiness and rest and...

לִקְדֻשָׁה וְלִמְנוּחָה וְ...

this Day of Atonement

אֶת יוֹם הַכִּפּוּרִים הַזֶּה

(whose primary purpose is) to forgive the punishment of the sin

לִמְחִילָה

and to forgive the actual sin

וְלִסְלִיחָה

and to atone completely (to such an extent that it is as if we had never sinned)

וּלְכַפָּרָה

and in that way pardon all of our sins

וְלִמְחָל בּוֹ אֶת כָּל עֲוֺנוֹתֵינוּ

ON SHABBOS SAY:

with love (because of Your love for us)

בְּאַהֲבָה

a day on which we are called and gather to sanctify ourselves in prayer

מִקְרָא קֹדֶשׁ

(and) it is a day that is a remembrance of our going out of Egypt.

זֵכֶר לִיצִיאַת מִצְרֶיִם.

And because of our sins we have
been exiled from our land (Israel)

וּמִפְּנֵי חֲטָאֵינוּ גָּלִינוּ מֵאַרְצֵנוּ

and we have been exiled even to a place
very distant from our fields (and therefore
cannot keep the laws dependent on the land)

וְנִתְרַחַקְנוּ מֵעַל אַדְמָתֵנוּ

and we (also) cannot
bring the sacrifices
that are an obligation on us

וְאֵין אֲנַחְנוּ יְכוֹלִים לַעֲשׂוֹת חוֹבוֹתֵינוּ

in the *Beis HaMikdash* (the Temple)
where You have chosen to rest Your Divine Presence

בְּבֵית בְּחִירָתֶךָ

in the House that is great in a physical sense
and holy in a spiritual sense

בַּבַּיִת הַגָּדוֹל וְהַקָּדוֹשׁ

on which Your name is called — for it is called
the House of God —

שֶׁנִּקְרָא שִׁמְךָ עָלָיו

[we cannot bring our sacrifices]
because of the hand of the enemy
that was sent to destroy Your Temple.

מִפְּנֵי הַיָּד שֶׁנִּשְׁתַּלְּחָה בְּמִקְדָּשֶׁךָ

Let it be a favorable time to let our prayers
enter the Heavens before You,

יְהִי רָצוֹן מִלְּפָנֶיךָ

Master of all,

יהוה

the Master of all strength, Who is able to do anything
and Who takes care of us with Divine Providence,

אֱלֹהֵינוּ

and the God Who took care of our Fathers
with Divine Providence (and made a covenant
with each of them),

וֵאלֹהֵי אֲבוֹתֵינוּ

the King Whose mercy is great,

מֶלֶךְ רַחֲמָן

that You should again have mercy on Israel
(and gather the exiles)

שֶׁתָּשׁוּב וּתְרַחֵם עָלֵינוּ

[and You should again have mercy] on the Temple
(that is destroyed)

וְעַל מִקְדָּשְׁךָ

with Your great mercy	בְּרַחֲמֶיךָ הָרַבִּים
and build the (future) Temple without delay	וְתִבְנֵהוּ מְהֵרָה
and You should never remove Your Presence from it and thereby the glory of the Third Temple will be greater than that of the previous ones.	וּתְגַדֵּל כְּבוֹדוֹ
(If we are like sons) You are our Father, and (if we are like servants) You are our King (so, please)	אָבִינוּ מַלְכֵּנוּ
reveal the honor of Your Kingdom on us without delay	גַּלֵּה כְּבוֹד מַלְכוּתְךָ עָלֵינוּ מְהֵרָה
and the glory of Your Kingdom should be revealed and seen upon us before the eyes of all the nations	וְהוֹפַע וְהִנָּשֵׂא עָלֵינוּ לְעֵינֵי כָּל חָי
and You should bring close to You all the Jews that were exiled among the nations close to the land of Israel	וְקָרֵב פְּזוּרֵינוּ מִבֵּין הַגּוֹיִם
and also those who were scattered to distant places You should gather, even from the ends of the earth	וּנְפוּצוֹתֵינוּ כַּנֵּס מִיַּרְכְּתֵי אָרֶץ
and bring us to Your city Zion with the sound of joyous songs	וַהֲבִיאֵנוּ לְצִיּוֹן עִירְךָ בְּרִנָּה
and to Jerusalem, where the Temple is, with ever-lasting joy.	וְלִירוּשָׁלַיִם בֵּית מִקְדָּשְׁךָ בְּשִׂמְחַת עוֹלָם
And then we will be able to bring (in the Temple) the obligatory *korbanos*	וְשָׁם נַעֲשֶׂה לְפָנֶיךָ אֶת קָרְבְּנוֹת חוֹבוֹתֵינוּ
that is, the *tamid* of the morning and the *tamid* of the afternoon in the order they are written in the Torah	תְּמִידִים כְּסִדְרָם
and the *korbanos mussaf* according to their laws that are written in the Torah.	וּמוּסָפִים כְּהִלְכָתָם

ON WEEKDAYS SAY:

And the *korban mussaf*
of this day of Yom Kippur

וְאֶת מוּסַף יוֹם הַכִּפּוּרִים הַזֶּה

ON SHABBOS SAY:

and the *korbanos mussaf*

וְאֶת מוּסְפֵי

of this Shabbos and this Yom Kippur

יוֹם הַשַּׁבָּת הַזֶּה וְיוֹם הַכִּפּוּרִים הַזֶּה

we will do all the preparations
of the sacrifices
and bring them on the Altar with love

נַעֲשֶׂה וְנַקְרִיב לְפָנֶיךָ בְּאַהֲבָה

as You commanded us

כְּמִצְוַת רְצוֹנֶךָ

as You wrote for us in Your Torah

כְּמוֹ שֶׁכָּתַבְתָּ עָלֵינוּ בְּתוֹרָתֶךָ

that Moshe wrote as a messenger
of Yours just as he heard from the
"mouth" of Your Glory

עַל יְדֵי מֹשֶׁה עַבְדֶּךָ מִפִּי כְבוֹדֶךָ

as it is written (for Shabbos — *Bamidbar* 28:9-10)
[for Rosh Hashanah — *Bamidbar* 29:1-2]:

כָּאָמוּר

ON SHABBOS ADD:

"And (the *korban mussaf* of) the day of Shabbos is

וּבְיוֹם הַשַּׁבָּת

two sheep within their first year,
without blemish,

שְׁנֵי כְבָשִׂים בְּנֵי שָׁנָה תְּמִימִם

and two-tenths of an *eifah*
(a measure) of the finest
wheat flour mixed with olive-oil for a *korban minchah*

וּשְׁנֵי עֶשְׂרֹנִים סֹלֶת מִנְחָה בְּלוּלָה בַשֶּׁמֶן

and wine to pour on the Altar for its *nesachim*.

וְנִסְכּוֹ.

This was the *olah* of the *korban mussaf*
for every Shabbos

עֹלַת שַׁבַּת בְּשַׁבַּתּוֹ

which was sacrificed after the *olah*
of the *korban tamid*

עַל עֹלַת הַתָּמִיד

and the wine that was brought with it and poured
on the Altar for its *nesachim*."

וְנִסְכָּהּ.

SOME ALSO SAY THIS PHRASE ON SHABBOS:

[This is the *korban mussaf*
of Shabbos, and the *korban*
mussaf of Yom Kippur as it is written in the Torah:]

[זֶה קָרְבַּן שַׁבָּת וְקָרְבַּן הַיּוֹם כָּאָמוּר]

"And on the tenth day
of this seventh month —
Tishrei (Yom Kippur)

וּבֶעָשׂוֹר לַחְדֶשׁ הַשְּׁבִיעִי הַזֶּה

you should have a day on which
you gather to make it holy with prayer

מִקְרָא קְדֶשׁ יִהְיֶה לָכֶם

and you should afflict yourselves
(by not eating or drinking)

וְעִנִּיתֶם אֶת נַפְשֹׁתֵיכֶם

any work you should not do.

כָּל מְלָאכָה לֹא תַעֲשׂוּ.

And (for the additional sacrifice)
you should bring a *korban olah*
for a pleasing aroma for the Master of all

וְהִקְרַבְתֶּם עֹלָה לַיהוה רֵיחַ נִיחֹחַ

one bull (from the beginning of its
second year until the end of its third year)

פַּר בֶּן בָּקָר אֶחָד

(and) one ram (more than thirteen months old)

אַיִל אֶחָד

(and) seven male sheep in their
first year

כְּבָשִׂים בְּנֵי שָׁנָה שִׁבְעָה

(all of which had to be) without blemish
(and then they would be favorable) for you."

תְּמִימִם יִהְיוּ לָכֶם.

And their accompanying
flour offerings and wine libations
are as it says in the Torah:

וּמִנְחָתָם וְנִסְכֵּיהֶם כִּמְדֻבָּר

"Three-tenths of an *eifah* (a measure)
of fine flour for the bull

שְׁלֹשָׁה עֶשְׂרֹנִים לַפָּר

"and two-tenths of an *eifah* of fine flour
for the ram

וּשְׁנֵי עֶשְׂרֹנִים לָאָיִל

and one-tenth on an *eifah* for each of the seven sheep וְעִשָּׂרוֹן לַכֶּבֶשׂ

and wine for each one according to the amount prescribed
in the Torah to pour on the Altar; וְיַיִן כְּנִסְכּוֹ

and two male goats within their first year
(one for the *mussaf* and one for the goat
on which the lot fell "for God")
to atone for *tumah*[4] in the Temple וּשְׁנֵי שְׂעִירִים לְכַפֵּר

and the two daily sacrifices (one in the
morning and one in the afternoon)
according to their law that the Torah writes. וּשְׁנֵי תְמִידִים כְּהִלְכָתָם.

ON SHABBOS ADD:

They will rejoice in the revelation of
Your Kingdom (in the future, in the world which
is completely Shabbos) **יִשְׂמְחוּ** בְמַלְכוּתְךָ

those who keep the Shabbos (the seventh day)
by abstaining from work שׁוֹמְרֵי שַׁבָּת

and who make Shabbos a day of delight
(with joyful rest, and delicious food and drinks) וְקוֹרְאֵי עֹנֶג

the nation (Israel) who sanctifies the Shabbos
(by abstaining from work) עַם מְקַדְּשֵׁי שְׁבִיעִי

they will all be satisfied, and also
delight in the spiritual good that
You will show in the future כֻּלָּם יִשְׂבְּעוּ וְיִתְעַנְּגוּ מִטּוּבֶךָ

because You have found favorable
the seventh day and You have made it
holy as a day of rest וּבַשְּׁבִיעִי רָצִיתָ בּוֹ וְקִדַּשְׁתּוֹ

since it is the most desirous of days חֶמְדַּת יָמִים

You have called it a name ("Shabbos" — which means rest) אוֹתוֹ קָרֵאתָ

to commemorate the act of creation
(and that You "rested" on Shabbos). זֵכֶר לְמַעֲשֵׂה בְרֵאשִׁית.

---

4. This refers to spiritual impurity, and like all *mussaf* goats, these come to atone for a
spiritually impure person who either entered the Temple or ate from an offering (*Rashi,
Bamidbar* 28:15).

The Master of all strength, Who is able to do anything and Who takes care of us with Divine Providence,	אֱלֹהֵינוּ
and the God who took care of our Fathers with Divine Providence	וֵאלֹהֵי אֲבוֹתֵינוּ
forgive our sins	מְחַל לַעֲוֹנוֹתֵינוּ

ON WEEKDAYS SAY:

on this Day of Atonement.	בְּיוֹם הַכִּפּוּרִים הַזֶּה

ON SHABBOS SAY:

on this [Shabbos and on this] Day of Atonement.	בְּיוֹם הַשַּׁבָּת הַזֶּה וּבְיוֹם הַכִּפּוּרִים הַזֶּה

Blot out [our sins]	מְחֵה
and remove entirely (leaving no vestige of)	וְהַעֲבֵר
our sins that were committed with intent	פְּשָׁעֵינוּ
and our sins that were committed without intention	וְחַטֹּאתֵינוּ
[wipe them out] from before Your eyes	מִנֶּגֶד עֵינֶיךָ
as it says (*Yeshayahu* 43:25):	כָּאָמוּר
"I forgave the generation of the Exodus their sins and I forgive in every generation your intentional sins	אָנֹכִי אָנֹכִי הוּא מֹחֶה פְשָׁעֶיךָ
for My sake (so that My Name should not be profaned among the nations if I destroy you)	לְמַעֲנִי
and what you have done unwillfully, I will not even remember (there will be no vestige of it)."	וְחַטֹּאתֶיךָ לֹא אֶזְכֹּר.
And it is also written (*Yeshayahu* 44:22):	וְנֶאֱמַר

"I have always blotted out
what you have done intentionally
like a wind dissipates a thick cloud (leaving some remnant)

מָחִיתִי כָעָב פְּשָׁעֶיךָ

and like a thin cloud gets scattered
(without leaving any trace)
so I have erased your unintentional sins

וְכֶעָנָן חַטֹּאתֶיךָ

therefore, return to Me
in repentance for I will redeem you."

שׁוּבָה אֵלַי כִּי גְאַלְתִּיךָ.

And it is also written (*Vayikra* 16:30):

וְנֶאֱמַר

"For on this day of Yom Kippur

כִּי בַיּוֹם הַזֶּה

God will forgive you (for your sins)
as if they never were

יְכַפֵּר עֲלֵיכֶם

in order to purify your souls
(from the tendency to repeat the sins)

לְטַהֵר אֶתְכֶם

(but) from all your sins

מִכֹּל חַטֹּאתֵיכֶם

it is incumbent upon you to cleanse
yourselves (with repentance)
before the Master of all."

לִפְנֵי יהוה תִּטְהָרוּ.

ON SHABBOS ADD:

The Master of all strength, Who is able to do anything
and Who takes care of us with Divine Providence,

אֱלֹהֵינוּ

and the God who took care of our Fathers
with Divine Providence

וֵאלֹהֵי אֲבוֹתֵינוּ

let our rest be pleasant before You

רְצֵה בִמְנוּחָתֵנוּ

---

make us holy from Above so that
we should do Your *mitzvos* properly

קַדְּשֵׁנוּ בְּמִצְוֹתֶיךָ

and give us Divine assistance
that all of our occupation should be
in Torah study

וְתֵן חֶלְקֵנוּ בְּתוֹרָתֶךָ

grant us good in a way that we will be
satisfied with what we have
(and not run after our desires)

שַׂבְּעֵנוּ מִטּוּבֶךָ

and cause us to rejoice through
the salvation that You will bring us

וְשַׂמְּחֵנוּ בִּישׁוּעָתֶךָ

ON SHABBOS ADD:

and give us as an inheritance
(the holiness that Shabbos inspires)

וְהַנְחִילֵנוּ

Master of all, the Master of all strength,
Who is able to do anything and Who takes
care of us with Divine Providence,

יהוה אֱלֹהֵינוּ

because of the love that You loved us
(when You gave us Shabbos)

בְּאַהֲבָה

and because of the desire You have for us (that You
want us to bring sacrifices even on Shabbos)

וּבְרָצוֹן

[give us as an inheritance] the inspiration
of Shabbos, the day that You made holy,

שַׁבַּת קָדְשֶׁךָ

and (through this inspiration) You should cause Israel
to have a complete rest on Shabbos

וְיָנוּחוּ בוֹ יִשְׂרָאֵל

for they sanctify Your Name
(by keeping Shabbos)

מְקַדְּשֵׁי שְׁמֶךָ

and (we ask that You) purify
our hearts that we should serve
You sincerely (without other motives)

וְטַהֵר לִבֵּנוּ לְעָבְדְּךָ בֶּאֱמֶת

[do all this] because You are
the Forgiver of Israel constantly

כִּי אַתָּה סָלְחָן לְיִשְׂרָאֵל

and You are the Pardoner of Israel
— who go in the straight path —

וּמָחֳלָן לְשִׁבְטֵי יְשֻׁרוּן

in every generation

בְּכָל דּוֹר וָדוֹר

and except for You we have
no other king who will
completely pardon and forgive us

וּמִבַּלְעָדֶיךָ אֵין לָנוּ מֶלֶךְ מוֹחֵל וְסוֹלֵחַ

(— only You).

(אֶלָּא אָתָּה)

You are the Source of Blessing, Master of all,	בָּרוּךְ אַתָּה יהוה
Who completely pardons and forgives the sins of the individual	מֶלֶךְ מוֹחֵל וְסוֹלֵחַ לַעֲוֹנוֹתֵינוּ
and (through that completely forgives the sins) of the entirety of the house of His nation, Israel	וְלַעֲוֹנוֹת עַמּוֹ בֵּית יִשְׂרָאֵל
and (You) remove our iniquities each and every year,[5]	וּמַעֲבִיר אַשְׁמוֹתֵינוּ בְּכָל שָׁנָה וְשָׁנָה
the King over all the inhabitants of the earth	מֶלֶךְ עַל כָּל הָאָרֶץ

ON WEEKDAYS SAY:

Who chose Israel and made them holier (than the other nations)	מְקַדֵּשׁ יִשְׂרָאֵל

ON SHABBOS SAY:

Who made the Shabbos holier (than the other days — and gave it to us as a present) and made Israel holier (than the other nations)	מְקַדֵּשׁ הַשַּׁבָּת וְיִשְׂרָאֵל

(and through Israel) He makes holy the Day of Atonement (to forgive our sins on it).	וְיוֹם הַכִּפּוּרִים.

עבודה
Return of the Temple Service

Be pleased[6]	רְצֵה
Master of all,	יהוה

---

5. One should feel a tremendous gratitude to the Almighty for the gift of Yom Kippur, the day on which He forgives our sins if we repent. Were the sins of the world to keep piling up year after year, the measure would be full and the world would be condemned to destruction. But after the sin of the Golden Calf was forgiven this day was established for forgiveness, and aids in the repentance process; and that is what the Sages mean (*Yoma* 86a): "Yom Kippur atones" (based on *Sefer HaChinuch, Mitzvah* 185).

6. Before reciting this blessing one should instill in his heart the love of all Jews, regardless of their origin or affiliation, for we ask here that God should be pleased with all of His nation Israel (*Darchei Chaim*). [The saintly Chofetz Chaim wrote (*Ahavas Yisrael*, Ch. 2) that we constantly pray for the rebuilding of the Temple, but we neglect to contemplate the cause of its destruction, which was hatred for an unjustifiable reason. Therefore if we want the Temple to be rebuilt we must first rectify this sin and love all Jews.]

the Master of all strength, Who is able to do anything and Who takes care of us with Divine Providence,	אֱלֹהֵינוּ
with Your nation, Israel (because they are praying for the rebuilding of the Temple)	בְּעַמְּךָ יִשְׂרָאֵל
and with their prayer (for the rebuilding of the Temple)	וּבִתְפִלָּתָם
and return the service of the Temple	וְהָשֵׁב אֶת הָעֲבוֹדָה
(even) to the Holy of Holies.	לִדְבִיר בֵּיתֶךָ
And the fire-offerings that they will bring	וְאִשֵּׁי יִשְׂרָאֵל
and the prayer of Israel (which is now in place of the offerings)	וּתְפִלָּתָם
because of Your love for the Jews	בְּאַהֲבָה
accept with desire	תְקַבֵּל בְּרָצוֹן
and help us that it should always be desirable	וּתְהִי לְרָצוֹן תָּמִיד
the service (whether offerings or prayers) of Israel, Your nation.	עֲבוֹדַת יִשְׂרָאֵל עַמֶּךָ
And let us merit to see (the *Shechinah* – Divine Presence) with our own eyes (i.e., soon, in our days)	וְתֶחֱזֶינָה עֵינֵינוּ
when You return Your Presence to the Temple (even if it is) in mercy (and not through our merits).	בְּשׁוּבְךָ לְצִיּוֹן בְּרַחֲמִים
You are the Source of Blessing, Master of all,	בָּרוּךְ אַתָּה יהוה
Who will return His Divine Presence to the Temple.	הַמַּחֲזִיר שְׁכִינָתוֹ לְצִיּוֹן.

הודאה
Thanking God[7]

We give thanks to You, acknowledging — **מוֹדִים** אֲנַחְנוּ לָךְ

that You are the Master of all — שָׁאַתָּה הוּא יהוה

the Master of all strength, Who is able to do anything and Who takes care of us with Divine Providence, — אֱלֹהֵינוּ

and the God Who took care of our Fathers with Divine Providence — וֵאלֹהֵי אֲבוֹתֵינוּ

(and that You will continue to take care of us) forever. — לְעוֹלָם וָעֶד

[You are] the Rock — Creator and Sustainer — of our lives — צוּר חַיֵּינוּ

[and You are] the Protector Who saves us from all troubles — מָגֵן יִשְׁעֵנוּ

You are the One [Who keeps us alive and saves us] in every generation. — אַתָּה הוּא לְדוֹר וָדוֹר

We will always express our thanks to You — נוֹדֶה לְּךָ

and we will tell Your praise to others — וּנְסַפֵּר תְּהִלָּתֶךָ

for our lives — each breath — that are given over into Your hand — עַל חַיֵּינוּ הַמְּסוּרִים בְּיָדֶךָ

and for our souls that are entrusted to You (while we sleep) — וְעַל נִשְׁמוֹתֵינוּ הַפְּקוּדוֹת לָךְ

and for the hidden miracles that You do for us every day — וְעַל נִסֶּיךָ שֶׁבְּכָל יוֹם עִמָּנוּ

and for Your wonders of "nature" (which You renew constantly) — וְעַל נִפְלְאוֹתֶיךָ

---

7. The *Beis Elokim* explains that the reason we bow at the beginning and end of this *brachah* is to show humility, recognizing our unworthiness for Hashem's special care, and realizing that our lives and all goodness come from Him.

and for Your favors (that You do for us constantly)	וְטוֹבוֹתֶיךָ
that You do in all parts of the day	שֶׁבְּכָל עֵת
in the evening, morning, and afternoon.	עֶרֶב וָבֹקֶר וְצָהֳרָיִם
You are the ultimate Good One	הַטּוֹב
for Your mercy has never finished – for You withhold punishment from those deserving it	כִּי לֹא כָלוּ רַחֲמֶיךָ
and You are the ultimate Merciful One (Who not only withholds punishment, but ...)	וְהַמְרַחֵם
Whose kindness never ends – for You even give these undeserving people additional kindnesses –	כִּי לֹא תַמּוּ חֲסָדֶיךָ
we have always put our hope in You.	מֵעוֹלָם קִוִּינוּ לָךְ
And for all of these wonders and favors that You do for us constantly	וְעַל כֻּלָּם
[Your Name] should be praised with the recognition that You are the Source of all Blessing	יִתְבָּרַךְ
and may Your Name (which represents Your acts) be exalted through the recognition of Your greatness	וְיִתְרוֹמַם שִׁמְךָ
since You are our King (Who takes care of us especially) [and we desire that Your Name be praised and exalted]	מַלְכֵּנוּ
constantly, every day,	תָּמִיד
forever and ever.	לְעוֹלָם וָעֶד
And inscribe for a good life (i.e., life that will be good for earning the World to Come)	**וּכְתוֹב לְחַיִּים טוֹבִים**
all the children of Your covenant.	**כָּל בְּנֵי בְרִיתֶךָ**

And all the living (those who will come back to life by the Revival of the Dead)	וְכֹל הַחַיִּים
will thank You constantly forever	יוֹדוּךָ סֶּלָה
and they will praise Your Name (which comes from Your deeds) truthfully, without any other motive	וִיהַלְלוּ אֶת שִׁמְךָ בֶּאֱמֶת
the Almighty	הָאֵל
Who saves us in all our troubles	יְשׁוּעָתֵנוּ
and Who helps us to succeed	וְעֶזְרָתֵנוּ
constantly, forever.	סֶלָה
You are the Source of Blessing, Master of all,	בָּרוּךְ אַתָּה יהוה
Whose Name is "The Good One" (for You are the ultimate good)	הַטּוֹב שִׁמְךָ
and to You alone it is fitting to give thanks (because You are the cause of all goodness).	וּלְךָ נָאֶה לְהוֹדוֹת.

שלום
Peace

Grant peace (which includes peace of mind, peace in one's house, peace between Jews, and peace in the country)	**שִׂים** שָׁלוֹם
(and grant what is) good for each person	טוֹבָה
and (grant) prosperity and success	וּבְרָכָה
(and) let us find favor in Your eyes and thereby find favor in the eyes of all who see us	חֵן
and grant our requests (even though we are not deserving)	וָחֶסֶד
and have mercy on us (not to punish us according to our wrongdoings)	וְרַחֲמִים

on those of us here (praying together)	עָלֵינוּ
and on all of Israel, Your nation.	וְעַל כָּל יִשְׂרָאֵל עַמֶּךְ
Since You are our Father, give us an abundance of goodness and success	בָּרְכֵנוּ אָבִינוּ
all of us like one (equally)	כֻּלָּנוּ כְּאֶחָד
with the "light of Your face" (which is a symbol of Your great love)	בְּאוֹר פָּנֶיךָ
because we already know from the Revelation at Sinai that with the "light of Your face" come great things:	כִּי בְאוֹר פָּנֶיךָ
You gave to us as a present (not because we were deserving),	נָתַתָּ לָּנוּ
Master of all,	יהוה
the Master of all strength, Who is able to do anything and Who takes care of us with Divine Providence,	אֱלֹהֵינוּ
the Torah that teaches us how to live	תּוֹרַת חַיִּים
and (through it) the love of doing kindness	וְאַהֲבַת חֶסֶד
and (You gave us with the Torah more opportunities for) reward in the World to Come (by fulfilling the many *mitzvos*)	וּצְדָקָה
and (as reward for keeping the Torah You give us also) an abundance of goodness and success (in this world)	וּבְרָכָה
and (in the merit of keeping the Torah You give us) special mercy	וְרַחֲמִים
and (as a reward for keeping the Torah You give us) a long, healthy life	וְחַיִּים
and (through the Torah we have) peace of body and mind (because all the ways of the Torah are peaceful).	וְשָׁלוֹם
And it should be good in Your eyes	וְטוֹב בְּעֵינֶיךָ

to give an abundance of goodness and success to Your nation, Israel	לְבָרֵךְ אֶת עַמְּךָ יִשְׂרָאֵל
in all parts of the day	בְּכָל עֵת
and in all hours of each part of the day	וּבְכָל שָׁעָה
with Your peace (which is a complete peace).	בִּשְׁלוֹמֶךָ

In the book of life	**בְּסֵפֶר חַיִּים**
of abundant goodness and success	**בְּרָכָה**
and peace between a man and his friend	**וְשָׁלוֹם**
and a good (ample and easy) livelihood	**וּפַרְנָסָה טוֹבָה**
may we be remembered	**נִזָּכֵר**
and may we be inscribed before You	**וְנִכָּתֵב לְפָנֶיךָ**
we (who are standing together praying)	**אֲנַחְנוּ**
and all of Your nation, Israel	**וְכָל עַמְּךָ בֵּית יִשְׂרָאֵל**
(let us be remembered and inscribed) for a truly good life (i.e., a life that will enable us to earn the World to Come)	**לְחַיִּים טוֹבִים**
and for peace within ourselves (that we should be satisfied with the materialistic things that we have).	**וּלְשָׁלוֹם.**

THERE ARE DIFFERENT CUSTOMS CONCERNING THE CONCLUSION OF THIS BLESSING AND EVERYONE SHOULD FOLLOW HIS CUSTOM. IF ONE DOES NOT KNOW HIS CUSTOM HE SHOULD RECITE THE VERSION ON THE RIGHT.

You are the Source of Blessing,	בָּרוּךְ אַתָּה	You are the Source of Blessing, Master of all,	בָּרוּךְ אַתָּה יהוה
Master of all,	יהוה	Who gives an abundance of goodness and success	הַמְבָרֵךְ
Who makes peace among all.	עוֹשֶׂה הַשָּׁלוֹם.	to His nation, Israel, with peace.	אֶת עַמּוֹ יִשְׂרָאֵל בַּשָּׁלוֹם.

וִידּוּי
Confession[8]

The Master of all strength, Who is able to do anything
and Who takes care of us with Divine Providence,

אֱלֹהֵֽינוּ

and the God who took care
of our Fathers with Divine Providence

וֵאלֹהֵי אֲבוֹתֵֽינוּ

let our prayers come before
Your Throne of Glory

תָּבֹא לְפָנֶֽיךָ תְּפִלָּתֵֽנוּ

and do not ignore that which
we say with humility before You

וְאַל תִּתְעַלַּם מִתְּחִנָּתֵֽנוּ

for we are not so brazen
and stubborn [to claim
that we are righteous]

שֶׁאֵין אֲנַֽחְנוּ עַזֵּי פָנִים וּקְשֵׁי עֹֽרֶף

to say before You,

לוֹמַר לְפָנֶֽיךָ

Master of all, the Master of all strength,
Who is able to do anything and
Who takes care of us with Divine Providence,

יהוה אֱלֹהֵֽינוּ

and the God who took care
of our Fathers with Divine Providence,

וֵאלֹהֵי אֲבוֹתֵֽינוּ

---

8. *Siddur Rokeach* says that *Viduy* (Confession) must be said with concentration, with a broken heart and with great sorrow; the penitent must admit what he has done and resolve to leave his bad ways. If one says it in this way, then perhaps he can hope that the Merciful One Whose Hand is open will have mercy on him.

Yesod VeShoresh HaAvodah writes that before saying the *Viduy* one should have in mind that he is fulfilling a positive biblical commandment, as it says (*Bamidbar* 5:7): "and they should confess the sins that they have done." And he writes further that **the main part of the Viduy is** the absolute and complete regret for having committed the sin and the acceptance to make fences to prevent oneself from succumbing to the sin again, for anyone who has sense will admit that confession that is not accompanied by repentance shows great *chutzpah* and brazenness.

According to *Seder HaYom* it is of paramount importance that the *Viduy* be said from the heart, not merely lip-service, for insincere *Viduy* increases one's sins, since he seems to think he is fooling the One Who knows all.

R' Chaim David Azulai [known as the *Chida*] writes that the essence of the *Viduy* is for the person to realize that he has absolutely sinned, and not seek excuses.

that we are righteous and have not sinned [we are not so brazen to say that]	צַדִּיקִים אֲנַחְנוּ וְלֹא חָטָאנוּ
but really we [and our forefathers] have sinned.	אֲבָל אֲנַחְנוּ [וַאֲבוֹתֵינוּ] חָטָאנוּ.

We have sinned so much that we deserve to be destroyed.	אָשַׁמְנוּ
We have been ungrateful for the good God has done for us (and have even responded to His goodness with evil).	בָּגַדְנוּ
We have stolen (this includes borrowing without permission, fooling someone ["stealing his mind"] and disturbing someone's sleep).	גָּזַלְנוּ
We have spoken disgracefully about others (this includes slander).	דִּבַּרְנוּ דֹפִי
We have caused perversion (this includes causing others to sin or preventing others from doing mitzvos).	הֶעֱוִינוּ
And we have judged the righteous as if they were evil (and not favorably).	וְהִרְשַׁעְנוּ
We have sinned intentionally.	זַדְנוּ
We have taken things away from others against their will (even if we have paid them more than it was worth).	חָמַסְנוּ
We have added one lie onto another in order to reinforce it.	טָפַלְנוּ שֶׁקֶר
We have given advice that was bad for the one who sought our advice.	יָעַצְנוּ רָע
We have not kept our promises (including those that we have made to God to better our ways).	כִּזַּבְנוּ

We have scoffed at people, at words of Torah, and at important things and actions (included in this is wasting time with idle chatter). **לַ**צְנוּ

We have known God and yet rebelled against Him (the worst of all sins). **מָ**רַדְנוּ

We have angered God with our sins. **נִ**אַצְנוּ

We have turned our hearts away from the service of God. **סָ**רַרְנוּ

We have sinned only to fulfill our desires. **עָ**וִינוּ

We have sinned because we denied God's existence. **פָּ**שַׁעְנוּ

We have caused others pain. **צָ**רַרְנוּ

We have been stubborn and have not accepted rebuke; we have not viewed personal hardships as a message to improve our ways. **קָ**שִׁינוּ עֹרֶף

We have done actions that make us considered wicked (like raising our hand to hit someone). **רָ**שַׁעְנוּ

We have corrupted ourselves with sins that are tantamount to immorality and idolatry. **שִׁ**חַתְנוּ

We have done acts that are abominable in the eyes of God (like actual immorality and idolatry). **תִּ**עַבְנוּ

We have strayed from the straight path of service to God. **תָּ**עִינוּ

We have done deceitful acts. **תִּ**עְתָּעְנוּ.

We have turned away from fulfilling Your positive commandments **סַרְנוּ** מִמִּצְוֹתֶיךָ

and from not fulfilling the good and pleasant positive commandments that You obligate us towards others וּמִמִּשְׁפָּטֶיךָ הַטּוֹבִים

and we have not gained by refraining
from doing Your *mitzvos* (for we have lost
much more than we have gained)

וְלֹא שָׁוָה לָנוּ

and You are righteous (justified)
in all the punishments
that You have brought on us[9]

וְאַתָּה צַדִּיק עַל כָּל הַבָּא עָלֵינוּ

because You have judged us truthfully

כִּי אֱמֶת עָשִׂיתָ

but we have been increasingly wicked.

וַאֲנַחְנוּ הִרְשָׁעְנוּ.

What can we say before Your Throne
of Glory to justify ourselves

מַה נֹּאמַר לְפָנֶיךָ

(to You) Who sits high in the Heavens
(and Whose eyes gaze over the entire world)

יוֹשֵׁב מָרוֹם

and what can we confess of our sins before You

וּמַה נְּסַפֵּר לְפָנֶיךָ

Who sits in the heavens (and knows all)

שׁוֹכֵן שְׁחָקִים

for all things, both those that are hidden
from people and those that are revealed,

הֲלֹא כָּל הַנִּסְתָּרוֹת וְהַנִּגְלוֹת

You already know.

אַתָּה יוֹדֵעַ.

You know the secrets of the universe

אַתָּה יוֹדֵעַ רָזֵי עוֹלָם

and all the actions people
have tried to conceal.

וְתַעֲלוּמוֹת סִתְרֵי כָּל חָי

You search out all the
inner thoughts of a person

אַתָּה חֹפֵשׂ כָּל חַדְרֵי בָטֶן

and examine one's motives and intentions
(to determine if the actions were premeditated,
done with joy, etc.).

וּבֹחֵן כְּלָיוֹת וָלֵב

---

9. *Siddur Maggid Tzedek* says that one should say this phrase very humbly and with sincerity, fully accepting God's judgment.

There is no thought that is hidden
from You

אֵין (כָּל) דָּבָר נֶעְלָם מִמֶּךָ

and there is no action that
escapes Your eyes

וְאֵין נִסְתָּר מִנֶּגֶד עֵינֶיךָ

and so [with this recognition],
we ask that it be a favorable time
to let our prayers come before You

וּבְכֵן יְהִי רָצוֹן מִלְּפָנֶיךָ

Master of all, the Master of all strength,
Who is able to do anything and Who takes
care of us with Divine Providence,

יהוה אֱלֹהֵינוּ

and the God who took care of
our Fathers with Divine Providence

וֵאלֹהֵי אֲבוֹתֵינוּ

that You forgive us for
the sins themselves that we
transgressed unintentionally

שֶׁתִּסְלַח לָנוּ עַל כָּל חַטֹּאתֵינוּ

and You pardon us
the insult to Your Honor
that we caused with our willful sins

וְתִמְחָל לָנוּ עַל כָּל עֲוֹנוֹתֵינוּ

and You atone (entirely
wipe out any trace) for our sins
that we did even rebelliously.

וּתְכַפֶּר לָנוּ עַל כָּל פְּשָׁעֵינוּ.

ONE SHOULD STRIKE THE LEFT SIDE OF THE CHEST (WHERE THE HEART IS)
WITH THE RIGHT FIST WHEN SAYING שֶׁחָטָאנוּ ("WE HAVE SINNED").
BY THE LAST GROUP (STARTING "AND FOR THE SINS FOR WHICH WE ARE OBLIGATED")
ONE SHOULD STRIKE THE CHEST WHEN SAYING שֶׁאָנוּ חַיָּבִים
("FOR WHICH WE ARE OBLIGATED") '[MEKOR CHAIM, KITZUR HALACHOS, CH. 607].

[Forgive, pardon and atone]
for the sins we have sinned before You
(Whose Honor fills the earth)

עַל חֵטְא שֶׁחָטָאנוּ לְפָנֶיךָ

with coercion (when we were not permitted to submit)

בְּאֹנֶס

and those we have done willingly (with desire).

וּבְרָצוֹן.

And for the sins we have sinned before You

וְעַל חֵטְא שֶׁחָטָאנוּ לְפָנֶיךָ

with a hardened heart (this includes
refraining from giving charity, or any form of cruelty).

בְּאִמּוּץ הַלֵּב.

For the sins we have sinned before You

עַל חֵטְא שֶׁחָטָאנוּ לְפָנֶיךָ

without thought (we have done things
without putting our minds to them,
including *mitzvos* not done expressly to serve God).

בִּבְלִי דָעַת.

And for the sins we have sinned before You

וְעַל חֵטְא שֶׁחָטָאנוּ לְפָנֶיךָ

with speech lacking proper contemplation
(like making vows or promising to do
something that we subsequently regret).

בְּבִטּוּי שְׂפָתָיִם.

For the sins we have sinned before You

עַל חֵטְא שֶׁחָטָאנוּ לְפָנֶיךָ

whether in a public place (without any sense of shame)
or in seclusion (ignoring the omnipresence of God).

בַּגָּלוּי וּבַסָּתֶר.

And for the sins we have sinned before You

וְעַל חֵטְא שֶׁחָטָאנוּ לְפָנֶיךָ

with immorality.

בְּגִלּוּי עֲרָיוֹת.

For the sins we have sinned before You

עַל חֵטְא שֶׁחָטָאנוּ לְפָנֶיךָ

by speaking too much (which inevitably causes sins)
and all sins of the mouth (including expressing a grudge).

בְּדִבּוּר פֶּה.

And for the sins we have sinned before You

וְעַל חֵטְא שֶׁחָטָאנוּ לְפָנֶיךָ

by purposely sinning against our friend
or causing him damage, while deceitfully
claiming that it was unintentional.

בְּדַעַת וּבְמִרְמָה.

For the sins we have sinned before You

עַל חֵטְא שֶׁחָטָאנוּ לְפָנֶיךָ

with forbidden thoughts
(like those of idolatry or atheism,
lustful thoughts or obsession with money).

בְּהִרְהוֹר הַלֵּב.

And for the sins we have sinned before You

וְעַל חֵטְא שֶׁחָטָאנוּ לְפָנֶיךָ

by causing our friend pain with hurtful
words or financial dishonesty.

בְּהוֹנָאַת רֵעַ.

For the sins we have sinned before You

עַל חֵטְא שֶׁחָטָאנוּ לְפָנֶיךָ

with confession said only with our mouth,
and not with sincere regret, nor commitment not to sin again.

בְּוִדּוּי פֶּה.

And for the sins we have sinned before You

וְעַל חֵטְא שֶׁחָטָאנוּ לְפָנֶיךָ

for having gathered for the purpose of lustfulness.

בִּוְעִידַת זְנוּת.

For the sins we have sinned before You

עַל חֵטְא שֶׁחָטָאנוּ לְפָנֶיךָ

whether with intention and knowledge of the sin,
or without intention or knowledge of the sin.

בְּזָדוֹן וּבִשְׁגָגָה.

And for the sins we have sinned before You

וְעַל חֵטְא שֶׁחָטָאנוּ לְפָנֶיךָ

by not giving honor, or even disgracing,
our parents, teachers and rabbis.

בְּזִלְזוּל הוֹרִים וּמוֹרִים.

For the sins we have sinned before You

עַל חֵטְא שֶׁחָטָאנוּ לְפָנֶיךָ

by forcing our friends, whether physically
or otherwise, to do our will.

בְּחֹזֶק יָד.

And for the sins we have sinned before You

וְעַל חֵטְא שֶׁחָטָאנוּ לְפָנֶיךָ

by causing a desecration to the honor of God
(by not thinking adequately before any action
about its repercussions).

בְּחִלּוּל הַשֵּׁם.

For the sins we have sinned before You

עַל חֵטְא שֶׁחָטָאנוּ לְפָנֶיךָ

with idle talk (which shows everyone how foolish he is,
wasting his time with meaningless chatter).

בְּטִפְשׁוּת פֶּה.

And for the sins we have sinned before You

וְעַל חֵטְא שֶׁחָטָאנוּ לְפָנֶיךָ

with impure lips (i.e. talking obscene
language or about indecent things).

בְּטֻמְאַת שְׂפָתָיִם.

For the sins we have sinned before You

עַל חֵטְא שֶׁחָטָאנוּ לְפָנֶיךָ

by inciting our evil inclination.

בְּיֵצֶר הָרָע.

And for the sins we have sinned before You

וְעַל חֵטְא שֶׁחָטָאנוּ לְפָנֶיךָ

by harming others in ways that they know
or in ways they don't know
(like slandering him behind his back).

בְּיוֹדְעִים וּבְלֹא יוֹדְעִים.

And for all the sins that we have mentioned

וְעַל כֻּלָּם

[You,] the God Who abundantly forgives, [please]

אֱלוֹהַּ סְלִיחוֹת

forgive us for the sins themselves

סְלַח לָנוּ

pardon us for the insult caused to Your Honor by our sins

מְחַל לָנוּ

(and) atone for us our sins as if they had never occurred.

כַּפֶּר לָנוּ.

For the sins we have sinned before You

עַל חֵטְא שֶׁחָטָאנוּ לְפָנֶיךָ

by giving or taking a bribe.

בְּכַפַּת שֹׁחַד.

And for the sins we have sinned before You

וְעַל חֵטְא שֶׁחָטָאנוּ לְפָנֶיךָ

by denying what was (i.e., plain lying)
and by not keeping our promises.

בְּכַחַשׁ וּבְכָזָב.

For the sins we have sinned before You

עַל חֵטְא שֶׁחָטָאנוּ לְפָנֶיךָ

by speaking or accepting disparaging
words about someone else, even if true.

בְּלָשׁוֹן הָרָע.

And for the sins we have sinned before You

וְעַל חֵטְא שֶׁחָטָאנוּ לְפָנֶיךָ

by scoffing at people, at words of Torah,
and at important things and actions.

בְּלָצוֹן.

For the sins we have sinned before You

עַל חֵטְא שֶׁחָטָאנוּ לְפָנֶיךָ

by dealing in business dishonestly
(e.g., deception or faulty measures).

בְּמַשָּׂא וּבְמַתָּן.

And for the sins we have sinned before You

וְעַל חֵטְא שֶׁחָטָאנוּ לְפָנֶיךָ

by eating and drinking (this includes
eating non-kosher foods or foods that had
insects; or eating without a blessing).

בְּמַאֲכָל וּבְמִשְׁתֶּה.

For the sins we have sinned before You

עַל חֵטְא שֶׁחָטָאנוּ לְפָנֶיךָ

by taking or paying interest (this includes
verbal interest, or paying more for credit).

בְּנֶשֶׁךְ וּבְמַרְבִּית.

And for the sins we have sinned before You

וְעַל חֵטְא שֶׁחָטָאנוּ לְפָנֶיךָ

(by walking) with an outstretched neck
(in a haughty manner; includes any act of overt haughtiness).

בִּנְטִיַּת גָּרוֹן.

For the sins we have sinned before You

עַל חֵטְא שֶׁחָטָאנוּ לְפָנֶיךָ

with a wink or motion of the eye
(which is sometimes enough to harm
others or entice them to sin).

בְּשִׂקּוּר עָיִן.

And for the sins we have sinned before You

וְעַל חֵטְא שֶׁחָטָאנוּ לְפָנֶיךָ

by saying words without concentration
(like praying, saying blessings,
or answering *Amen* without thinking).

בְּשִׂיחַ שִׂפְתוֹתֵינוּ.

For the sins we have sinned before You

עַל חֵטְא שֶׁחָטָאנוּ לְפָנֶיךָ

by looking down at people because of our haughtiness.

בְּעֵינַיִם רָמוֹת.

And for the sins we have sinned before You

וְעַל חֵטְא שֶׁחָטָאנוּ לְפָנֶיךָ

by being brazen towards our rabbis or
towards anyone greater than us.

בְּעַזּוּת מֵצַח.

And for all the sins that we have mentioned

וְעַל כֻּלָּם

[You,] the God Who abundantly forgives, [please]

אֱלוֹהַּ סְלִיחוֹת

forgive us for the sins themselves

סְלַח לָנוּ

pardon us for the insult caused to Your Honor by our sins מְחַל לָנוּ

(and) atone for us our sins as if they had never occurred. כַּפֶּר לָנוּ.

For the sins we have sinned before You עַל חֵטְא שֶׁחָטָאנוּ לְפָנֶיךָ

by throwing off the yoke of Heaven or even the yoke
of one *mitzvah* (like the yoke of learning Torah). בִּפְרִיקַת עֹל.

And for the sins we have sinned before You וְעַל חֵטְא שֶׁחָטָאנוּ לְפָנֶיךָ

by perversion of judgment
(including questioning the justice of God). בִּפְלִילוּת.

For the sins we have sinned before You עַל חֵטְא שֶׁחָטָאנוּ לְפָנֶיךָ

by entrapping a friend (even if no harm resulted). בִּצְדִיַּת רֵעַ.

And for the sins we have sinned before You וְעַל חֵטְא שֶׁחָטָאנוּ לְפָנֶיךָ

with a begrudging eye, feeling unhappy
when things go well for others (this also refers
to one who does not want to do good for others). בְּצָרוּת עָיִן.

For the sins we have sinned before You עַל חֵטְא שֶׁחָטָאנוּ לְפָנֶיךָ

by acting light-headedly (without fear of Heaven)
while doing *mitzvos* or in holy places
(like a synagogue). בְּקַלּוּת רֹאשׁ.

And for the sins we have sinned before You וְעַל חֵטְא שֶׁחָטָאנוּ לְפָנֶיךָ

by having been stubborn, not accepting
rebuke or not looking at personal hardships
as a message to improve our ways. בְּקַשְׁיוּת עֹרֶף.

For the sins we have sinned before You עַל חֵטְא שֶׁחָטָאנוּ לְפָנֶיךָ

with feet running to do evil. בְּרִיצַת רַגְלַיִם לְהָרַע.

And for the sins we have sinned before You וְעַל חֵטְא שֶׁחָטָאנוּ לְפָנֶיךָ

by tale-bearing
(i.e., going from one to another relating information
which causes ill will between people) or accepting the tale.

בִּרְכִילוּת.

For the sins we have sinned before You

עַל חֵטְא שֶׁחָטָאנוּ לְפָנֶיךָ

by swearing falsely or in vain.

בִּשְׁבוּעַת שָׁוְא.

And for the sins we have sinned before You

וְעַל חֵטְא שֶׁחָטָאנוּ לְפָנֶיךָ

by hating other Jews without a valid reason.

בְּשִׂנְאַת חִנָּם.

For the sins we have sinned before You

עַל חֵטְא שֶׁחָטָאנוּ לְפָנֶיךָ

by not acting properly with money that was
entrusted to us (such as in a partnership,
or a loan that was not repaid on time).

בִּתְשׂוּמֶת יָד.

And for the sins we have sinned before You

וְעַל חֵטְא שֶׁחָטָאנוּ לְפָנֶיךָ

with a confusion of heart.

בְּתִמְהוֹן לֵבָב.

And for all the sins that we have mentioned

וְעַל כֻּלָּם

[You,] the God Who abundantly forgives, [please]

אֱלוֹהַ סְלִיחוֹת

forgive us for the sins themselves

סְלַח לָנוּ

pardon us for the insult caused to Your Honor by our sins

מְחַל לָנוּ

(and) atone for us our sins as if they had never occurred.

כַּפֶּר לָנוּ.

And for the sins for which
we are obligated to bring

וְעַל חֲטָאִים שֶׁאָנוּ חַיָּבִים עֲלֵיהֶם

a *korban olah*
(e.g., for transgressing a positive command, like *Tefillin*,
or standing up fully for someone over seventy).

עוֹלָה.

And for the sins for which
we are obligated to bring

וְעַל חֲטָאִים שֶׁאָנוּ חַיָּבִים עֲלֵיהֶם

a *korban chatas* (for committing a sin unintentionally, that had it been done intentionally would be punished by *kares*, e.g., desecrating Shabbos).

חַטָּאת.

And for the sins for which we are obligated to bring

וְעַל חֲטָאִים שֶׁאָנוּ חַיָּבִים עֲלֵיהֶם

a *korban oleh veyored* [that varies according to the wealth of the sinner] (e.g., for unintentionally entering the Temple when impure).

קָרְבַּן עוֹלֶה וְיוֹרֵד.

And for the sins for which we are obligated to bring

וְעַל חֲטָאִים שֶׁאָנוּ חַיָּבִים עֲלֵיהֶם

a *korban asham* for a certain sin (e.g., swearing falsely about someone else's money in his hand) or possible sin.

אָשָׁם וַדַּאי וְתָלוּי.

And for the sins for which we incur

וְעַל חֲטָאִים שֶׁאָנוּ חַיָּבִים עֲלֵיהֶם

lashes for rebellion (e.g., for violating a Rabbinic prohibition or refusing to do a positive commandment).

מַכַּת מַרְדּוּת.

And for the sins for which we incur

וְעַל חֲטָאִים שֶׁאָנוּ חַיָּבִים עֲלֵיהֶם

forty lashes (for one who transgresses a biblical prohibition, e.g., rounding off the corners of a man's head).

מַלְקוּת אַרְבָּעִים.

And for the sins for which we are obligated

וְעַל חֲטָאִים שֶׁאָנוּ חַיָּבִים עֲלֵיהֶם

to die young at the hands of the Heavenly Court (e.g., one who renders a decision in front of his rabbi; or emits semen in vain).

מִיתָה בִּידֵי שָׁמָיִם.

And for the sins for which we are obligated

וְעַל חֲטָאִים שֶׁאָנוּ חַיָּבִים עֲלֵיהֶם

to be cut off from the World to Come
and die childless (e.g., one who intentionally
cohabits with a *niddah,* or eats on Yom Kippur).

כָּרֵת וַעֲרִירִי.

And for the sins for
which we incur

וְעַל חֲטָאִים שֶׁאָנוּ חַיָּבִים עֲלֵיהֶם

one of the four types of death
administered by *beis din* (a Jewish court of law):

אַרְבַּע מִיתוֹת בֵּית דִּין —

stoning (e.g., for desecrating Shabbos intentionally
or for homosexual relations)

סְקִילָה

burning (e.g., for relations with a woman and her daughter)

שְׂרֵפָה

beheading (e.g., for murder)

הֶרֶג

and strangling (e.g., for hitting one's parents
or having relations with a married woman).

וְחֶנֶק

[and we ask forgiveness] for not doing
one of the 248 positive commandments

עַל מִצְוַת עֲשֵׂה

and for any of the 365 negative
commandments that we have violated

וְעַל מִצְוַת לֹא תַעֲשֶׂה

whether it was one that could be
corrected by doing a positive act
(like returning an object he stole)

בֵּין שֶׁיֵּשׁ בָּהּ קוּם עֲשֵׂה

or whether it was of those that
do not have a positive act to rectify it
(like most transgressions, e.g., immorality).

וּבֵין שֶׁאֵין בָּהּ קוּם עֲשֵׂה

[We ask forgiveness for both]
the sins that are revealed to us

אֶת הַגְּלוּיִם לָנוּ

and those that are not revealed to us.

וְאֶת שֶׁאֵינָם גְּלוּיִם לָנוּ

Those that are revealed to us

אֶת הַגְּלוּיִם לָנוּ

we have already said before You
(in our confession)

כְּבָר אֲמַרְנוּם לְפָנֶיךָ

and we have confessed them to You;

וְהוֹדֵינוּ לְךָ עֲלֵיהֶם

and those that are not revealed to us

וְאֶת שֶׁאֵינָם גְּלוּיִם לָנוּ

they are still revealed
and known to You, Who knows all
[and we ask forgiveness for them, too]

לְפָנֶיךָ הֵם גְּלוּיִם וִידוּעִים

as it says (*Devarim* 29:28):

כַּדָּבָר שֶׁנֶּאֱמַר

"The sins that are hidden from the one who did them
(i.e., he did them unintentionally and unknowingly)

הַנִּסְתָּרֹת

are for the Master of all, the Master of all
strength Who is able to do anything and Who takes
care of us with Divine Providence (to atone for us),

לַיהוה אֱלֹהֵינוּ

but the sins that are revealed

וְהַנִּגְלֹת

are for us and our children forever
to repent for them to achieve atonement

לָנוּ וּלְבָנֵינוּ עַד עוֹלָם

(and) to keep all of these words
of the Torah (i.e., all the *mitzvos*)."

לַעֲשׂוֹת אֶת כָּל דִּבְרֵי הַתּוֹרָה הַזֹּאת.

[So, please forgive us] because
You are the Forgiver of Israel constantly

כִּי אַתָּה סָלְחָן לְיִשְׂרָאֵל

and You are the Pardoner of Israel
—who go in the straight path —

וּמָחֳלָן לְשִׁבְטֵי יְשֻׁרוּן

in every generation

בְּכָל דּוֹר וָדוֹר

and except for You,

וּמִבַּלְעָדֶיךָ

we have no other king
who will completely pardon and forgive us

אֵין לָנוּ מֶלֶךְ מוֹחֵל וְסוֹלֵחַ

(— only You).

(אֶלָּא אָתָּה).

The Master of all strength, Who is able to do anything
and Who takes care of me with Divine Providence,

אֱלֹהַי

before I was formed I was not worthy to be created	עַד שֶׁלֹּא נוֹצַרְתִּי אֵינִי כְדַאי
and now that I have been formed	וְעַכְשָׁו שֶׁנּוֹצַרְתִּי
it is as if I was never formed (for the world has not gained by my existence).	כְּאִלּוּ לֹא נוֹצַרְתִּי
I am like dust while I am still alive (for I do not have sufficient good deeds)	עָפָר אֲנִי בְּחַיָּי
and I will surely be so in my death (when I will no longer be able to perform *mitzvos*).	קַל וָחְמֶר בְּמִיתָתִי
(Therefore) I stand before You	הֲרֵי אֲנִי לְפָנֶיךָ
like a vessel full of embarrassment and shame.	כִּכְלִי מָלֵא בוּשָׁה וּכְלִמָּה.
May it be a time of favor before Your Throne of Glory	יְהִי רָצוֹן מִלְּפָנֶיךָ
Master of all, the Master of all strength, Who is able to do anything and Who takes care of me with Divine Providence,	יהוה אֱלֹהַי
and the God who took care of my Fathers with Divine Providence	וֵאלֹהֵי אֲבוֹתַי
that You help me so that I should not sin anymore (by removing the causes of sin and daily preoccupations)	שֶׁלֹּא אֶחֱטָא עוֹד
and that which I have already sinned before You	וּמַה שֶׁחָטָאתִי לְפָנֶיךָ
cleanse with Your great mercy	מְרֵק בְּרַחֲמֶיךָ הָרַבִּים
but not through terrible suffering or difficult illnesses (rather through minor pains).	אֲבָל לֹא עַל יְדֵי יִסּוּרִים וַחֲלָיִם רָעִים.

תחנונים
Personal Requests

The Master of all strength, Who is able to do anything and Who takes care of me with Divine Providence,

אֱלֹהַי

help me to guard my tongue from speaking bad about others (*lashon hara*)

נְצוֹר לְשׁוֹנִי מֵרָע

and [help me to guard] my lips from speaking deceit or falsehood

וּשְׂפָתַי מִדַּבֵּר מִרְמָה

and help me so that my soul should be silent (and even in thought I should not get angry) at those who curse me

וְלִמְקַלְלַי נַפְשִׁי תִדּוֹם

and help me so that my soul should be like dust (very humble) before everyone (and not mind insults).

וְנַפְשִׁי כֶּעָפָר לַכֹּל תִּהְיֶה

Open up my heart so that it should be receptive and understand Your Torah

פְּתַח לִבִּי בְּתוֹרָתֶךָ

and help my soul eagerly pursue Your *mitzvos*
and all those who want to harm me (whether in mundane matters or spiritual matters, i.e., to cause me to sin)

וּבְמִצְוֹתֶיךָ תִּרְדּוֹף נַפְשִׁי

וְכֹל הַחוֹשְׁבִים עָלַי רָעָה

quickly annul their plan

מְהֵרָה הָפֵר עֲצָתָם

and ruin their thought (even before they make plans).

וְקַלְקֵל מַחֲשַׁבְתָּם

Act (take us out of exile) for the sake of Your Name, which is desecrated now among the gentiles

עֲשֵׂה לְמַעַן שְׁמֶךָ

act (take us out of exile) for the sake of Your right hand, which You have now withdrawn in our exile

עֲשֵׂה לְמַעַן יְמִינֶךָ

act (take us out of exile)
for the sake of Your Holiness
(so that all will know that You lead us with holiness)

עֲשֵׂה לְמַעַן קְדֻשָּׁתֶךְ

act (take us out of exile)
for the sake of Your Torah
(so the Torah can be studied properly and completely)

עֲשֵׂה לְמַעַן תּוֹרָתֶךְ

and in order that Your dear ones, Israel,
should be released from all troubles

לְמַעַן יֵחָלְצוּן יְדִידֶיךָ

save them with (the wonders and miracles that
are attributed to) Your right hand

הוֹשִׁיעָה יְמִינְךָ

and answer (even) me in this prayer.

וַעֲנֵנִי.

Let the words of my prayer
be desirable to You[10]

יִהְיוּ לְרָצוֹן אִמְרֵי פִי

and also the thoughts of my heart which
I cannot express [should be desirable] before You,
Master of all,

וְהֶגְיוֹן לִבִּי לְפָנֶיךָ

יהוה

My Rock, upon Whom I rely for all my requests

צוּרִי

and Who will be my Redeemer.

וְגֹאֲלִי.

ONE SHOULD BOW AND GO BACK THREE STEPS
LIKE A SERVANT DEPARTING FROM HIS MASTER

The One Who makes peace in Heaven
(among the angels)

עֹשֶׂה [הַ]שָּׁלוֹם בִּמְרוֹמָיו

may He make peace (for those on earth,
who are naturally quarrelsome)

הוּא יַעֲשֶׂה שָׁלוֹם

on those of us here (praying together)

עָלֵינוּ

and on all of Israel

וְעַל כָּל יִשְׂרָאֵל

---

10. *Seder HaYom* writes that one should say this verse with great concentration, for it will help considerably that his prayers should not go unanswered (quoted also in *Mishnah Berurah* 122:8).

and (you, the angels who escort me,) agree to my prayer, and say Amen!	וְאִמְרוּ אָמֵן.
May it be Your desire,	**יְהִי רָצוֹן** מִלְפָנֶיךָ
Master of all,	יהוה
the Master of all strength, Who is able to do anything and Who takes care of us with Divine Providence,	אֱלֹהֵינוּ
and the God Who took care of our Fathers with Divine Providence,	וֵאלֹהֵי אֲבוֹתֵינוּ
that You should rebuild the Temple (so that we will be able to do the ultimate *avodah* — service to You)	שֶׁיִּבָּנֶה בֵּית הַמִּקְדָּשׁ
quickly and in our lifetime	בִּמְהֵרָה בְיָמֵינוּ
and help us so that all our toil should be in learning Your Torah.	וְתֵן חֶלְקֵנוּ בְּתוֹרָתֶךָ
And there, in the Temple, we will bring offerings (the ultimate service) with reverence	וְשָׁם נַעֲבָדְךָ בְּיִרְאָה
as [they brought offerings and served in reverence] in the earlier days (of Moshe)	כִּימֵי עוֹלָם
and as they did in the previous years (of Shlomo *HaMelech*).	וּכְשָׁנִים קַדְמוֹנִיּוֹת.
And then, it will be pleasing to the Master of all	וְעָרְבָה לַיהוה
the offerings that will be brought in the Temple (which is in the portion of Yehudah in Jerusalem)	מִנְחַת יְהוּדָה וִירוּשָׁלָיִם
as [the offerings were pleasing] in the earlier days (of Moshe)	כִּימֵי עוֹלָם
and as they were in the previous years (of Shlomo *HaMelech*).	וּכְשָׁנִים קַדְמוֹנִיּוֹת.

Ne'ilah

"**N**e'ilah is the sealing of the final judgment which was written on Rosh Hashanah, whether for good or for bad. One should recite this prayer very carefully, for the climax of the entire *Aseres Yemei Teshuvah* is Yom Kippur, and **the climax of the entire Yom Kippur is *Ne'ilah*,** because everything is decided according to the conclusion, and if not now, when? Therefore, even if one is weak due to the fast, he should strengthen himself to pray with a pure and clear mind, and accept upon himself the steps of repentance sincerely. One who seeks to be purified will be helped from Above, and he will be sealed in the Book of Good Life" (*Mishnah Berurah* 623:3).

Ne'ilah — Closing Prayer for the Day of Atonement[1]

When I call in the name of the Master of all	**כִּי** שֵׁם יהוה אֶקְרָא
you should ascribe greatness to the Master of all strength, Who is able to do anything and Who takes care of us with Divine Providence.	הָבוּ גֹדֶל לֵאלֹהֵינוּ.
Master of all — in particular, My Master	אֲדֹנָי
please open my lips (because I am afraid and ashamed to open them)	שְׂפָתַי תִּפְתָּח
and [help me pray with concentration, so] my mouth will [be able to] tell Your true praise.	וּפִי יַגִּיד תְּהִלָּתֶךָ.

אבות
Our God and the God of Our Fathers,
Who Created Everything, and Protected Abraham[2]

You are the source of blessing (an expression of praise)	**בָּרוּךְ** אַתָּה
Master of all (Who always was, is, and will be)	יהוה
the Master of all strength, Who is able to do anything and Who takes care of us with Divine Providence,	אֱלֹהֵינוּ

---

1. We add this additional prayer on Yom Kippur to arouse God's mercy at this time of the closing of the Gates of Heaven, so that all of our prayers should be accepted favorably, and our request to atone for our sins be fulfilled (Seder HaYom).

Yesod VeShoresh HaAvodah writes that one should exert himself greatly to say this prayer with concentration, and infuse his heart with concern and fear over the frightful judgment being sealed at this time in the Heavens. And how good it would be if one would shed a few tears to arouse mercy in the Upper World.

2. One must be very careful to concentrate when saying this brachah, because otherwise he does not fulfill his obligation to pray. In the time of the Gemara one would have had to repeat the Shemoneh Esrei if he had not concentrated. Nowadays, however, when we are not sure that the second time will yield the proper concentration either, we do not repeat the Shemoneh Esrei; therefore one has to be exceedingly careful to concentrate for the first brachah or there is no remedy to rectify his prayer. [Nevertheless, if one did not concentrate for the first brachah he should still finish the prayer (Kehillos Yaakov, Brachos, Ch. 26).]

and the God Who took care of our Fathers with Divine Providence (and made a covenant with each of them)	וֵאלֹהֵי אֲבוֹתֵינוּ
the God Who made a covenant with our father Abraham (who excelled in kindness)	אֱלֹהֵי אַבְרָהָם
the God Who made a covenant with our father Isaac (who excelled in service of God)	אֱלֹהֵי יִצְחָק
and the God Who made a covenant with our father Jacob (who excelled in learning Torah)	וֵאלֹהֵי יַעֲקֹב
He is the Almighty (all power is His, especially in exercising the attribute of mercy)	הָאֵל
Who is the Great One (all greatness is His, especially in exercising the attribute of kindness)	הַגָּדוֹל
(and) He is the Strong One (all strength is His, especially in exercising the attribute of judgment)	הַגִּבּוֹר
and He alone deserves to be feared (because no being has the ability to do good or bad except Him)	וְהַנּוֹרָא
for He is the supreme God Who is the ultimate cause of everything	אֵל עֶלְיוֹן
Who always does kindnesses that are purely good	גּוֹמֵל חֲסָדִים טוֹבִים
and He recreates everything, constantly, every day	וְקוֹנֶה הַכֹּל
and every day He recalls for our benefit the kindnesses performed by the forefathers	וְזוֹכֵר חַסְדֵי אָבוֹת
and He constantly brings the Redeemer closer	וּמֵבִיא גּוֹאֵל
to the forefathers' children's children (even though the merit of the forefathers might already be used up)	לִבְנֵי בְנֵיהֶם

for the sake of His Name (which will be sanctified at the time of the Redemption)	לְמַעַן שְׁמוֹ
[and He will also bring the Redeemer] because of His great love for the Jewish people.	בְּאַהֲבָה
Remember us for life in this world (in order that we may earn the World to Come by doing *mitzvos* here)	**זָכְרֵנוּ לְחַיִּים**
King, Who desires life (and not death for a sinner, but rather that he should repent)[3]	**מֶלֶךְ חָפֵץ בַּחַיִּים**
and seal us[4] in the Book of the Righteous, for life	**וְחָתְמֵנוּ בְּסֵפֶר הַחַיִּים**
for Your sake, in order that we may serve You	**לְמַעַנְךָ**
the Master of all strength, Who is able to do anything and is the One Who apportions life to all.	**אֱלֹהִים חַיִּים**
He is the King over all	מֶלֶךְ
Who is the Helper (to help one succeed)	עוֹזֵר
and the Savior (from trouble)	וּמוֹשִׁיעַ
and the Protector (to prevent trouble from coming).	וּמָגֵן
You are the Source of Blessing,	בָּרוּךְ אַתָּה
Master of all,	יהוה
the Protector of Abraham (and because of Abraham He continues His protection over us).	מָגֵן אַבְרָהָם.

---

3. R' Hirtz Shatz in his *Siddur* writes that when one says these words he should think that if he only repents he will live, and should resolve to do *teshuvah*.

4. Since this is the last prayer before the sealing of the judgment, we ask that we be successful in our judgment and be sealed for life (*Seder HaYom*).

גְבוּרוֹת
The Mighty Acts of God
and the Revival of the Dead

You alone are eternally Strong	**אַתָּה** גִּבּוֹר לְעוֹלָם
Master of all	אֲדֹנָי
You even revive the dead (which shows the greatest strength, contradicting all laws of nature)	מְחַיֵּה מֵתִים אַתָּה
[and] You have an abundance of strength with which to save.	רַב לְהוֹשִׁיעַ
He provides all the living with their food and other needs in kindness (not because they are deserving)	מְכַלְכֵּל חַיִּים בְּחֶסֶד
He revives the dead with great mercy (searching for merits with which they would deserve revival)	מְחַיֵּה מֵתִים בְּרַחֲמִים רַבִּים
He supports those who are falling (whether physically, emotionally, or financially)	סוֹמֵךְ נוֹפְלִים
and He heals the sick from all types of illnesses (even when doctors have given up hope)	וְרוֹפֵא חוֹלִים
and He opens the bonds of those who are restricted (e.g., giving movement to our limbs when we awaken)	וּמַתִּיר אֲסוּרִים
and He will keep His promise to those sleeping in the dust (the dead), to revive them.	וּמְקַיֵּם אֱמוּנָתוֹ לִישֵׁנֵי עָפָר
Who is like You (who can do as many mighty deeds, which are infinite, even for one person)?	מִי כָמוֹךָ
— You, to Whom all mighty deeds belong! —	בַּעַל גְּבוּרוֹת

And who is comparable to You in even one of Your mighty deeds (which are of the highest quality)?

וּמִי דוֹמֶה לָּךְ

You are the King over all

מֶלֶךְ

Who causes death and revival in many respects (such as sleep and awakening, poverty and wealth)

מֵמִית וּמְחַיֶּה

and, like the sprouting of a seed, You bring the Salvation (the Revival of the Dead).

וּמַצְמִיחַ יְשׁוּעָה

Who is like You, who has as much mercy on his sons as You, the Merciful Father, have for us

מִי כָמוֹךְ אַב הָרַחֲמִים

(and) remembers His creatures, out of mercy, for life.

זוֹכֵר יְצוּרָיו לְחַיִּים בְּרַחֲמִים

And (from the mighty deeds that we mentioned) we see that You are surely trusted to revive the dead.

וְנֶאֱמָן אַתָּה לְהַחֲיוֹת מֵתִים

You are the Source of Blessing, Master of all,

בָּרוּךְ אַתָּה יהוה

the Reviver of all the dead (from Adam until the time of the Revival).[5]

מְחַיֵּה הַמֵּתִים.

קְדוּשַׁת הַשֵּׁם
Return of the Glory of God's Kingdom (to Zion)

You, Yourself, are holy (different and separate from everything)

אַתָּה קָדוֹשׁ

and Your Name (which comes from Your many acts) reveals holiness

וְשִׁמְךָ קָדוֹשׁ

and the holy ones — Israel —

וּקְדוֹשִׁים

---

5. Even though many bodies have decomposed over thousands of years, and some have been burned and their dust has been scattered, and others have drowned at sea, Hashem with His great might will recognize and recompose the bodies and return to them their original souls (*Yesod VeShoresh HaAvodah*).

(when *Mashiach* comes) will praise You
every day, forever.

בְּכָל יוֹם יְהַלְלוּךְ סֶלָה.

And then (in the time of *Mashiach*)
[may it be speedily in our days]

וּבְכֵן

[You shall] put Your fear
(which will be a catalyst for repentance)

תֵּן פַּחְדְּךָ

Master of all

יהוה

the Master of all strength, Who is able to do anything
and Who takes care of us with Divine Providence,

אֱלֹהֵינוּ

on all Your works (which refers to the Jewish people)

עַל כָּל מַעֲשֶׂיךָ

and (put) Your dread

וְאֵימָתְךָ

on all that You have created
(which refers to the gentiles)

עַל כָּל מַה שֶׁבָּרֵאתָ

and then all the Jews will fear You

וְיִירָאוּךָ כָּל הַמַּעֲשִׂים

and all the nations of the world will
bow down to You in subjugation

וְיִשְׁתַּחֲווּ לְפָנֶיךָ כָּל הַבְּרוּאִים

and all of mankind will make one group

וְיֵעָשׂוּ כֻלָּם אֲגֻדָּה אַחַת

to do Your will with a
complete heart (submitting all
their tendencies to Divine service).

לַעֲשׂוֹת רְצוֹנְךָ בְּלֵבָב שָׁלֵם

As we already know (Your power from the
Exodus from Egypt)

כְּמוֹ שֶׁיָּדַעְנוּ

Master of all

יהוה

the Master of all strength, Who is able to do anything
and Who takes care of us with Divine Providence,

אֱלֹהֵינוּ

(where You revealed) that dominion is Yours

שֶׁהַשִּׁלְטוֹן לְפָנֶיךָ

and strength (in the constant running of the world) is in Your (left) hand	עֹז בְּיָדְךָ
and might (to do miracles) is in Your right hand	וּגְבוּרָה בִּימִינֶךָ
and (when You again reveal this in the time of *Mashiach*) Your Name will be revered	וְשִׁמְךָ נוֹרָא
on all the nations of the world.	עַל כָּל מַה שֶּׁבָּרֵאתָ.
And, then, Master of all, give honor to Your nation, Israel	**וּבְכֵן** תֵּן כָּבוֹד יהוה לְעַמֶּךָ
(and cause everyone to) praise those who fear You	תְּהִלָּה לִירֵאֶיךָ
and (give) to those who cling to You the good for which they rely on You	וְתִקְוָה [טוֹבָה] לְדוֹרְשֶׁיךָ
and (give) to those who yearn for Your salvation, the ability to praise You as they desire (without fear)	וּפִתְחוֹן פֶּה לַמְיַחֲלִים לָךְ
(and then when they no longer fear anyone) there will be an inner joy in the land of Israel (with the ingathering of the exiles)	שִׂמְחָה לְאַרְצֶךָ
and there will be open joy in Your city, Jerusalem, (where the glory of the Divine Presence will be felt most)	וְשָׂשׂוֹן לְעִירֶךָ
and then the kingdom of the family of David Your servant will sprout forth (with the coming of *Mashiach*)	וּצְמִיחַת קֶרֶן לְדָוִד עַבְדֶּךָ
and the influence of the son of Yishai (father of David) Your appointed one (*Mashiach*) will spread	וַעֲרִיכַת נֵר לְבֶן יִשַׁי מְשִׁיחֶךָ
(and we ask that this should happen) speedily in our days (so that we should witness the return of the honor of God).	בִּמְהֵרָה בְיָמֵינוּ.

And then (when *Mashiach* has come)

וּבְכֵן

the righteous will see (that the glory
of God has returned) and they will have inner joy

צַדִּיקִים יִרְאוּ וְיִשְׂמֶחוּ

and the upright ones (who do everything
just for the sake of Heaven) will be
inspired to dance from joy

וִישָׁרִים יַעֲלֹזוּ

and the pious (who do more than
they are required to do by the Torah)
will raise their voices in jubilant song

וַחֲסִידִים בְּרִנָּה יָגִילוּ

and all those who do injustice and iniquity
will close their mouths

וְעוֹלָתָה תִּקְפָּץ פִּיהָ

and all evil will vanish like smoke

וְכָל הָרִשְׁעָה כֻּלָּהּ כֶּעָשָׁן תִּכְלֶה

when you remove evil
kingdoms from the earth.

כִּי תַעֲבִיר מֶמְשֶׁלֶת זָדוֹן מִן הָאָרֶץ.

And (then it will be apparent)
that You alone, the Master of all,
are the only King

וְתִמְלוֹךְ אַתָּה יהוה לְבַדֶּךָ

on all Your works (the Jews and the other nations)

עַל כָּל מַעֲשֶׂיךָ

(and Your rule will be especially
evident) in the Temple, the place
of the manifestation of the Divine Presence,

בְּהַר צִיּוֹן מִשְׁכַּן כְּבוֹדֶךָ

and in Jerusalem which is designated
as Your holy city

וּבִירוּשָׁלַיִם עִיר קָדְשֶׁךָ

as it is written in Your holy words
(*Tehillim* 146:10):

כַּכָּתוּב בְּדִבְרֵי קָדְשֶׁךָ

"God will reign forever

יִמְלֹךְ יהוה לְעוֹלָם

(that is,) the Master of all strength
and the One able to do anything,
Who dwells particularly in Zion (the Temple)

אֱלֹהַיִךְ צִיּוֹן

(He will reign) for all generations

לְדֹר וָדֹר

(therefore, Israel) praise God."

הַלְלוּיָהּ.

You are holy (different and separate from everything)

קָדוֹשׁ אַתָּה

and Your Name (which is evident from
Your many acts) causes awe

וְנוֹרָא שְׁמֶךָ

and there is no other power except You

וְאֵין אֱלוֹהַּ מִבַּלְעָדֶיךָ

as it is written (*Yeshayahu* 5:16):

כַּכָּתוּב

"And the Master of all, Who is the ruler over
all the Heavenly and earthly legions, will be exalted

וַיִּגְבַּהּ יהוה צְבָאוֹת

when He does judgment on all

בַּמִּשְׁפָּט

and the Almighty, Who is holy (different
and separate from everything),

וְהָאֵל הַקָּדוֹשׁ

will become more holy in our eyes through
the kindness He does with us."

נִקְדַּשׁ בִּצְדָקָה

You are the Source of Blessing, Master of all

בָּרוּךְ אַתָּה יהוה

the King, Who is holier than all else.

הַמֶּלֶךְ הַקָּדוֹשׁ.

קְדֻשַׁת הַיּוֹם
The Holiness of the Day
Atoning of Our Sins

You chose us (the Nation
of Israel) from all nations
(when You took us out of Egypt)

אַתָּה בְחַרְתָּנוּ מִכָּל הָעַמִּים

You showed Your love for us
(by giving us the Torah)

אָהַבְתָּ אוֹתָנוּ

and You showed that You desired us (by giving us the special protection of the Clouds of Glory even though we had sinned with the Golden Calf)

וְרָצִיתָ בָּנוּ

and You elevated us from all languages (by giving us the holy language — Hebrew — which is spoken in Heaven)

וְרוֹמַמְתָּנוּ מִכָּל הַלְּשׁוֹנוֹת

and You made us holy by giving us the *mitzvos* which permeate us with holiness

וְקִדַּשְׁתָּנוּ בְּמִצְוֹתֶיךָ

and You have brought us close, our King, to Your service

וְקֵרַבְתָּנוּ מַלְכֵּנוּ לַעֲבוֹדָתֶךָ

and Your Name which is great (as we see from Your acts)

וְשִׁמְךָ הַגָּדוֹל

and holy (as we see from Your directing the world with a mastery beyond our comprehension)

וְהַקָּדוֹשׁ

You have called on us — for we are called the Nation of God.

עָלֵינוּ קָרֶאתָ.

And the Master of all, the Master of all strength, Who is able to do anything and Who takes care of us with Divine Providence, gave us

וַתִּתֶּן לָנוּ יהוה אֱלֹהֵינוּ

with love (because of His love for us)

בְּאַהֲבָה

ON SHABBOS ADD:

with love You gave us this Shabbos day [which is called a great gift]

אֶת יוֹם הַשַּׁבָּת הַזֶּה

(whose primary purpose is) for holiness and rest, and...

... וְלִמְנוּחָה וְ

this Day of Atonement

אֶת יוֹם הַכִּפּוּרִים הַזֶּה

(whose primary purpose is) to forgive the punishment of the sin

לִמְחִילָה

and to forgive the actual sin

וְלִסְלִיחָה

and to atone completely (to such an extent that it is as if we had never sinned)	וּלְכַפְּרָה
and in that way pardon all of our sins	וְלִמְחָל בּוֹ אֶת כָּל עֲוֹנוֹתֵינוּ

ON SHABBOS SAY:

with love (because of Your love for us)	בְּאַהֲבָה
a day on which we are called and gather to sanctify ourselves in prayer	מִקְרָא קֹדֶשׁ
(and) it is a day that is a remembrance of our going out of Egypt.	זֵכֶר לִיצִיאַת מִצְרָיִם.
The Master of all strength, Who is able to do anything and Who takes care of us with Divine Providence,	אֱלֹהֵינוּ
and the God Who took care of our Fathers with Divine Providence	וֵאלֹהֵי אֲבוֹתֵינוּ
may our remembrance and consideration go up	יַעֲלֶה
and come	וְיָבֹא
and reach	וְיַגִּיעַ
and be seen in a good way	וְיֵרָאֶה
and be accepted with desire	וְיֵרָצֶה
and be heard well	וְיִשָּׁמַע
and be considered	וְיִפָּקֵד
and be remembered forever	וְיִזָּכֵר
our remembrance (i.e., our special relationship with You)	זִכְרוֹנֵנוּ
And Your special consideration to do good for us	וּפִקְדוֹנֵנוּ

and the remembrance of the covenants You made with our Fathers	וְזִכְרוֹן אֲבוֹתֵינוּ
and the remembrance of the promise to bring *Mashiach,* a descendant of David Your servant,	וְזִכְרוֹן מָשִׁיחַ בֶּן דָּוִד עַבְדֶּךָ
and the remembrance of Jerusalem, the city of Your Holiness, which is now in ruins	וְזִכְרוֹן יְרוּשָׁלַיִם עִיר קָדְשֶׁךָ
and the remembrance of Your nation, the House of Israel, which is now in exile	וְזִכְרוֹן כָּל עַמְּךָ בֵּית יִשְׂרָאֵל
(may all of these remembrances) come before You	לְפָנֶיךָ
for salvation (for all of Israel)	לִפְלֵיטָה
for good (for all of Israel)	לְטוֹבָה
to find favor in Your eyes and in everyone's eyes	לְחֵן
and to grant us our requests (even though we are not deserving)	וּלְחֶסֶד
and for mercy (not punishing us according to our wrongdoings)	וּלְרַחֲמִים
and for life (for all of Israel)	לְחַיִּים
and for peace (for all of Israel)	וּלְשָׁלוֹם
on this Day of Atonement.	בְּיוֹם הַכִּפּוּרִים הַזֶּה
Remember us, Master of all	זָכְרֵנוּ יהוה
the Master of all strength, Who is able to do anything and Who takes care of us with Divine Providence,	אֱלֹהֵינוּ
on this day of Yom Kippur to give everyone whatever is good for him	בּוֹ לְטוֹבָה

and consider us on this day for prosperity and success	וּפָקְדֵנוּ בוֹ לִבְרָכָה
and save us on this day (of judgment) so that we will merit life.	וְהוֹשִׁיעֵנוּ בוֹ לְחַיִּים
And with Your previous promise to save us and to have mercy on us	וּבִדְבַר יְשׁוּעָה וְרַחֲמִים
have mercy on us because You are our Creator, and favor us (with salvation)	חוּס וְחָנֵּנוּ
and have mercy on us because of our lowly nature and save us, even though we are undeserving	וְרַחֵם עָלֵינוּ וְהוֹשִׁיעֵנוּ
because our eyes are looking to You in hope	כִּי אֵלֶיךָ עֵינֵינוּ
because You are the Almighty King over all	כִּי אֵל מֶלֶךְ
and You are gracious and merciful (even to the undeserving).	חַנּוּן וְרַחוּם אָתָּה.

The Master of all strength, Who is able to do anything and Who takes care of us with Divine Providence,	**אֱלֹהֵינוּ**
and the God who took care of our Fathers with Divine Providence	וֵאלֹהֵי אֲבוֹתֵינוּ
forgive our sins	מְחַל לַעֲוֹנוֹתֵינוּ

ON WEEKDAYS SAY:

on this Day of Atonement.	בְּיוֹם הַכִּפּוּרִים הַזֶּה.

ON SHABBOS SAY:

on this Shabbos and on this Day of Atonement.	בְּיוֹם הַשַּׁבָּת הַזֶּה וּבְיוֹם הַכִּפּוּרִים הַזֶּה

Blot out [our sins]	מְחֵה
and remove entirely (leaving no vestige of)	וְהַעֲבֵר

our sins that were committed with intent

פְּשָׁעֵינוּ

and our sins that were committed
without intention

וְחַטֹּאתֵינוּ

[wipe them out] from before Your eyes

מִנֶּגֶד עֵינֶיךָ

as it says (*Yeshayahu* 43:25):

כָּאָמוּר

"I forgave the generation of the
Exodus their sins and I forgive
in every generation your intentional sins

אָנֹכִי אָנֹכִי הוּא מֹחֶה פְשָׁעֶיךָ

for My sake (so that My Name should not be profaned
among the nations if I destroy you)

לְמַעֲנִי

and what you have done unwillfully,
I will not even remember
(there will be no vestige of it)."

וְחַטֹּאתֶיךָ לֹא אֶזְכֹּר.

And it is also written (*Yeshayahu* 44:22):

וְנֶאֱמַר:

"I have always blotted out what you have
done intentionally like a wind dissipates
a thick cloud (leaving some remnant)

מָחִיתִי כָעָב פְּשָׁעֶיךָ

and like a thin cloud gets scattered
(without leaving any trace)
so I have erased your unintentional sins

וְכֶעָנָן חַטֹּאתֶיךָ

therefore, return to Me
in repentance for I will redeem you."

שׁוּבָה אֵלַי כִּי גְאַלְתִּיךָ.

And it is also written (*Vayikra* 16:30):

וְנֶאֱמַר

"For on this day of Yom Kippur

כִּי בַיּוֹם הַזֶּה

God will forgive you (for your sins)
as if they never were

יְכַפֵּר עֲלֵיכֶם

in order to purify your souls
(from the tendency to repeat the sins)

לְטַהֵר אֶתְכֶם

(but) from all your sins

מִכֹּל חַטֹאתֵיכֶם

it is incumbent upon you to cleanse
yourselves (with repentance)
before the Master of all."

לִפְנֵי יהוה תִּטְהָרוּ.

ON SHABBOS ADD:

The Master of all strength, Who is able to do anything
and Who takes care of us with Divine Providence,

אֱלֹהֵינוּ

and the God who took care of our Fathers
with Divine Providence

וֵאלֹהֵי אֲבוֹתֵינוּ

let our rest be pleasant before You

רְצֵה בִמְנוּחָתֵנוּ

---

make us holy from Above so that
we should do Your *mitzvos* properly

קַדְּשֵׁנוּ בְּמִצְוֹתֶיךָ

and give us Divine assistance that all of our
occupation should be in Torah study

וְתֵן חֶלְקֵנוּ בְּתוֹרָתֶךָ

grant us good in a way that we will be
satisfied with what we have
(and not run after our desires)

שַׂבְּעֵנוּ מִטּוּבֶךָ

and cause us to rejoice through
the salvation that You will bring us

וְשַׂמְּחֵנוּ בִּישׁוּעָתֶךָ

ON SHABBOS ADD:

and give us as an inheritance (the holiness that Shabbos inspires)

וְהַנְחִילֵנוּ

Master of all, the Master of all strength, Who is able to do
anything and Who takes care of us with Divine Providence,

יהוה אֱלֹהֵינוּ

because of the love that You loved us (when You gave us Shabbos)

בְּאַהֲבָה

and because of the desire You have for us
(that You want us to bring sacrifices even on Shabbos)

וּבְרָצוֹן

[give us as an inheritance] the inspiration
of Shabbos, the day that You made holy,

שַׁבַּת קָדְשֶׁךָ

and (through this inspiration) You should
cause Israel to have a complete rest on Shabbos

וְיָנוּחוּ בוֹ/בָם יִשְׂרָאֵל

for they sanctify Your Name (by keeping Shabbos).

מְקַדְּשֵׁי שְׁמֶךָ

And (we ask that You) purify our hearts that we should serve You sincerely (without other motives)	וְטַהֵר לִבֵּנוּ לְעָבְדְּךָ בֶּאֱמֶת
[do all this] because You are the Forgiver of Israel constantly	כִּי אַתָּה סָלְחָן לְיִשְׂרָאֵל
and You are the Pardoner of Israel — who go in the straight path —	וּמָחֳלָן לְשִׁבְטֵי יְשֻׁרוּן
in every generation	בְּכָל דּוֹר וָדוֹר
and except for You	וּמִבַּלְעָדֶיךָ
we have no other king who will completely pardon and forgive us	אֵין לָנוּ מֶלֶךְ מוֹחֵל וְסוֹלֵחַ
(— only You).	(אֶלָּא אָתָּה)
You are the Source of Blessing, Master of all,	בָּרוּךְ אַתָּה יהוה
Who completely pardons and forgives the sins of the individual	מֶלֶךְ מוֹחֵל וְסוֹלֵחַ לַעֲוֹנוֹתֵינוּ
and (through that completely forgives the sins) of the entirety of the house of His nation, Israel	וְלַעֲוֹנוֹת עַמּוֹ בֵּית יִשְׂרָאֵל
and (You) remove our iniquities	וּמַעֲבִיר אַשְׁמוֹתֵינוּ
each and every year,[6]	בְּכָל שָׁנָה וְשָׁנָה
the King over all the inhabitants of the earth	מֶלֶךְ עַל כָּל הָאָרֶץ

---

6. One should feel a tremendous gratitude towards the Almighty for the gift of Yom Kippur, the day on which He forgives our sins, if we repent. Were the sins of the world to keep piling up year after year, the measure would soon be full and the world would be condemned to destruction. But after the sin of the Golden Calf was forgiven, this day was established for forgiveness, and aids in the repentance process; and that is what is meant by "Yom Kippur atones" (*Yoma* 86a) [based on *Sefer HaChinuch*, *Mitzvah* 185].

ON WEEKDAYS SAY:

Who chose Israel and made them
holier (than the other nations)

מְקַדֵּשׁ יִשְׂרָאֵל

ON SHABBOS SAY:

Who made the Shabbos holier
(than the other days — and gave it
to us as a present) and made Israel holier (than the other nations)

מְקַדֵּשׁ הַשַּׁבָּת וְיִשְׂרָאֵל

(and through Israel) He makes holy
the Day of Atonement (to forgive our sins on it).

וְיוֹם הַכִּפּוּרִים.

עבודה
Return of the Temple Service

Be pleased[7]

רְצֵה

Master of all,

יהוה

the Master of all strength, Who is able to do anything
and Who takes care of us with Divine Providence,

אֱלֹהֵינוּ

with Your nation, Israel (because they are
praying for the rebuilding of the Temple)

בְּעַמְּךָ יִשְׂרָאֵל

and with their prayer (for the rebuilding of the Temple)

וּבִתְפִלָּתָם

and return the service of the Temple

וְהָשֵׁב אֶת הָעֲבוֹדָה

(even) to the Holy of Holies.

לִדְבִיר בֵּיתֶךָ

And the fire-offerings that they will bring

וְאִשֵּׁי יִשְׂרָאֵל

and the prayer of Israel
(which is now in place of the offerings)

וּתְפִלָּתָם

because of Your love for the Jews

בְּאַהֲבָה

---

7. Before reciting this blessing one should instill in his heart the love of all Jews,
regardless of their origin or affiliation, for we ask here that God be pleased with all of His
nation Israel (*Darchei Chaim*). [The saintly Chofetz Chaim wrote (*Ahavas Yisrael,* Ch.
2) that we constantly pray for the rebuilding of the Temple, but we neglect to contemplate the cause of its destruction, which was hatred for an unjustifiable reason. Therefore if we want the Temple to be rebuilt we must first rectify this sin and love all Jews.]

accept with desire	תְּקַבֵּל בְּרָצוֹן
and help us that it should always be desirable	וּתְהִי לְרָצוֹן תָּמִיד
the service (whether offerings or prayers) of Israel, Your nation.	עֲבוֹדַת יִשְׂרָאֵל עַמֶּךָ
And let us merit to see (the *Shechinah* – Divine Presence) with our own eyes (i.e., soon, in our days)	וְתֶחֱזֶינָה עֵינֵינוּ
when You return Your Presence to the Temple (even if it is) in mercy (and not through our merits).	בְּשׁוּבְךָ לְצִיּוֹן בְּרַחֲמִים
You are the Source of Blessing, Master of all,	בָּרוּךְ אַתָּה יהוה
Who will return His Divine Presence to the Temple.	הַמַּחֲזִיר שְׁכִינָתוֹ לְצִיּוֹן.

הודאה
Thanking God[8]

We give thanks to You, acknowledging	**מוֹדִים** אֲנַחְנוּ לָךְ
that You are the Master of all	שָׁאַתָּה הוּא יהוה
the Master of all strength, Who is able to do anything and Who takes care of us with Divine Providence,	אֱלֹהֵינוּ
and the God Who took care of our Fathers with Divine Providence	וֵאלֹהֵי אֲבוֹתֵינוּ
(and that You will continue to take care of us) forever.	לְעוֹלָם וָעֶד
[You are] the Rock – Creator and Sustainer – of our lives	צוּר חַיֵּינוּ
[and You are] the Protector Who saves us from all troubles	מָגֵן יִשְׁעֵנוּ

---

8. The *Beis Elokim* explains that the reason we bow at the beginning and end of this *brachah* is to show humility, recognizing our unworthiness for Hashem's special care, and realizing that our lives and all goodness come from Him.

You are the One [Who keeps us alive and saves us] in every generation.	אַתָּה הוּא לְדוֹר וָדוֹר
We will always express our thanks to You	נוֹדֶה לְּךָ
and we will tell Your praise to others	וּנְסַפֵּר תְּהִלָּתֶךָ
for our lives – each breath – that are given over into Your hand	עַל חַיֵּינוּ הַמְּסוּרִים בְּיָדֶךָ
and for our souls that are entrusted to You (while we sleep)	וְעַל נִשְׁמוֹתֵינוּ הַפְּקוּדוֹת לָךְ
and for the hidden miracles that You do for us every day	וְעַל נִסֶּיךָ שֶׁבְּכָל יוֹם עִמָּנוּ
and for Your wonders of "nature" (which You renew constantly)	וְעַל נִפְלְאוֹתֶיךָ
and for Your favors (that You do for us constantly)	וְטוֹבוֹתֶיךָ
that You do in all parts of the day	שֶׁבְּכָל עֵת
in the evening, morning, and afternoon.	עֶרֶב וָבְקֶר וְצָהֳרָיִם
You are the ultimate Good One	הַטּוֹב
for Your mercy has never finished – for You withhold punishment from those deserving it	כִּי לֹא כָלוּ רַחֲמֶיךָ
and You are the ultimate Merciful One (Who not only withholds punishment, but ...)	וְהַמְרַחֵם
Whose kindness never ends – for You even give these undeserving people additional kindnesses –	כִּי לֹא תַמּוּ חֲסָדֶיךָ
we have always put our hope in You.	מֵעוֹלָם קִוִּינוּ לָךְ
And for all of these wonders and favors that You do for us constantly	וְעַל כֻּלָּם

[Your Name] should be praised with the recognition that You are the Source of all Blessing	יִתְבָּרֵךְ
and may Your Name (which represents Your acts) be exalted through the recognition of Your greatness	וְיִתְרוֹמַם שִׁמְךָ
since You are our King (Who takes care of us especially) [and we desire that Your Name be praised and exalted]	מַלְכֵּנוּ
constantly, every day,	תָּמִיד
forever and ever.	לְעוֹלָם וָעֶד
And seal for a good life (i.e., life that will be good for earning the World to Come)	**וַחֲתוֹם לְחַיִּים טוֹבִים**
all the children of Your covenant.	**כָּל בְּנֵי בְרִיתֶךָ**
And all the living (those who will come back to life by the Revival of the Dead)	וְכֹל הַחַיִּים
will thank You constantly forever	יוֹדוּךָ סֶּלָה
and they will praise Your Name (which comes from Your deeds) truthfully, without any other motive	וִיהַלְלוּ אֶת שִׁמְךָ בֶּאֱמֶת
the Almighty	הָאֵל
Who saves us in all our troubles	יְשׁוּעָתֵנוּ
and Who helps us to succeed	וְעֶזְרָתֵנוּ
constantly, forever.	סֶלָה
You are the Source of Blessing, Master of all,	בָּרוּךְ אַתָּה יהוה
Whose Name is "The Good One" (for You are the ultimate good)	הַטּוֹב שִׁמְךָ
and to You alone it is fitting to give thanks (because You are the cause of all goodness).	וּלְךָ נָאֶה לְהוֹדוֹת.

שלום
Peace

Grant peace (which includes peace of mind, peace in one's house, peace between Jews, and peace in the country)	**שִׂים** שָׁלוֹם
(and grant what is) good for each person	טוֹבָה
and (grant) prosperity and success	וּבְרָכָה
(and) let us find favor in Your eyes and thereby find favor in the eyes of all who see us	חֵן
and grant our requests (even though we are not deserving)	וָחֶסֶד
and have mercy on us (not to punish us according to our wrongdoings)	וְרַחֲמִים
on those of us here (praying together)	עָלֵינוּ
and on all of Israel, Your nation.	וְעַל כָּל יִשְׂרָאֵל עַמֶּךָ
Since You are our Father, give us an abundance of goodness and success	בָּרְכֵנוּ אָבִינוּ
all of us like one (equally)	כֻּלָּנוּ כְּאֶחָד
with the "light of Your face" (which is a symbol of Your great love)	בְּאוֹר פָּנֶיךָ
because we already know from the Revelation at Sinai that with the "light of Your face" come great things:	כִּי בְאוֹר פָּנֶיךָ
You gave to us as a present (not because we were deserving),	נָתַתָּ לָנוּ
Master of all,	יהוה
the Master of all strength, Who is able to do anything and Who takes care of us with Divine Providence,	אֱלֹהֵינוּ

the Torah that teaches us how to live	תּוֹרַת חַיִּים
and (through it) the love of doing kindness	וְאַהֲבַת חֶסֶד
and (You gave us with the Torah more opportunities for) reward in the World to Come (by fulfilling the many *mitzvos*)	וּצְדָקָה
and (as reward for keeping the Torah You give us also) an abundance of goodness and success (in this world)	וּבְרָכָה
and (in the merit of keeping the Torah You give us) special mercy	וְרַחֲמִים
and (as a reward for keeping the Torah You give us) a long, healthy life	וְחַיִּים
and (through the Torah we have) peace of body and mind (because all the ways of the Torah are peaceful).	וְשָׁלוֹם
And it should be good in Your eyes	וְטוֹב בְּעֵינֶיךָ
to give an abundance of goodness and success to Your nation, Israel	לְבָרֵךְ אֶת עַמְּךָ יִשְׂרָאֵל
in all parts of the day	בְּכָל עֵת
and in all hours of each part of the day	וּבְכָל שָׁעָה
with Your peace (which is a complete peace).	בִּשְׁלוֹמֶךָ
In the book of life	**בְּסֵפֶר חַיִּים**
of abundant goodness and success	**בְּרָכָה**
and peace between a man and his friend	**וְשָׁלוֹם**
and a good (ample and easy) livelihood	**וּפַרְנָסָה טוֹבָה**
may we be remembered	**נִזָּכֵר**
and may we be sealed before You	**וְנֵחָתֵם לְפָנֶיךָ**
we (who are standing together praying)	**אֲנַחְנוּ**

and all of Your nation, Israel

וְכָל עַמְּךָ בֵּית יִשְׂרָאֵל

(let us be remembered and sealed)
for a truly good life (i.e., a life that will
enable us to earn the World to Come)

לְחַיִּים טוֹבִים

and for peace within ourselves
(that we should be satisfied with
the materialistic things that we have).

וּלְשָׁלוֹם.

THERE ARE DIFFERENT CUSTOMS CONCERNING THE CONCLUSION OF THIS BLESSING;
AND EVERYONE SHOULD FOLLOW HIS CUSTOM. IF ONE DOES NOT KNOW HIS CUSTOM
HE SHOULD RECITE THE VERSION ON THE RIGHT.

You are the Source of Blessing, בָּרוּךְ אַתָּה	You are the Source of בָּרוּךְ אַתָּה יהוה Blessing, Master of all,
Master of all, יהוה	Who gives an abundance of הַמְבָרֵךְ goodness and success
Who makes עוֹשֶׂה הַשָּׁלוֹם. peace among all.	to His nation, Israel, אֶת עַמּוֹ יִשְׂרָאֵל with peace. בַּשָּׁלוֹם.

וִידוּי
Confession[9]

The Master of all strength, Who is able to do anything
and Who takes care of us with Divine Providence,

אֱלֹהֵינוּ

and the God who took care
of our Fathers with Divine Providence

וֵאלֹהֵי אֲבוֹתֵינוּ

---

9. *Siddur Rokeach* says that *Viduy* (Confession) must be said with concentration, with a broken heart and with great sorrow; the penitent must admit what he has done and resolve to leave his bad ways. If one says it in this way, then perhaps he can hope that the Merciful One Whose Hand is open will have mercy on him.

Yesod VeShoresh HaAvodah writes that before saying the *Viduy* one should have in mind that he is fulfilling a positive biblical commandment, as it says (*Bamidbar* 5:7): "and they should confess the sins that they have done." And he writes further that **the main part of the Viduy is** the absolute and complete regret for having committed the sin and the acceptance to make fences to prevent oneself from succumbing to the sin again, for anyone who has sense will admit that confession that is not accompanied by repentance shows great *chutzpah* and brazenness.

According to *Seder HaYom* it is of paramount importance that the *Viduy* be said from the heart, not merely lip-service, for insincere *Viduy* increases one's sins, since he seems to think he is fooling the One Who knows all.

R' Chaim David Azulai [known as the *Chida*] writes that the essence of the *Viduy* is for the person to realize that he has absolutely sinned, and not seek excuses.

let our prayers come before Your Throne of Glory	תָּבֹא לְפָנֶיךָ תְּפִלָּתֵנוּ
and do not ignore that which we say with humility before You	וְאַל תִּתְעַלַּם מִתְּחִנָּתֵנוּ
for we are not so brazen and stubborn [to claim that we are righteous]	שֶׁאֵין אֲנַחְנוּ עַזֵּי פָנִים וּקְשֵׁי עֹרֶף
to say before You,	לוֹמַר לְפָנֶיךָ
Master of all, the Master of all strength, Who is able to do anything and Who takes care of us with Divine Providence,	יהוה אֱלֹהֵינוּ
and the God who took care of our Fathers with Divine Providence,	וֵאלֹהֵי אֲבוֹתֵינוּ
that we are righteous and have not sinned [we are not so brazen to say that]	צַדִּיקִים אֲנַחְנוּ וְלֹא חָטָאנוּ
but really we [and our forefathers] have sinned.	אֲבָל אֲנַחְנוּ [וַאֲבוֹתֵינוּ] חָטָאנוּ.
We have sinned so much that we deserve to be destroyed.	אָשַׁמְנוּ
We have been ungrateful for the good God has done for us (and have even responded to His goodness with evil).	בָּגַדְנוּ
We have stolen (this includes borrowing without permission, fooling someone ["stealing his mind"] and disturbing someone's sleep).	גָּזַלְנוּ
We have spoken disgracefully about others (this includes slander).	דִּבַּרְנוּ דֹפִי
We have caused perversion (this includes causing others to sin or preventing others from doing *mitzvos*).	הֶעֱוִינוּ

And we have judged the righteous as if they were evil (and not favorably).	וְהִרְשַׁעְנוּ
We have sinned intentionally.	זַדְנוּ
We have taken things away from others against their will (even if we have paid them more than it was worth).	חָמַסְנוּ
We have added one lie onto another in order to reinforce it.	טָפַלְנוּ שֶׁקֶר
We have given advice that was bad for the one who sought our advice.	יָעַצְנוּ רָע
We have not kept our promises (including those that we have made to God to better our ways).	כִּזַּבְנוּ
We have scoffed at people, at words of Torah, and at important things and actions (included in this is wasting time with idle chatter).	לַצְנוּ
We have known God and yet rebelled against Him (the worst of all sins).	מָרַדְנוּ
We have angered God with our sins.	נִאַצְנוּ
We have turned our hearts away from the service of God.	סָרַרְנוּ
We have sinned only to fulfill our desires.	עָוִינוּ
We have sinned because we denied God's existence.	פָּשַׁעְנוּ
We have caused others pain.	צָרַרְנוּ
We have been stubborn and have not accepted rebuke; we have not viewed personal hardships as a message to improve our ways.	קִשִּׁינוּ עֹרֶף
We have done actions that make us considered wicked (like raising our hand to hit someone).	רָשַׁעְנוּ

We have corrupted ourselves with sins that are tantamount to immorality and idolatry.	שִׁחַתְנוּ
We have done acts that are abominable in the eyes of God (like actual immorality and idolatry).	תִּעַבְנוּ
We have strayed from the straight path of service to God.	תָּעִינוּ
We have done deceitful acts.	תִּעְתָּעְנוּ.

We have turned away from fulfilling Your positive commandments	סַרְנוּ מִמִּצְוֹתֶיךָ
and from not fulfilling the good and pleasant positive commandments that You obligate us towards others	וּמִמִּשְׁפָּטֶיךָ הַטּוֹבִים
and we have not gained by refraining from doing Your *mitzvos* (for we have lost much more than we have gained)	וְלֹא שָׁוָה לָנוּ
and You are righteous (justified) in all the punishments that You have brought on us[10]	וְאַתָּה צַדִּיק עַל כָּל הַבָּא עָלֵינוּ
because You have judged us truthfully	כִּי אֱמֶת עָשִׂיתָ
but we have been increasingly wicked.	וַאֲנַחְנוּ הִרְשָׁעְנוּ.

What can we say before Your Throne of Glory to justify ourselves	מַה נֹּאמַר לְפָנֶיךָ
(to You) Who sits high in the Heavens (and Whose eyes gaze over the entire world)	יוֹשֵׁב מָרוֹם
and what can we confess of our sins before You	וּמַה נְּסַפֵּר לְפָנֶיךָ

---

10. *Siddur Maggid Tzedek* says that one should say this phrase very humbly and with sincerity, fully accepting God's judgment.

Who sits in the heavens (and knows all)

שׁוֹכֵן שְׁחָקִים

for all things, both those that
are hidden from people
and those that are revealed,

הֲלֹא כָל הַנִּסְתָּרוֹת וְהַנִּגְלוֹת

You already know.

אַתָּה יוֹדֵעַ.

מה אנו מה חיינו
What Are We and What Is Our Life[11]

You give sinners the free choice
to do evil (if one wants to sin, he is able to,
but is not helped to sin)

אַתָּה נוֹתֵן יָד לַפּוֹשְׁעִים

yet Your right hand is extended
to help those who repent (for one
who wants to be pure, God helps).

וִימִינְךָ פְּשׁוּטָה לְקַבֵּל שָׁבִים

And You, Master of all, the Master of all
strength, Who is able to do anything and Who
takes care of us with Divine Providence, taught us

וַתְּלַמְּדֵנוּ יהוה אֱלֹהֵינוּ

to confess before You
all of our sins (for one who admits
his sin to God receives mercy)

לְהִתְוַדּוֹת לְפָנֶיךָ עַל כָּל עֲוֹנוֹתֵינוּ

so that we should refrain from the
iniquities of our hands (which we recognize
by confessing)

לְמַעַן נֶחְדַּל מֵעֹשֶׁק יָדֵינוּ

and then You will accept us
by virtue of our complete repentance

וּתְקַבְּלֵנוּ בִּתְשׁוּבָה שְׁלֵמָה לְפָנֶיךָ

---

11. *Seder HaYom* explains that we say this prayer to increase God's mercy and to appease
the attribute of strict justice, although a sinner does not deserve the opportunity to
repent, since he has angered the King of kings. Nevertheless, because of God's infinite
mercy, and in recognition of the sinner's lowliness and the insignificance of his actions
(the idea of the words מָה אָנוּ מָה חַיֵּינוּ, "What are we and what is our life?"), God prepared
a way for us to repent so that we will deserve life. We thus beseech the Almighty to accept
our repentance with pity, and to seal us in the Book of Good Life.

as if we had brought sacrifices like those
that were burned on the Altar and those
brought for appeasement before You[12]

כְּאִשִּׁים וּכְנִיחוֹחִים

because of the words that You said
(*Hoshea* 14:3) [promising that repentance
will be accepted like sacrifices]

לְמַעַן דְּבָרֶיךָ אֲשֶׁר אָמָרְתָּ

(for) if we were to bring sacrifices
to atone for our sins, the amount of our
obligation would be endless

אֵין קֵץ לְאִשֵּׁי חוֹבוֹתֵינוּ

and there is no number to the
multitude of sacrifices we would have
to bring to appease for all our guilt.

וְאֵין מִסְפָּר לְנִיחוֹחֵי אַשְׁמָתֵנוּ

And You know

וְאַתָּה יוֹדֵעַ

that our ultimate end is
to be consumed by worms

שֶׁאַחֲרִיתֵנוּ רִמָּה וְתוֹלֵעָה

therefore (recognizing our lowliness,)
You have given us many ways to achieve
forgiveness (including confession).

לְפִיכָךְ הִרְבֵּיתָ סְלִיחָתֵנוּ

What is our significance (that we stand before You)?

מָה אָנוּ

What is the significance of our life
(which is as fleeting as a passing shadow)?

מֶה חַיֵּינוּ

What is the significance of our acts of kindness
(in comparison to Yours)?

מֶה חַסְדֵּנוּ

What is the significance of our acts of charity
(since all the money we have is really God's)?

מַה צִּדְקֵנוּ

12. R' Shamshon Raphael Hirsch writes that sacrifices burned on the fire of the Altar
represent one's total devotion, the utilization of all of one's energies for the ''fire'' of
God's law [an expression from *Devarim* 33:2], so that one may be cleansed, enlightened
and revived thereby. And the sacrifices brought for appeasement represent our dedica-
tion to live our lives solely for the fulfillment of His will. Therefore, we ask God to accept
our resolve to repent on this day, as expressed with our confessions, as sacrifices that
were burned upon the Altar and brought for appeasement.

[What can a person do to save himself; all the more, to save others?] [מַה יִּשְׁעֵנוּ]

What is the significance of our strength (since in the Hand of God is the real strength)? מַה כֹּחֵנוּ

What is the significance of our might to fight with others (since in the Hand of God is the real might)? מַה גְּבוּרָתֵנוּ.

(Since our deeds are insignificant) what can we say before You? מַה נֹּאמַר לְפָנֶיךָ

Master of all, the Master of all strength, Who is able to do anything and Who takes care of us with Divine Providence, יהוה אֱלֹהֵינוּ

and the God who took care of our Fathers with Divine Providence וֵאלֹהֵי אֲבוֹתֵינוּ

are not all the mighty ones like nothing before You (their strength is worthless for they could suddenly die) הֲלֹא כָל הַגִּבּוֹרִים כְּאַיִן לְפָנֶיךָ

and are not the famous people as if they never existed (before You) וְאַנְשֵׁי הַשֵּׁם כְּלֹא הָיוּ

and are not the wise people as if devoid of knowledge (in Your eyes) וַחֲכָמִים כִּבְלִי מַדָּע

and are not the understanding people as if they were without intelligence (compared to You)? וּנְבוֹנִים כִּבְלִי הַשְׂכֵּל

For most of the actions of man (except Torah and *mitzvos*) are worthless [before You] כִּי רֹב מַעֲשֵׂיהֶם תֹּהוּ

and the days of their lives are meaningless before You (to Whom a thousand years are like one day) וִימֵי חַיֵּיהֶם הֶבֶל לְפָנֶיךָ

and the superiority of a man over an animal is insignificant וּמוֹתַר הָאָדָם מִן הַבְּהֵמָה אָיִן

when he wastes his life with the vanities of this world (and not with Torah and *mitzvos*).[13]	כִּי הַכֹּל הָבֶל.
(Even though man's superiority is insignificant) You separated people from animals at the time of Creation	**אַתָּה** הִבְדַּלְתָּ אֱנוֹשׁ מֵרֹאשׁ
and you endowed him with special intelligence in order that he should stand before You in service	וַתַּכִּירֵהוּ לַעֲמוֹד לְפָנֶיךָ
for (even though man is a lowly creature) who can tell You what to do (although the angels tried to dissuade You)	כִּי מִי יֹאמַר לְךָ מַה תִּפְעָל
and even if man is righteous, what does he give You (for everything is Yours and You do not need him).	וְאִם יִצְדַּק מַה יִּתֶּן לָךְ
And the Master of all, the Master of all strength, Who is able to do anything and Who takes care of us with Divine Providence, gave us	וַתִּתֶּן לָנוּ יהוה אֱלֹהֵינוּ
with love (because of His love for us)	בְּאַהֲבָה
this Day of Atonement	אֶת יוֹם הַכִּפֻּרִים הַזֶּה
as a last time to change the decree of Rosh Hashanah	קֵץ
and (a day to) waive the punishment of sins	וּמְחִילָה
and to forgive the actual sins	וּסְלִיחָה

---

13. This is a verse in *Koheles* (3:19). The *Midrash* (*Eliyahu Zuta* 24) comments on this verse that after an animal dies it is at rest, but a person after death must stand in judgment, where he is shown all of his deeds and is judged for them (*Rokeach*).

The Heavenly judgment is twofold: "Know ... before Whom you will give *justification* and *reckoning*" (*Avos* 3:1). דִּין, *justification,* is defense for the sin itself, and חֶשְׁבּוֹן, *reckoning,* is a calculation of the *mitzvos* one could have done in the time that he had sinned (*Vilna Gaon,* quoted by *Chofetz Chaim* [in his Introduction, Positive Command 12]. See *Meshech Chochmah* [*Devarim* 30:20] who also quotes this explanation and applies it to Yom Kippur itself, stressing the urgent need to utilize this day to the fullest and not squander its unique potential for atonement).

of all of our sins

עַל כָּל עֲוֹנוֹתֵינוּ

in order that we should refrain
from sinning – particularly from stealing[14] —

לְמַעַן נֶחְדַּל מֵעשֶׁק יָדֵינוּ

and so that we should
return completely and
keep the laws that You desire

וְנָשׁוּב אֵלֶיךָ לַעֲשׂוֹת עַל חֻקֵּי רְצוֹנְךָ

with all our heart.

בְּלֵבָב שָׁלֵם

And You should thereby
have mercy on us,
with Your abundant mercy,

וְאַתָּה בְּרַחֲמֶיךָ הָרַבִּים רַחֵם עָלֵינוּ

for You do not want
the destruction of the world
(but rather that everyone do teshuvah)

כִּי לֹא תַחְפּוֹץ בְּהַשְׁחָתַת עוֹלָם

as it says (Yeshayahu 55:6):

שֶׁנֶּאֱמַר

"Seek out God when He is available
(to individuals and congregations i.e.,
during the Ten Days of Repentance)

דִּרְשׁוּ יהוה בְּהִמָּצְאוֹ

call out to Him in prayer when
He is close."

קְרָאֻהוּ בִּהְיוֹתוֹ קָרוֹב.

And it also says (ibid. v. 7):

וְנֶאֱמַר

"A wicked person should leave his evil way
(both his actions and his words)
and not sin anymore

יַעֲזֹב רָשָׁע דַּרְכּוֹ

---

14. Yesod VeShoresh HaAvodah writes that if a person knows that he possesses an item that was acquired through some form of thievery, he should resolve now to do complete teshuvah; he should make a serious commitment to correct this sin and return that which he has stolen immediately after Yom Kippur. One can discern the severity of stealing from the fact that the Men of the Great Assembly, who composed this prayer, explicitly mentioned here this sin, as opposed to all others. Also, the fate of the generation of the Mabul (Flood) was sealed only because of the sin of stealing. [Also, the Yesod VeShoresh HaAvodah writes (10:2) that there is no sin that prevents a person's prayers from going up to the highest Heaven as much as the sin of stealing!]

| and the sinful man should abandon his bad thoughts[15] | וְאִישׁ אָוֶן מַחְשְׁבֹתָיו |

and he should repent (out of love) to the Master of All, and He will have mercy on him

וְיָשֹׁב אֶל יהוה וִירַחֲמֵהוּ

and (at least repent in fear) to the Master of all strength, Who is able to do anything and Who takes care of us with Divine Providence,

וְאֶל אֱלֹהֵינוּ

for He abundantly forgives even one who has sinned a lot."

כִּי יַרְבֶּה לִסְלֹוחַ.

And You, the God Who abundantly forgives,

וְאַתָּה אֱלֹוהַּ סְלִיחוֹת

Who is gracious (giving to those who beseech Him even if they are undeserving)

חַנּוּן

and merciful (Who has mercy on sinners to be lenient in their punishment when they call out to Him)

וְרַחוּם

slow to anger (not punishing sinners quickly, in order to give them time to repent)

אֶרֶךְ אַפַּיִם

and abundantly kind (leaning towards kindness even to those who do not have sufficient merits to protect themselves)

וְרַב חֶסֶד

[and truthful to pay reward to those who do His will]

[וֶאֱמֶת]

and increasingly does good to people (for God gives great reward in the World to Come)

וּמַרְבֶּה לְהֵיטִיב

---

15. A person should not say that he need only repent for transgressions committed by physical actions, such as immorality or robbery. Just as a person must repent for such sins, so too must he repent for his improper attitudes and characteristics, such as: anger, hatred, jealousy, mockery, pursuit of money or honor, the pursuit of good food, and other improper attitudes. And **these sins are worse** than those transgressed by actions, for when one is steeped in such an outlook it is very hard to extricate oneself from it. Thus we quote the verse, "A wicked person should leave his evil way, and the sinful man should abandon his bad thoughts" (*Rambam, Hilchos Teshuvah* 7:3). (See *Rokeach* who interprets this as referring specifically to heretical thoughts.)

and You want the repentance of the wicked	וְרוֹצֶה אַתָּה בִּתְשׁוּבַת רְשָׁעִים
and you do not desire that they should die because of their sins	וְאֵין אַתָּה חָפֵץ בְּמִיתָתָם
as it says (*Yechezkel* 33:11):	שֶׁנֶּאֱמַר
"Say to the children of Israel:	אֱמֹר אֲלֵיהֶם
I swear, says the Master of all, the Master of all strength Who is able to do anything,	חַי אָנִי נְאֻם אֲדֹנָי יֱהֹוִה [אֱלֹהִים – read]
I do not desire the death of the wicked	אִם אֶחְפֹּץ בְּמוֹת הָרָשָׁע
but that he should repent from his evil way, and live (for repentance saves from death);	כִּי אִם בְּשׁוּב רָשָׁע מִדַּרְכּוֹ וְחָיָה
repent from your sins, and repent from your evil ways (so that you should not sin in the future)	שׁוּבוּ שׁוּבוּ מִדַּרְכֵיכֶם הָרָעִים
why should you cause yourselves death by refusing to repent?"	וְלָמָּה תָמוּתוּ בֵּית יִשְׂרָאֵל.
And it also says (*Yechezkel* 18:23):	וְנֶאֱמַר
"Do I want the death of the wicked because of their sins,	הֶחָפֹץ אֶחְפֹּץ מוֹת רָשָׁע
says the Master of all, the Master of all strength Who is able to do anything,	נְאֻם אֲדֹנָי יֱהֹוִה [אֱלֹהִים – read]
is it not that the sinner repents from his evil ways (that I want), so that he should live?"	הֲלֹא בְּשׁוּבוֹ מִדְּרָכָיו וְחָיָה.
And it also says (ibid. v. 32):	וְנֶאֱמַר
"For I do not desire the death of the one who deserves death,	כִּי לֹא אֶחְפֹּץ בְּמוֹת הַמֵּת

says the Master of all, the Master of all strength Who is able to do anything,	נְאֻם אֲדֹנָי יֱהֹוִה [read – אֱלֹהִים]
therefore, repent from your sins, and you will live.''[16]	וְהָשִׁיבוּ וִחְיוּ.
[So, please forgive us] because You are the Forgiver of Israel constantly	כִּי אַתָּה סָלְחָן לְיִשְׂרָאֵל
and You are the Pardoner of Israel – who go in the straight path –	וּמְחֳלָן לְשִׁבְטֵי יְשֻׁרוּן
in every generation	בְּכָל דּוֹר וָדוֹר
and except for You,	וּמִבַּלְעָדֶיךָ
we have no other king who will completely pardon and forgive us	אֵין לָנוּ מֶלֶךְ מוֹחֵל וְסוֹלֵחַ
(– only You).	אֶלָּא אָתָּה.
The Master of all strength, Who is able to do anything and Who takes care of me with Divine Providence,	אֱלֹהַי
before I was formed I was not worthy to be created	עַד שֶׁלֹּא נוֹצַרְתִּי אֵינִי כְדַאי
and now that I have been formed	וְעַכְשָׁו שֶׁנּוֹצַרְתִּי
it is as if I was never formed (for the world has not gained by my existence).	כְּאִלּוּ לֹא נוֹצַרְתִּי

---

16. Regarding the verse, ''The words of His palate are sweet'' (*Shir HaShirim* 5:16), the *Midrash* (*Shir HaShirim Rabbah* 6) lists several verses from Scripture which illustrate this concept, including those cited here (*Yechezkel* 33:11 and 18:32) and comments, ''Is there a sweeter palate than this?''

Reishis Chochmah (*Teshuvah,* Ch. 1) writes: ''The penitent should be inspired to repent out of love, for since God in His love provided him with the ways of repentance, it is fitting that the person should love Him and do His desire.'' In other words, when one contemplates God's magnanimity in enabling us to do *teshuvah* and to totally wipe out our sins, no matter how many or great they are, we recognize the great love that God has for us, and His great desire to forgive us and let us continue living. This thought alone should inspire us to repent, mend our ways, and to serve Him with love for the rest of our lives.

I am like dust while I am still alive
(for I do not have sufficient good deeds)

עָפָר אֲנִי בְּחַיָּי

and I will surely be so in my death
(when I will no longer be able
to perform *mitzvos*).

קַל וָחְמֶר בְּמִיתָתִי.

(Therefore) I stand before You

הֲרֵי אֲנִי לְפָנֶיךָ

like a vessel full of embarrassment and shame.

כִּכְלִי מָלֵא בוּשָׁה וּכְלִמָּה

May it be a time of favor before
Your Throne of Glory

יְהִי רָצוֹן מִלְּפָנֶיךָ

Master of all, the Master of all strength,
Who is able to do anything and Who takes care
of me with Divine Providence,

יהוה אֱלֹהַי

and the God who took care
of my Fathers with Divine Providence

וֵאלֹהֵי אֲבוֹתַי

that You help me so that I should not
sin anymore (by removing the causes of sin
and daily preoccupations)

שֶׁלֹּא אֶחֱטָא עוֹד

and that which I have already
sinned before You

וּמַה שֶׁחָטָאתִי לְפָנֶיךָ

cleanse with Your great mercy

מָרֵק בְּרַחֲמֶיךָ הָרַבִּים

but not through
terrible suffering
or difficult illnesses (rather through minor pains).

אֲבָל לֹא עַל יְדֵי יִסּוּרִים וָחֳלָיִם רָעִים.

תחנונים
Personal Requests

The Master of all strength, Who is able to do anything and
Who takes care of me with Divine Providence,

אֱלֹהַי

help me to guard my tongue from speaking bad
about others (*lashon hara*)

נְצוֹר לְשׁוֹנִי מֵרָע

and [help me to guard] my lips
from speaking deceit or falsehood

וּשְׂפָתַי מִדַּבֵּר מִרְמָה

and help me so that my soul
should be silent (and even in thought
I should not get angry) at those who curse me

וְלִמְקַלְלַי נַפְשִׁי תִדּוֹם

and help me so that my soul
should be like dust (very humble)
before everyone (and not mind insults).

וְנַפְשִׁי כֶּעָפָר לַכֹּל תִּהְיֶה

Open up my heart so that it should be
receptive and understand Your Torah

פְּתַח לִבִּי בְּתוֹרָתֶךָ

and help my soul eagerly pursue
Your *mitzvos*

וּבְמִצְוֹתֶיךָ תִּרְדּוֹף נַפְשִׁי

and all those who want to harm me
(whether in mundane matters or spiritual
matters, i.e., to cause me to sin)

וְכֹל הַחוֹשְׁבִים עָלַי רָעָה

quickly annul their plan

מְהֵרָה הָפֵר עֲצָתָם

and ruin their thought
(even before they make plans).

וְקַלְקֵל מַחֲשַׁבְתָּם

Act (take us out of exile)
for the sake of Your Name,
which is desecrated now among the gentiles

עֲשֵׂה לְמַעַן שְׁמֶךָ

act (take us out of exile)
for the sake of Your right hand,
which You have now withdrawn in our exile

עֲשֵׂה לְמַעַן יְמִינֶךָ

act (take us out of exile)
for the sake of Your Holiness
(so that all will know that You lead us with holiness)

עֲשֵׂה לְמַעַן קְדֻשָּׁתֶךָ

act (take us out of exile)
for the sake of Your Torah
(so the Torah can be studied properly and completely)

עֲשֵׂה לְמַעַן תּוֹרָתֶךָ

and in order that Your dear ones, Israel,
should be released from all troubles

לְמַעַן יֵחָלְצוּן יְדִידֶיךָ

save them with (the wonders and miracles that
are attributed to) Your right hand

הוֹשִׁיעָה יְמִינְךָ

and answer (even) me in this prayer.

וַעֲנֵנִי.

Let the words of my prayer
be desirable to You[17]

יִהְיוּ לְרָצוֹן אִמְרֵי פִי

and also the thoughts of my heart which
I cannot express [should be desirable] before You,

וְהֶגְיוֹן לִבִּי לְפָנֶיךָ

Master of all,

יהוה

My Rock, on Whom I rely for all my requests

צוּרִי

and Who will be my Redeemer.

וְגֹאֲלִי.

ONE SHOULD BOW AND GO BACK THREE STEPS
LIKE A SERVANT DEPARTING FROM HIS MASTER

The One Who makes peace in Heaven
(among the angels)

עֹשֶׂה [הַ]שָׁלוֹם בִּמְרוֹמָיו

may He make peace (for those on earth,
who are naturally quarrelsome)

הוּא יַעֲשֶׂה שָׁלוֹם

on those of us here (praying together)

עָלֵינוּ

and on all of Israel

וְעַל כָּל יִשְׂרָאֵל

and (you, the angels who escort me,)
agree to my prayer, and say Amen!

וְאִמְרוּ אָמֵן.

May it be Your desire,

יְהִי רָצוֹן מִלְּפָנֶיךָ

Master of all,

יהוה

---

17. *Seder HaYom* writes that one should say this verse with great concentration, for it
will help considerably that his prayers should not go unanswered (quoted also in *Mishnah Berurah* 122:8).

the Master of all strength, Who is able to do anything and Who takes care of us with Divine Providence,	אֱלֹהֵינוּ
and the God Who took care of our Fathers with Divine Providence,	וֵאלֹהֵי אֲבוֹתֵינוּ
that You should rebuild the Temple (so that we will be able to do the ultimate *avodah* — service to You)	שֶׁיִּבָּנֶה בֵּית הַמִּקְדָּשׁ
quickly and in our lifetime	בִּמְהֵרָה בְיָמֵינוּ
and help us so that all our toil should be in learning Your Torah.	וְתֵן חֶלְקֵנוּ בְּתוֹרָתֶךָ
And there, in the Temple, we will bring offerings (the ultimate service) with reverence	וְשָׁם נַעֲבָדְךָ בְּיִרְאָה
as [they brought offerings and served in reverence] in the earlier days (of Moshe)	כִּימֵי עוֹלָם
and as they did in the previous years (of Shlomo *HaMelech*).	וּכְשָׁנִים קַדְמוֹנִיּוֹת.
And then, it will be pleasing to the Master of all	וְעָרְבָה לַיהוה
the offerings that will be brought in the Temple (which is in the portion of Yehudah in Jerusalem)	מִנְחַת יְהוּדָה וִירוּשָׁלָיִם
as [the offerings were pleasing] in the earlier days (of Moshe)	כִּימֵי עוֹלָם
and as they were in the previous years (of Shlomo *HaMelech*).	וּכְשָׁנִים קַדְמוֹנִיּוֹת.

Kedushah

Kedushah for Rosh Hashanah Shacharis

As it is written by Your prophet Yeshayahu (6:3):	כַּכָּתוּב עַל יַד נְבִיאֶךְ
The Serafim[1] angels call to each other for permission to praise God and then each one says:	וְקָרָא זֶה אֶל זֶה וְאָמַר
"Holy is God in the Heavens	**קָדוֹשׁ**
Holy is God on earth	**קָדוֹשׁ**
Holy is God forever and ever	**קָדוֹשׁ**
the Master of all	**יהוה**
Who is the ruler over all the Heavenly and earthly legions	**צְבָאוֹת**
the whole world is filled with His Glory."	**מְלֹא כָל הָאָרֶץ כְּבוֹדוֹ.**
Then, after the Serafim have said this verse ("Holy etc.")	אָז
(the Ofanim and Chayos angels respond) with a great trembling sound	בְּקוֹל רַעַשׁ גָּדוֹל
mighty and powerful	אַדִּיר וְחָזָק
they make a sound heard	מַשְׁמִיעִים קוֹל
raising themselves towards the sound of the Serafim	מִתְנַשְּׂאִים לְעֻמַּת שְׂרָפִים
opposite the Serafim, they say "Baruch" (Yechezkel 3:12):	לְעֻמָּתָם בָּרוּךְ יֹאמֵרוּ:

1. Although there are ten levels of angels (Rambam, Hilchos Yesodei HaTorah 2:7), the verses of Kedushah are said by the three types indicated in the blessings before Shema in Shacharis, namely: Serafim, Ofanim and Chayos.

"(Praised as) the Source of Blessing is the Glory of God	בָּרוּךְ כְּבוֹד יהוה
from the place where His Glory is (although its exact place is unknown)."	מִמְּקוֹמוֹ.
From Your place, our King, You should show the splendor of Your Divine Presence	מִמְּקוֹמְךָ מַלְכֵּנוּ תוֹפִיעַ
and reveal Your Kingship over us (and judge the descendants of Esav)	וְתִמְלֹךְ עָלֵינוּ
because we are yearning for You.	כִּי מְחַכִּים אֲנַחְנוּ לָךְ
When will You fulfill Your promise to reign in Zion?	מָתַי תִּמְלֹךְ בְּצִיּוֹן
May it happen soon and in our lifetime (so that we should witness the return of the Glory of God)	בְּקָרוֹב בְּיָמֵינוּ
and may You dwell (in Zion) forever.	לְעוֹלָם וָעֶד תִּשְׁכּוֹן
Reveal Yourself in greatness (by taking revenge against Your enemies)	תִּתְגַּדַּל
and reveal Your holiness	וְתִתְקַדַּשׁ
in the midst of Your city, Jerusalem,	בְּתוֹךְ יְרוּשָׁלַיִם עִירְךָ
for all generations	לְדוֹר וָדוֹר
and forever and ever.	וּלְנֵצַח נְצָחִים
And may our eyes merit to see when You will be recognized as the King of the whole world	וְעֵינֵינוּ תִרְאֶינָה מַלְכוּתֶךָ
as it says in the songs of Your might	כַּדָּבָר הָאָמוּר בְּשִׁירֵי עֻזֶּךָ
that were written by David, Your righteous anointed one (*Tehillim* 146:10):	עַל יְדֵי דָוִד מְשִׁיחַ צִדְקֶךָ.

"God will reign forever   יִמְלֹךְ יהוה לְעוֹלָם

(that is,) the Master of all strength   אֱלֹהַיִךְ צִיּוֹן
and the One able to do anything,
Who dwells particularly in Zion (the Temple)

(He will reign) for all generations   לְדֹר וָדֹר

(therefore, Israel) praise God."   הַלְלוּיָהּ.

Kedushah for Rosh Hashanah *Mussaf*
and for All Prayers on Yom Kippur

As it is written by Your prophet *Yeshayahu* (6:3):	כַּכָּתוּב עַל יַד נְבִיאֶךְ
The *Serafim*[1] angels call to each other for permission to praise God and then each one says:	וְקָרָא זֶה אֶל זֶה וְאָמַר
"Holy is God in the Heavens	**קָדוֹשׁ**
Holy is God on earth	**קָדוֹשׁ**
Holy is God forever and ever	**קָדוֹשׁ**
the Master of all	**יהוה**
who is the ruler over all the Heavenly and earthly legions	**צְבָאוֹת**
the whole world is filled with His Glory."	**מְלֹא כָל הָאָרֶץ כְּבוֹדוֹ.**
His Glory fills the entire world	כְּבוֹדוֹ מָלֵא עוֹלָם
(when) His ministering angels (hear the *Serafim* say "the whole world is filled with His Glory" they) ask each other	מְשָׁרְתָיו שׁוֹאֲלִים זֶה לָזֶה
where is the set place of His Glory?	אַיֵּה מְקוֹם כְּבוֹדוֹ
Opposite the *Serafim*, the *Ofanim* and *Chayos* angels say "*Baruch*" (*Yechezkel* 3:12):	לְעֻמָּתָם בָּרוּךְ יֹאמֵרוּ׃

---

1. Although there are ten levels of angels (*Rambam, Hilchos Yesodei HaTorah* 2:7), the verses of *Kedushah* are said by the three types indicated in the blessings before *Shema* in *Shacharis*, namely: *Serafim, Ofanim* and *Chayos*.

"(Praised as) the Source of Blessing
is the Glory of God

בָּרוּךְ כְּבוֹד יהוה

from the place where His Glory is
(although its exact place is unknown)."

מִמְּקוֹמוֹ.

From His place may He turn to us
with mercy

מִמְּקוֹמוֹ הוּא יִפֶן בְּרַחֲמִים

and be gracious to Israel, the nation
that declares the Oneness of His Name

וְיָחוֹן עַם הַמְיַחֲדִים שְׁמוֹ

evening and morning

עֶרֶב וָבְקֶר

every day, constantly,

בְּכָל יוֹם תָּמִיד

twice daily, with love

פַּעֲמַיִם בְּאַהֲבָה

they say "Shema" (Devarim 6:4):

שְׁמַע אוֹמְרִים:

"Hear, understand and accept
(the yoke of Heaven), Israel

שְׁמַע יִשְׂרָאֵל

(that) the Master of all,
the Master of all strength,
Who is able to do anything and
Who takes care of us with Divine Providence,

יהוה אֱלֹהֵינוּ

He is the Master of all, the One and Only."

יהוה אֶחָד.

He is the Master of all strength, Who is able to do
anything and Who takes care of us with
Divine Providence,

הוּא אֱלֹהֵינוּ

He is our Father (Who takes us and carries us
as a father does to his son)

הוּא אָבִינוּ

He is our King (Who rules over us
and all our descendants)

הוּא מַלְכֵּנוּ

and He saves us from all those
that rise up against us

הוּא מוֹשִׁיעֵנוּ

and He, in His mercy, will let us
hear again (as we did at the Exodus
from Egypt)

וְהוּא יַשְׁמִיעֵנוּ בְּרַחֲמָיו שֵׁנִית

in front of all the living

לְעֵינֵי כָּל חָי

"to be for you for a God

לִהְיוֹת לָכֶם לֵאלֹהִים

I am the Master of all, the Master of all
strength Who is able to do anything and
Who takes care of you with Divine Providence."[2]

אֲנִי יהוה אֱלֹהֵיכֶם.

The Mighty, our Mighty One

אַדִּיר אַדִּירֵנוּ

the Master of all, Who is our Master,

יהוה אֲדֹנֵינוּ

**how mighty is Your Name
in the entire world.**

מָה אַדִּיר שִׁמְךָ בְּכָל הָאָרֶץ.

**And then (at the
time of the redemption),
the nations will realize that the
Master of all is the ruler of the entire world**

וְהָיָה יהוה לְמֶלֶךְ עַל כָּל הָאָרֶץ

**on that day
(the gentiles will leave
their gods and realize that)
the Master of all is one (and there is no other god)**

בַּיּוֹם הַהוּא יִהְיֶה יהוה אֶחָד

**and His Name will be mentioned by all
(and no other god's name will be mentioned
in the world).**

וּשְׁמוֹ אֶחָד.

And in Your Holy Writings
(that were said with Divine inspiration)

וּבְדִבְרֵי קָדְשְׁךָ

---

2. R' Shlomo of Worms writes that this is the verse at the end of the *Shema*, that is, the end of the third paragraph of *Shema* (*Bamidbar* 15:41) normally recited in the *Shacharis*. It was included in the *Kedushah* of *Mussaf*, together with the first verse of the *Shema*, as a commemoration of the time when a Persian king forbade the Jews from reciting the *Shema* and he put guards in the synagogues to insure that they wouldn't say it. However, after *Shacharis* the guards left, and *Shema* was therefore added in the *Kedushah* of *Mussaf* so that everyone should remember it.

it is written saying (*Tehillim* 146:10):	כָּתוּב לֵאמֹר׃
"God will reign forever	**יִמְלֹךְ יהוה לְעוֹלָם**
(that is,) the Master of all strength and the One able to do anything, Who dwells particularly in Zion (the Temple)	**אֱלֹהַיִךְ צִיּוֹן**
(He will reign) for all generations	**לְדֹר וָדֹר**
(therefore, Israel) praise God."	**הַלְלוּיָהּ׃**

Kedushah for Rosh Hashanah *Minchah*

Let us declare holy Your Name in this world	נְקַדֵּשׁ אֶת שִׁמְךָ בָּעוֹלָם
just as the angels proclaim Its holiness	כְּשֵׁם שֶׁמַּקְדִּישִׁים אוֹתוֹ
in the upper Heavens (called *Aravos*)	בִּשְׁמֵי מָרוֹם
as it is written by Your prophet (*Yeshayahu* 6:3):	כַּכָּתוּב עַל יַד נְבִיאֶךָ
The *Serafim* angels call to each other for permission to praise God and then each one says:	וְקָרָא זֶה אֶל זֶה וְאָמַר
"Holy is God in the Heavens	**קָדוֹשׁ**
Holy is God on earth	**קָדוֹשׁ**
Holy is God forever and ever	**קָדוֹשׁ**
the Master of all	**יהוה**
Who is the ruler over all the Heavenly and earthly legions	**צְבָאוֹת**
the whole world is filled with His Glory."	**מְלֹא כָל הָאָרֶץ כְּבוֹדוֹ.**
Opposite the *Serafim,* they say *"Baruch"* (*Yechezkel* 3:12):	לְעֻמָּתָם בָּרוּךְ יֹאמֵרוּ:
"(Praised as) the Source of Blessing is the Glory of God	**בָּרוּךְ כְּבוֹד יהוה**
from the place where His Glory is (although its exact place is unknown)."	**מִמְּקוֹמוֹ.**
And in Your Holy Writings (that were said with Divine inspiration)	וּבְדִבְרֵי קָדְשְׁךָ

it is written saying (*Tehillim* 146:10):

כָּתוּב לֵאמֹר

"God will reign forever

יִמְלֹךְ יהוה לְעוֹלָם

**(that is,) the Master of all strength
and the One able to do anything,
Who dwells particularly in Zion (the Temple)**

אֱלֹהַיִךְ צִיּוֹן

(He will reign) for all generations

לְדֹר וָדֹר

(therefore, Israel) praise God."

הַלְלוּיָהּ.

Appendices

Bibliography

◄§ Appendix I:

בָּרוּךְ אַתָּה

Two of the words most frequently said in prayer are *"Baruch atah."* These words are in the formula of each and every one of the one hundred *brachos* we say every day, either at the beginning or at the end, yet their meaning is very enigmatic. Since the first known English translation of the *siddur,* written in 1766 by Isaac Pinto (1715 − 1787) in New York (for those of the "British Dominions in America"), the translation has been "**Blessed art Thou**" (except that since the time of the American Revolution we have modernized it, changing it to "Blessed are You").

What does "Blessed art Thou" mean? Many people will tell you that it means "You should be blessed (have an abundance)," and consequently they call every *brachah* a "blessing," as if we are blessing God. However, none of the definitions in the *Oxford Dictionary* agree with this.[1] The most appropriate definition found there is: "The object of adoring reverence, worthy to be praised by men," and accordingly, "Blessed art Thou" means "You are worthy of being praised." But is that really what *"Baruch Atah"* means?

The true meaning of the word *"baruch"* is actually a dispute among the *Rishonim.* The foremost commentator on prayer among the *Rishonim,* the *Avudraham* [R' David ben Yosef Avudraham (14th cent.)] (p. 33), writes that *"baruch* is not a verb, but is like *rachum* (the Merciful One) and *chanun* (the Gracious One), and means that He Himself is the **Source of Blessing**." The *Sefer HaChinuch* [attributed to R' Aharon HaLevi (13th cent.)] (*mitzvah* 430) elaborates, stating that when we say *"baruch"* we are not blessing God, because He needs no blessing, for He is the Master of all; rather, it is a thanks to God in recognition that He is the Source of all Blessing. This is also the

---

1. The *Oxford English Dictionary* has four definitions for the word "**blessed**": (1) consecrated by a religious rite; (2) the object of adoring reverence, worthy to be praised by men; (3) enjoying supreme felicity (happiness); (4) bringing, or accompanied by, happiness. See there "**bless, v.1**" that the development of the word was "influenced by being chosen to translate Heb. ברך! " See "**bless**" definition 5a ("thanksgiving or acknowledgment of gracious beneficence or goodness"), which is correct, but not given for "**blessed.**"

opinion of R' Avraham ibn Ezra [1090 – 1164] (*Shemos* 18:10); R' Bachai ben Asher [14th cent.] (*Kad Hakemach – Brachah*); *Shushan Sodos* [author unknown – 14th cent.] (Karetz 1824, p. 53a); R' Yom Tov Lipman Milhoizen [14th – 15th cent.] (S*efer HaNitzachon,* Ch. 131); and R' Yosef Albo [15th cent.] (*Sefer HaIkkarim* 2:26).

A similar opinion, which explains the word *baruch* as expressing praise or thanks (but not specifying for what), is found in many *Rishonim and Geonim,* foremost of whom is *Rashi* (*Ezra* 7:27), who says "*Baruch Hashem*" is Ezra's way of expressing thanks to God. The famous lexicographer, the *Radak* [R' David Kimchi (1160 – 1235)] (*Sefer HaShorashim L'Radak – Baraich*), writes that when people give a *brachah* to God, it is a form of praise. Of the same opinion are R' Yonah ibn Janach [990 – 1050] (*Sefer HaShorashim – Baraich*), who writes that it is praise and thanks; R' Chananel ben Chushiel [985 – 1057] (quoted in *Or Zarua, Hil. Krias Shema,* Ch. 8); and R' Chizkiyah ben Manoach [13th cent.] (*Chizkuni Bereishis* 24:27).

There is also a *Midrash* (*Osiyos d'Rabbi Akiva,* ver. 2) supporting this, which states, "The letter '*beis*' came to God and said: Master of the World, would You like to create Your world with me, for with me people will *praise You* every day, as it stays, '*Baruch*'. . .?"

There is, however, another view in the *Rishonim,* and that is the famous opinion of the *Rashba* [R' Shlomo ben Aderes (1235 – 1310)] (*Chidushei Aggados, Brachos* 7a), who writes, "Don't think that a *brachah* is a form of thanksgiving, for a *brachah* is an expression denoting increase and abundance, as in the verse (*Shemos* 23:25), 'And He will bless your bread and your water'; so too in the verse (*Tehillim* 119:12), 'Blessed are You God; teach me Your laws' [*Baruch atah Hashem lamdeini chukecha*] . . . [Saying the *brachah*] causes God to increase mercy on His creations." However, R' Yaakov ben Chaviv [1445 – 1516] (*Ein Yaakov, HaKoseiv,* ibid.), already challenged this, stating, "If only someone could explain to me how '*Baruch atah*' fits into the words to mean that God should increase and add on to our good (the *Rashba's* explanation)!"

Although most *Rishonim* hold that "*baruch*" means praise or is an expression of praise, the *Nefesh HaChaim* [R' Chaim of Volozhin (1749 – 1821)] (2:2) mentions this approach of the *Rashba* as part of his explanation of the word "*baruch,*" which he says (2:4) means that there should be an increase of God's influence (showering of good) in the world, that is, literally blessing God. He also cites the *Zohar* in support of his view. However, one of the main proofs for his thesis is the *Gemara* (*Brachos* 7a) that the *Rashba* was explaining, yet that *Gemara* is adequately explained by R' Chananel and the *Shushan Sodos,* each one according to his interpretation of "*baruch.*"

Perhaps this dispute can be muted by citing the words of Rabbeinu Bachai (*Devarim* 8:10). After he quotes the "plain meaning" which he wrote in *Kad HaKemach,* that a *brachah* is a form of thanks in recognition that God is the Source of Blessing, he writes that according to the way of *kabbalah* a *brachah* can be understood differently, and he goes on to explain like the *Rashba.*

Therefore, we see that the word *"baruch"* can be explained on different levels. The simple meaning is that given by the vast majority of *Rishonim* : **an expression of thanks or praise to God Who is the Source of Blessing.**[2] Since this *sefer* is on a simple level, and not a *kabbalistic* one, I have used this explanation.

2. R' Shabsi Sofer wrote similarly in his *siddur,* "that **He is the Source and the Influence of blessings** [and he writes the Yiddish word for Blesser — *ein bentcher*], and so wrote the *Avudraham.* "

⋘ Appendix II:
Ten Suggestions on How to Merit a Favorable Judgment[1]

1.

We must have a sincere, strong desire to repent to God, including a firm commitment to correct our ways and actions in the future. Also, we must plead for Divine assistance for a complete repentance.

2.

We must strengthen our faith in the principle of Kingship, that is, recognize that there is no one else but God.

3.

We must approach Rosh Hashanah with the recognition that we have nothing, and that on our own, we have no hope of passing the judgment. When God sees that we come before Him humbly and with fear, then we may merit favor in His eyes, and that is our biggest hope on this day of judgment.

4.

The nature of a person is to think that his life is secure and assured, however, a person should exert himself to realize that he must ask for life. And for what kind of life? A life that is *"lema'ancha* — for Your sake" — a life so that we may serve You.

5.

We should seize every opportunity to grow in Torah and fear of Heaven to prepare for Rosh Hashanah. Were we to feel that we are like paupers asking for alms at the door, we would grab every *mitzvah* that we have the ability to do, even a small one . . . and being careful even in small *mitzvos* strengthens the whole principle of Kingship.

---

1. Adapted from the *Or Yechezkel — Sichos Elul* by R' Yechezkel Levenstein, *zt"l*.

6.

The *Gemara* (*Rosh Hashanah* 17a) states that anyone who overlooks injustices done to him, will be forgiven for all of his sins. If we are not exacting with others, then God will not be exacting with us, for the way of [Divine] judgment is measure for measure.

7.

The best suggestion for an individual to emerge with a favorable judgment is to try to be part of the community. How does one accomplish that? When one has a desire to do something beneficial for the community, whether in material or spiritual matters, helps other individuals, and prays for all of Israel, then he becomes as one with the community, and has hope to be inscribed for a good year.

8.

On the day of Rosh Hashanah itself we must be very careful not to transgress any sin or to exhibit bad character traits, such as anger, and certainly not to be haughty. And we must take care not to disturb others during prayer.

9.

The greatest danger when one stands in judgment is to think, "Though I walk as my heart sees fit, I will have peace" [*Devarim* 29:18; the punishment for that thought is described in the following verse, "God will not want to forgive him"]. The way to avoid that thought is by contemplating the great punishment for sins, and to contrast this with the great reward that awaits the righteous in the World to Come; concerning that he will be brought to judgment on Rosh Hashanah.

10.

Part of our responsibility on Rosh Hashanah is to accept upon ourselves the service of God without limit, an absolute commitment to do the will of God without condition. And at least on Rosh Hashanah one should feel himself totally subservient to the will of God. If we do that, then we will have hope to merit a *"Kesivah VaChasimah Tovah"* ("a decree written down and sealed for our good").

ᴥ§ Bibliography[1]

R' Aharon ben R' Yecheil (19th cent.) Wrote commentary on *Siddur* called *Nehorah HaSholaim* and a commentary on the *Machzor* entitled ***Korban Aharon.***

Albo, R' Yosef (15th cent.) Wrote an important philosophical work in which he clarifies the fundamental principles of Torah faith, called ***Sefer HaIkkarim.***

R' Alexander Ziskind of Horodna (1740-1794) Known for his extreme piety; wrote down the proper thought or intention which one should have for every action and prayer, in his ***Yesod VeShoresh HaAvodah.***

Altschuler, R' David and R' Yechiel Hillel (18th cent.) R' David started the famous, concise and simple two-part commentary on the Prophets and Writings by the name of ***Metzudas David*** and ***Metzudas Tzion,*** which was completed by his son R' Yechiel Hillel.

R' Asher ben Yechiel (1250-1327) One of the leading halachic authorities of the Middle Ages; he wrote a classic halachic commentary on the Talmud, known as the ***Rosh*** (the acronym of his name) as well as many other works; had to flee Germany and settled in Toledo, Spain; he was recognized as the Torah leader of his generation.

Avudraham, R' David ben Yosef (14th cent.) A disciple of the *Tur;* wrote the prime commentary on *tefillah* from the Middle Ages, known as the ***Avudraham,*** which explains both the simple meaning and the deeper concepts of prayer, as well as many laws and customs of prayer.

Azkari, R' Elazar (1533-1600) Lived in Tzefas; wrote a work of *mussar* in which he categorizes the *mitzvos* according to the parts of the body to which they apply, called ***Sefer Chareidim.***

Azulai, R' Chaim Yosef David (1724-1806) Known as the ***Chida*** (the acronym of his name), author of numerous books on all topics of the Torah, including *Birkei Yosef* on the *Shulchan Aruch.*

R' Bachai ben Asher (1263-1340) Wrote a comprehensive Torah commentary (***Rabbeinu Bachai***) which includes the simple meaning and kabbalistic explanations.

R' Bachai ben Yosef ibn Pakuda (11th cent.) Wrote one of the first works of *mussar,* entitled ***Chovos HaLevavos*** [Duties of the Heart], which is regarded as one of the foremost *mussar* works till today.

Bachrach, R' Ya'ir Chaim (1638-1702) Author of the famous responsa *Chavos Ya'ir;* also authored a work on the *Shulchan Aruch* called ***Mekor***

---

1. Some of the earlier dates may **not** be completely accurate. For all dates, I have relied a great deal on the excellent work *"Challenge of Sinai"* by Rabbi Zechariah Fendel, Hashkafa Publications, 1978.

Chaim, part of which has just recently been found and published.

Beis Elokim see Trani, R' Moshe.

Blazer, R' Yitzchak (1837-1907) One of the primary disciples of R' Yisrael Salanter; Rabbi of St. Petersburg, Russia, and was therefore known by the name *R' Itzele Peterburger;* author of **Kochvei Or.**

Chasman, R' Leib (1869-1935) *Mashgiach* of Chevron Yeshivah; his discourses were collected and published in **Or Yahel.**

Chayei Adam see Danzig, R' Avraham.

Chofetz Chaim — R' Yisrael Meir HaKohen of Radin (1838-1933) His first book was entitled **Chofetz Chaim** (concerning the laws of *lashon hara)* after which he was subsequently known. Also author of numerous other works, including **Mishnah Berurah,** which is recognized as the primary halachic work dealing with the daily laws as well as the laws of Shabbos and *Yom Tov.* Famous for his great piety and wisdom; recognized leader of Torah Jewry in his generation.

Chovos HaLevavos see R' Bachai ben Yosef.

Danzig, R' Avraham (1748-1820) A *dayan* in Vilna who wrote two very popular, concise works of Jewish law: *Chayei Adam* on *Orach Chaim,* and *Chochmas Adam* on *Yoreh De'ah.*

Dover Shalom see Landau, R' Yitzchak Eliyahu.

R' Elazar ben Yehudah from Worms (1160-1237) A leading scholar and mystic of Medieval Germany. Wrote his famous work on *halachah* and ethics, **Rokeach,** after which he was called. Also wrote a commentary on the Torah and on the *Siddur,* both of which include the simple meaning as well as mystical meanings, which have just recently been published.

R' Eliyahu di Vidosh (16th cent.) One of the great Torah scholars and Kabbalists who lived in Tzefas, Israel during its golden era in the 16th cent.; famous for his tremendous *mussar* work **Reishis Chochmoh;** also wrote **Totzos Chaim.**

R' Eliyahu of Vilna — the Vilna Gaon (1720-1797) Considered the greatest Torah scholar in many centuries; his writings cover the spectrum of the Written and Oral law, including *Kabbalah,* and are known by the acronym for his name — "Gra" (e.g., **Chidushei HaGra**).

Emden, R' Yaakov (1697-1776) Known as the **Ya'avetz** (the acronym for his name — Yaakov ben Tzvi); one of the outstanding Torah scholars of his generation; author of numerous works including a commentary on the entire *Siddur.*

Epstein, R' Baruch (1860-1942) Author of numerous works the most famous being *Torah Temimah* on the Torah. Also wrote a work on the *Siddur* called **Baruch She'amar.**

Epstein, R' Yechiel Michel (17th cent.) Author of halachic and *mussar* work **Kitzur Shelah,** which is primarily condensed from the *sefer Sh'nei Luchos HaBris* (acronym "Shelah"), without the *Kabbalah,* and has many additions from other works.

Epstein, R' Yechiel Michel (1829 – 1908) Rabbi of Navardok, Poland and a prominent halachic decisor; author of *Aruch HaShulchan.*

Eybschuetz, R' Yonasan (1690-1764) One of the outstanding Torah scholars of his generation; Rabbi of the combined communities of Hamburg, Altona and Wandsbek; author of many works including *Urim VeTumim* (on *Shulchan Aruch Choshen Mishpat*) and *Yaaros Devash* (long sermons of *mussar*).

Feinstein, R' Moshe (1895-1986) *Rosh Yeshivah* of Mesivta Tiferes Jerusalem in N.Y. and the Yeshivah of Staten Island; the leading halachic decisor of his time, and the foremost leader of Orthodox Jewry in America; author of *Igros Moshe* (responsa) and *Dibros Moshe* (on the Talmud).

Friedlander, R' Chaim (1923-1986) One of the *Mashgichim* in Ponevez Yeshivah following the death of R' Yechezkel Levenstein; author of *Sifsei Chaim.* Also published many of the works of R' Moshe Chaim Luzzatto.

Gemara This refers to the Babylonian Talmud [redacted about 425 c.e.], which is the final body of the transmission of the Oral Torah given at Har Sinai. All subsequent *halachah* is derived from the teachings of the *Gemara,* otherwise known as the *Talmud,* which is accepted as the definitive legal interpretation of the Torah.

Gordon, R' Aryeh Leib (19th cent.) Author of the commentary *Iyun Tefillah* printed in the popular *Siddur Otzar HaTefillos;* known as an expert in Hebrew grammar.

Hirsch, R' Shamshon Raphael (1808-1888) Rabbi in Frankfurt-am-Main; great leader of German Orthodox Jewry and battler against Reform movement; author of many works including *Horeb* (a comprehensive analysis of Jewish laws and observances), a commentary on the Torah and *Tehillim;* and a *Commentary on the siddur.*

R' Hirtz *Shatz* (the Chazzan) wrote a commentary on the *Siddur* gathered from many sources, including Kabbalistic ones; printed in 1560 in Tohegan.

Kanievsky, R' Yaakov Yisrael (1899-1985) Known as *The Steipler* (because of his hometown); famous for his great piety and wisdom; people came from all over the world to Bnei Brak, Israel, to seek his blessing; author of *Kehillos Yaakov* (on the Talmud) and *Karyana D'Igarta* (a collection of his letters).

Korban Aharon see R' Aharon ben R' Yechiel.

Kotler, R' Aharon (1892-1962) *Rosh Yeshivah* of Kletk, Poland and later of Beth Medrash Govoha in Lakewood; a foremost Torah leader of his time and propounder of the primacy of Torah. Many of his lectures and discourses have been published in *Mishnas R' Aharon.*

Kronglas, R' Dovid (1910-1972) *Mashgiach* of Yeshivas Ner Yisrael in Baltimore; author of *Divrei Dovid* and *Sichos Chochmah U'Mussar.*

Landau, R' Yechezkel (1713-1793) Rabbi of Prague and one of the major halachic authorities in his days; wrote the famous responsa called *Noda*

BiYehudah, after which he became known. Also wrote *Tzlach* (on the Talmud), among other works.

Landau, R' Yitzchak Eliyahu (1801-1876) *Dayan* of Vilna; wrote commentary on *Siddur* called *Dover Shalom* printed in *Siddur Otzar HaTefillos.*

Levenstein, R' Yechezkel (1885-1974) Prominent *mussar* personality; *Mashgiach* of the Mir Yeshivos in Poland, Shanghai, New York and Jerusalem, before becoming *Mashgiach* of Ponevez Yeshivah in Bnei Brak in 1954. Many of his discourses and letters have been collected in the six-volume *Or Yechezkel.*

Lipshitz, R' Yisrael (1782-1860) Wrote a commentary on the entire *Mishnah* called *Tiferes Yisrael* (*Yachin U'Boaz*).

Lopian, R' Elya (1876-1970) Prominent *mussar* personality; *Mashgiach* of Kfar Chassidim in Israel; his discourses were collected in *Lev Eliyahu.*

Luzzatto, R' Moshe Chaim (1707-1746) Author of the primary *mussar* text, *Mesillas Yesharim;* also wrote many other *sefarim,* primarily on *Kabbalah,* including *Yalkut Yedi'os HaEmes.*

Maggid Tzedek see R' Pinchas from Plutsk.

Margolis, R' Efraim Zalman (1760-1828) Great scholar and businessman from Broad (then Austria); author of numerous works including *Mateh Efraim,* a major work on the laws and customs of the High Holidays.

R' Meir Simchah HaKohen (1843-1926) Rabbi of Dvinsk for 40 years; an illus-

trious Torah scholar; author of the classic *Or Same'ach* on the Rambam's *Yad HaChazakah,* and *Meshech Chochmah* on the Torah.

Meiri see R' Menachem ben Shlomo.

Meltsen, R' Yitzchak (19th – 20th cent.) Wrote commentary on the *Siddur* called *Siach Yitzchak* which was printed in *Siddur Ishei Yisrael* (known also as the *Siddur HaGra*).

R' Menachem ben Aharon (ca. 1310-1385) A disciple of R' Yehudah ben HaRosh; wrote an all-encompassing work on laws and ethics by the name of *Tzeidah LaDerech.*

R' Menachem ben Shlomo Meiri (1249-1315) Wrote a very lucid commentary on the Talmud called *Beis HaBechirah,* as well as other *sefarim,* including *Chibur HaTeshuvah,* a large work concerning repentance.

Mesillas Yesharim, see Luzzatto, R' Moshe Chaim.

Midrash A general term, usually denoting the non-legalistic teachings of the Sages, generally written according the the order of the Torah. They were written during the period of the *Tana'im, Amora'im* and *Geonim.* The main ones are: *Midrash Rabbah* and *Midrash Tanchuma* [we have also cited *Pesikta Rabbasi, Pesikta d'Rav Kahana, Eliyahu Zuta* and *Midrash Tehillim* (also known as *Midrash Shocher Tov*)].

Mishnah Berurah see Chofetz Chaim.

R' Moshe ben Maimon – *Rambam* (1135-1204) One of the leading Torah scholars of the Middle Ages; wrote comprehensive code of Jewish Law, encompassing the entire Torah, called *Mishneh Torah* or *Yad HaChazakah,* which has remained one of the most important texts of *halacha* till this day. Also wrote a commentary on the *Mishnah,* and a famous work on Jewish philosophy, *Moreh Nevuchim,* among others.

R' Moshe ben Nachman – *Ramban* (1194-1270) One of the leading Torah scholars of the Middle Ages and master of *Kabbalah;* wrote many works, most notably, a commentary on several tractates of the Talmud, and an extensive commentary on the Torah which is one of the foundations of Jewish thought till this day.

R' Moshe ben Yehudah Machir (16th-17th cent.) Lived in Tzefas; wrote *Seder HaYom,* a work on laws and customs for daily life as well as the entire year, which includes an explanation of several prayers.

Orchos Tzaddikim (c. 14th cent.) One of the classic *mussar* works, drawing mainly from earlier works; written anonymously in the period of the later *Rishonim.*

Papo, R' Eliezer (1785-1827) Wrote famous *mussar* work *Pele Yo'eitz,* among other *sefarim.*

R' Pinchas from Plutsk (18th cent.) known as the *Maggid of Plutsk;* wrote a commentary on *Siddur* called *Maggid Tzedek* (Shklov, 1788), used extensively by the *Eitz Yosef* commentary in *Siddur Otzar HaTefillos.*

Rashi acronym for R' Shlomo Yitzchaki (1040-1105). Known as the "Teacher of all of Israel" for he wrote the primary

commentary on the entire Torah and Talmud [with Divine inspiration (according to the *Shelah*)]. His concise, clear commentaries are considered absolutely basic to the understanding of these texts until this very day.

Rokeach see R' Elazar ben Yehudah.

Ruderman, R' Yaakov Yitzchak (1900-1987) Founder and *Rosh Yeshivah* of Yeshivas Ner Yisrael in Baltimore, which he headed for over fifty years; author of *Avodas Levi.*

Salanter, R' Yisrael Lipkin (1810-1883) One of the outstanding Torah scholars of his generation, founder of the *mussar* movement, which stresses morals based on traditional ethical literature. His teaching had a tremendous impact, so much so, that all yeshivos have incorporated a session of *mussar* into their daily schedule. Some of his letters were printed in *Or Yisrael.*

Seder HaYom see R' Moshe ben Yehudah Machir.

Sefer HaChinuch [some attribute to R' Aharon HaLevi] (13th cent.) Classic work on the 613 Commandments including their laws and rationale.

Shaarei Teshuvah see R' Yonah.

Shalmei Tzibbur, a compilation of laws and customs of prayer written by R' Yisrael Yaakov Algazi (1679-1756), who was a Rabbi and kabbalist in Jerusalem; also wrote several other works.

R' Shlomo ben Aderes (1235-1310) Leading rabbi in Spain in the late 13th cent.; famous for his many classical works, primarily his commentary on the Talmud and his thousands of responsa on all aspects of the Torah, known as **Teshuvos HaRashba.**

R' Shlomo ben Shimshon from Worms (d. 1096) Contemporary of Rashi; wrote a commentary on the *Siddur,* the earliest Ashkenazic commentary that we know of, which was first printed recently (1972) under the name **Siddur R' Shlomo MiGermiza.** He was killed in a sanctification of God's Name, together with his wife and daughters, during the first Crusades.

Shulchan Aruch see R' Yosef Caro.

Siddur Avodas Yisrael Published by R' Seligmann Yitzchak Baer (1825-1897), follower of the school of R' Wolf Heidenheim (1757-1832) [the noted grammarian]. Known for its authoritative, precise text of the *tefillos,* as well as its scholarly commentary. Printed in Roedelheim in 1868.

Siddur Chasidei Ashkenaz Contains a commentary on much of the *Siddur* from the *Chasidei Ashkenaz* [Pious Men of Germany] of the 12th cent. Just recently printed, together with *Siddur R' Shlomo MiGermiza.*

Siddur Otzar HaTefillos A treasury of commentaries on the *Siddur,* primarily *Eitz Yosef* [by R' Chanoch Zundel ben R' Yosef (d.1867)] and *Iyun Tefillah* (see Gordon, R' Aryeh Leib); first published in 1915.

Sofer, R' Moshe (1762-1839) Known as **Chasam Sofer** after the *sefarim* which he wrote by that name; Rabbi and *Rosh Yeshivah* in Pressburg, Hungary; leader of Hungarian Jewry and a main halachic decisor in his generation.

Sofer, R' Shabsi (end of 16th cent. – beg. of 17th cent.) Great scholar and expert in Hebrew grammar who was asked by the great Sages of his generation (including the *Maharsha* and *Bach*) to write a *Siddur* with the accurate text to be used by all cities (in a great part of Europe). It was never printed with all its explanations until recently (1994).

Tiferes Yisrael see R' Yisrael Lipshitz.

Trani, R' Moshe ben Yosef (1500 – 1580) Contemporary of R' Yosef Caro; wrote commentary on Rambam by the name of *Kiryas Sefer,* and a famous work on *Hashkafah* (Jewish ideology) called **Beis Elokim.** Also wrote responsa known by the acronym of his name *Teshuvos Mabit.*

Tur see R' Yaakov ben HaRosh.

Wolbe, R' Shlomo (Contemporary) One of the foremost *mussar* personalities of our generation; author of the popular *mussar* work **Alei Shur** (2 vol.).

R' Yaakov ben HaRosh (1270- 1343) Wrote a systematic code of Jewish Law, called *Arba'ah Turim* or **Tur** for short, which included all halachic material relevant to Jewish life in the Diaspora. It became the foundation for the order of the *Shuchan Aruch.* He also wrote commentaries on the Torah.

R' Yehudah ben Yakar (13th cent.) One of the teachers of the Ramban, wrote a commentary on the *Siddur,* which was used extensively by the *Avudraham.*

R' Yehuda HaChassid (1148-1217) One of the leaders of the *Chasidei Ashkenaz* [Pious Men of Germany]; wrote the classic work of *mussar, halachah* and customs called **Sefer Chasidim.**

Yesod VeShoresh HaAvodah See R' Alexander Ziskind.

R' Yitzchak ben Yosef of Corbeil (1206-1280) Wrote a concise code of law revolving around the 613 *mitzvos* called **Smak** (the acronym for *Sefer Mitvos Katan*).

R' Yonah *HaChassid* of Gerondi (ca.1200-1263) One of the leaders of Sephardic Jewry in his generation; known for his great piety. Wrote many works, but is most famous for his commentary to *Pirkei Avos* and his compendium on repentance called **Shaarei Teshuvah,** which is regarded as one of the primary *mussar* works till today.

R' Yosef Caro (1488-1575) Author of the universally accepted code of Jewish law, *Shulchan Aruch,* which is a concise work of all the laws which are relevant today. Also wrote *Beis Yosef* on the *Tur* which formed the foundation of the **Shulchan Aruch,** and *Kesef Mishneh* on the *Mishneh Torah of the* Rambam.

Ziv, R' Simchah Zissel (1824-1898) Known as *The Alter of Kelm;* founder and head of the famous Talmud Torah in Kelm, Lithuania, which became the chief center for the spread of the *mussar* movement. He was one of the foremost disciples of R' Yisrael Salanter. Many of his letters were collected in **Chochmah U'Mussar.**

This volume is part of
THE ARTSCROLL SERIES®
an ongoing project of
translations, commentaries and expositions
on Scripture, Mishnah, Talmud, Halachah,
liturgy, history, the classic Rabbinic writings,
biographies and thought.

For a brochure of current publications
visit your local Hebrew bookseller
or contact the publisher:

Mesorah Publications, ltd

4401 Second Avenue
Brooklyn, New York 11232
(718) 921-9000
www.artscroll.com